George Douglas Campbell Argyll

Scotland as it was and as it is

Vol 2

George Douglas Campbell Argyll

Scotland as it was and as it is
Vol 2

ISBN/EAN: 9783743346161

Manufactured in Europe, USA, Canada, Australia, Japa

Cover: Foto ©ninafisch / pixelio.de

Manufactured and distributed by brebook publishing software (www.brebook.com)

George Douglas Campbell Argyll

Scotland as it was and as it is

CONTENTS OF VOL. II.

CHAPTER I.
                                                                  PAGE
THE RESPONSE OF OWNERSHIP,   1

CHAPTER II.
BEFORE THE DAWN,   61

CHAPTER III.
THE BURST OF INDUSTRY,   144

CHAPTER IV.
THE FRUITS OF MIND,   229

APPENDIX,   323

ILLUSTRATIONS.

CAWDOR CASTLE (AFTER A SKETCH BY GEORGE REID, R.S.A.)	*Vignette*
"QUINAIG" (RANGE OF MOUNTAINS, SUTHERLAND),	112
"SUILVEN" (SUTHERLAND),	132
BEN MORE, MULL (VOLCANIC MOUNTAIN),	164
LOCH MAREE (ROSS-SHIRE),	266

CHAPTER I.

THE RESPONSE OF OWNERSHIP.

THERE is a theory very prevalent in the popular literature of Scotland that the last Jacobite Rebellion, which arose in July 1745 and was quelled on the Moor of Culloden in April 1746, marks the date of a great change in the landed tenures of the Highlands. The notion is, that before that date the old native population of the country lived in some condition of Arcadian bliss, founded on the relation between Celtic Clansmen and their Chiefs, whilst subsequent to that date their position became soon changed, and lowered into the modern relation between Tenant and Landlord, or between Owners and Occupiers of the soil.

The facts and documents which have been already dealt with in these pages, prove that this theory is a dream built up out of two separate delusions. One of these delusions is in respect to the true nature of the change which was involved in the passage from Celtic dues and services to rents fixed by contract or agreement. The other delusion is in respect to the causes of that change,—

to the areas of country over which it passed, and to the dates at which it became established. As regards the nature of that change, the theory not only mistakes but reverses the facts, whilst as regards the districts it affected, and the times of its arising, the popular idea is not less erroneous.

Systematic hardship and oppression was inseparable from the condition of the native population under the unlimited exactions of Celtic Feudalism. The change from those exactions to definite and stipulated rents, lasting for definite and stipulated times, was not a change for the worse, but a change immeasurably for the better. On the other hand, the last Jacobite Rebellion—"The Forty-Five," as it is still called in Scotland—marks no epoch in the history and progress of that change, which is to be compared in importance with other epochs of much older date. The Jacobite Rebellion of 1745 catches the superficial eye merely because it happens to have been the last occasion on which the Clans were marshalled in open war against the Government. But wars and rebellions of this kind were quite separate from those standing and permanent evils of the Clan system which affected most powerfully the condition of the people. Open wars against the Government—occurring almost always at distant intervals, and never of long duration,—had no other effect than some local devastations, and the loss of a few hundred lives. It was the perennial feuds between Clan and Clan, or rather between Chief and Chief,—it was the numerous, nameless, and desolating usages of daily life under the full-blown system of Celtic Feudalism, that kept down the people, and prevented the possibility of any advance in industry or in wealth. The change from this system to the system of definite agricultural rents dates, in the Eastern and in the Middle Lowlands of Scotland, from the foundation of the Monarchy,—from the first introduction of Law, and from the first settlement of the races out of whose amalgamation Scotland grew. The history of its progress is the history of our civilisation. In the Border Highlands the great epoch of its accomplishment is that of the Union of the Crowns. In the Western Highlands and the Hebrides the most memorable date is 1609, only a few years later, when the Celtic usages were condemned as the root of the misery and barbarism which confessedly prevailed, and when the fundamental demands of peace and of law were recorded in the "Statutes of Iona." From that date all over the Western Highlands it made somewhat slow, but, on the whole, steady and continuous progress, in proportion as the rebellious Clans were broken up, and those Chiefs became firmly established who were loyal to the Government. Their interest and inclination alike induced them to merge their lawless character as Chiefs, in their lawful character as the protectors and promoters of peaceful industry, in virtue of being great Owners and improvers of the soil.

The distances of History are foreshortened to us

like the distances of Space. We forget the long intervals of time that really separate events which, in perspective, seem now close together. Thus to us looking back it seems as if almost the whole time between the Union of the Crowns and the second Jacobite Rebellion in 1745 was a time full of wars. And so it was—but with long intervals between those wars, during which the silent processes of change and of advance had time to lay down and to consolidate the growing structures of Society. Thirty-six years elapsed between the accession of James I. and the first shedding of blood in the great Civil Wars of his son's reign, in 1639. During the whole of that interval progress was being made in the civilisation of the Highlands. The worst period of those wars for that portion of the country, was the period occupied by the brilliant but savage and unscrupulous campaign of Montrose, and this only lasted about eighteen months, from April 1644, when he erected his standard at Dumfries, to September 1645, when he was finally defeated by General Leslie at Philiphaugh. It is a memorable fact, too, that in this campaign the original nucleus of the army of Montrose was not composed of Scoto-Celts, but of the Irish Celts, whom he recruited through the Macdonalds of Antrim,—whom he joined only after a journey in disguise in the heart of the Highlands,—and without whose help he does not appear to have had, or to have hoped for, any prospect of success. They were employed to ravage the western portions of Argyllshire upon their way.

The courage, resource, and agility of Montrose, with the enjoyments of violence and plunder which were held out to all his followers, did at last rouse the passions and attract the cupidity of some Northern Clans, so that before his defeat his army is said to have accumulated to the number of 6000 men. But their dispersion, as usual, was complete; and when, after an interval of six years, Montrose made his last and fatal attempt in 1650, he again made it trusting to a body of German mercenaries whom he landed in the North. But the Highlanders did not flock to his standard, and it was a Chief of the purest Celtic blood—Macleod of Assynt,—who surrendered him, or in Jacobite language, "betrayed" him to the Government.

Again, after this rebellion there was a long interval of repose in the Highlands, and during part of it, under the rule of the great Protector, for seven or eight years, from 1650 to 1658, an important stride was made towards the final settlement and civilisation of the country. The master eye and the master hand of Cromwell saw and touched the root-evil of the Clans; and he made his dealings with it so conspicuous that they have caught the eye even of compilers who, with no special knowledge of this subject, write School Primers upon the History of the time. Thus we are told in one of these, with some looseness of expression, but with substantial truth, that "in order to improve the state of the people, all feudal dues were taken away. A fixed rent in money was substituted for all the services and restrictions to which the land had been hitherto liable."[1]

The Restoration in 1660 restored everything that was corrupt and bad wherever its power reached, and we have seen the wicked purpose with which its appeal to Celtic Feudalism was made in 1677. But the work of the "Highland Host" lasted only for a few months, and no raiding expedition of this kind could affect the permanent causes which were steadily at work all over the Highlands ever since the Clans had ceased to fight among themselves. The Rebellion which was raised in 1685 by my own unfortunate ancestor, the ninth Earl of Argyll, attempting, in concert with the Duke of Monmouth in England, to anticipate by a few years the Great Revolution which was at hand, was a Rebellion suppressed in a few weeks. He brought no bands of Irish Celts to ravage his native country. He brought no Dutch or German mercenaries to fight the battles of Scottish freedom. He achieved no immediate success to attract plundering Caterans always ready to flock to those who promised booty. He represented a Cause and not a Person. The Cause was one which Highlanders had never valued. His own lands had already become largely occupied by peaceful Farmers, whilst only a remainder of the Subtenants belonged to the old idle and fighting classes. Celtic Feudalism therefore completely failed him. He did not appeal either to the rude,

[1] I quote from the *History of Scotland*, by Margaret Macarthur—an excellent Book of its class, belonging to the series edited by Edward A. Freeman, D.C.L.

or to the sentimental, incitements which alone had ever moved it. He was joined by a mere handful—about 1800 men—and nothing came of his attempt except the sacrifice of his own life, and the ravage of his own estates. Yet he spoke in the light of prophecy when in his last hours he said, " I have a strong impression on my spirit that deliverance will come very suddenly."[1]

Three years later, the great Revolution of 1688, which was peaceably accomplished elsewhere, involved once more that appeal to the Clans—with as usual an Irish contingent—which was raised by John Graham of Claverhouse, Viscount Dundee. In 1689, at Killiecrankie, the Highlanders showed what they could do in fighting. But the death of their leader was, as usual, fatal to them, for mere fighting is only one part of the art of war. This rising again was speedily suppressed, but for several years a great part of the Highlands continued in a troubled state—till in 1692, the Government insisted on the formal submission of every suspected Chief. In that year the massacre of the Macdonalds of Glencoe cast indelible disgrace on the Government of King William. But the execration with which this deed was denounced when its real nature came to be understood, is a satisfactory indication of the change which had been long in progress. Such a revival, imitation, and even exaggeration by a civilised Government, of the worst features of Celtic intertribal treachery and murder, revolted the public

---

[1] Macaulay's *History of England*, vol. i. p. 563-4.

conscience, and the feeling it excited brings out as nothing else could do, how fast and far Society had advanced from the typical Epoch of the Clans. It is remarkable, however, that this atrocious murder was perpetrated and defended, not as a mere act of vengeance against men who were rebels, but as a sentence of execution against men who were irreclaimable marauders. And this, beyond all doubt, they actually were. Macaulay has expended all the resources of his eloquence in explaining how impossible it was that they could be anything else, living as they did in Glencoe. "All the science and industry of a peaceful age," he says, "can extract nothing valuable from that wilderness: but in an age of violence and rapine the wilderness itself was valued on account of the shelter which it afforded to the plunderer and the plunder. Nothing could be more natural than that the Clan to which this rugged desert belonged should have been noted for predatory habits. For, among the Highlanders, generally, to rob was thought at least as honourable an employment as to cultivate the soil; and of all the Highlanders the Macdonalds of Glencoe had the least productive soil, and the most convenient and secure den of robbers."[1] This great crime, which has justly entailed upon its perpetrators the severest judgment of posterity, was due to the combination of two of the strongest incitements which existed at the time, first, the indignation of a civilised Government against men who, in the midst of a

[1] Macaulay's *History of England*, vol. iv. p. 192.

peaceful society, lived avowedly and notoriously a life of plunder; and secondly, the fierce and vindictive passions of a neighbouring Clan, to whose hands the punishment was committed, and whose lands and houses had been ravaged and destroyed by the unhappy victims. The massacre of Glencoe is therefore to be regarded as one of the last, and one of the most signal examples of the old evils which we have traced from the days of the Wolf of Badenoch, in the power of Celtic Feudalism to rouse ferocious passions—in the cruel and treacherous deeds which men comparatively civilised and enlightened could persuade themselves to defend and even to adopt when they came into contact with it.

Another interval of twenty-three years separates the massacre of Glencoe from the first Jacobite rising of the Eighteenth Century, in 1715. This rising was so short, and so easily suppressed, that its effects were altogether evanescent, and can hardly have interrupted in the smallest degree the gradual and steady processes of change which were happily bringing to an end the terrible abuses and miseries of the Clans. The Rebellion was suppressed within Five Months. There were the usual incidents—the treachery of Chiefs—the gallantry of their Highland followers. The Earl of Mar attended a Levee of George I. on the day before he left London to raise the standard of the Pretender in the valley of the Dee. In their invasion of England, where, as is well known, they penetrated as far as Preston, they were miserably led. On the other hand, at the

Battle of Sheriffmuir, the Clans fought with their accustomed courage, and won quite half of the honours of the day. But for more than a single battle the military power of Celtic Feudalism was nearly gone. Their surrender in England at Preston, and their dispersion in Scotland, after Sheriffmuir, mark the low point to which it had already fallen.

Again, we have another long interval, from the Rebellion of 1715 to that of "The Forty-Five," an interval of no less than thirty years—or, as it is usually reckoned, a whole generation. This is one of those many intervals between conspicuous events, over which the eye of the historian often passes with a careless and unobservant glance, seeing nothing that catches his attention, or at least nothing of a large class of facts which, nevertheless, are of far higher interest and importance than the cycle of rebellions. Now it is in respect to this interval of time—an interval during which a whole generation was born and rose to manhood, before the last of our civil wars—before "The Forty-Five"—that I am in possession of documents which singularly illustrate the continuity of Scottish history, and the identity of the processes of change through which our civilisation had been steadily advancing over the whole Kingdom from the days of Malcolm Canmore.

Having now indicated the period to which these documents refer, and its importance in an historical point of view, I must add a few words in explanation of the men whose evidence they contain. The management of great Baronial Estates in those days was an object of ambition among men of the highest position in society. It was an employment which had all the dignity, and variety of interest, and extent of power, which belonged to the government of a Province. Smaller Proprietors of land of the oldest families, Clansmen nearly related to their Chief, and men of high public positions, even on the Bench and at the Bar, were among the number of those who undertook such duties, and who devoted to them all the knowledge and culture of their day. Such was the character and position of the two men whose narratives and reports I am about to cite.

Nor is it less important to observe the position of the districts respecting which their evidence is supplied. We have seen how long and how late the worst evils of Celtic Feudalism lingered in those Western Isles of Scotland, which had always been most inaccessible to the central government, and amongst which savage intertribal wars had for many generations kept the people in poverty, and the Kingdom in frequent uneasiness and alarm. We have seen, nevertheless, from the Conferences of Iona, held in 1609, that all these habits and customs were confessed and acknowledged by the Chiefs themselves to be barbarous and illegal, and that reversion to the system of regular rents and of tenures known to the law, was the admitted remedy, and the promised reform. We have seen that in Kintyre the system of agricultural Leases and generally all the relations of Landlord and Tenant came naturally into full operation the moment that district was freed from the Clan Donnel, the last representatives of the old Lords of the Isles, and of a family which for centuries had upheld and handed down the picturesque but savage customs and traditions of the Clans. We have seen, too, that the tenure by Lease which had been enjoyed for centuries, even in the Hebrides, by the blood-relations of the Chiefs, was now in that district extended to those poorer men who constituted the great bulk of the population, but who formerly were only Subtenants, without any tenure except that which arose out of the necessity of having men who could render "services." These services never were exclusively military. The spade-plough[1] was more constantly needed than the sword or the pike. They included every kind of labour, and every kind of exaction by which the produce of labour could be made to support the power, or minister to the rude but lavish and wasteful expenditure of the Chiefs. This great process of the emergence of law and order from under the overlying burden of Celtic violence and confusion, is a process which we have thus seen in its earliest results, but which hitherto we have not seen in the details and methods of its operation. Yet it is these details which are the most interesting facts of all in the history of civilisation—the steps by which so great

---

[1] The "caseroim," the ancient implement of Celtic agriculture— a heavy spade driven by the foot. The word means "crooked foot."

a reform was made—the action of those who were agents in it—the exact condition of things with which they had to deal—and the nature of the powers which were the instruments of their work.

All this is precisely the information supplied to us by papers connected with the management of certain estates which fell into the possession of the Clan Campbell, along with or soon after the acquisition of Kintyre. These estates were purely Hebridean—lying in the Islands of Mull and of Iona, and in the adjoining peninsula of Morven, with one of the outer Islands, Tyree, which had from the most ancient times been closely connected with Iona. All these lands had for centuries been dominated by the Clan Maclean, whose brave but fierce and lawless Chiefs now sleep in numbers beneath the sheltering stones, and the rude knightly effigies of the Reilig Oran.[1] In 1732, about half-way between the two Jacobite risings of 1715 and 1745, Campbell of Stonefield, Sheriff of the County, was sent to examine and report on their condition. From that Report we learn that these lands were universally held in Lease by gentlemen who were themselves either members of the Clan Campbell, or in some cases were Macleans, or by others who, according to the common habit of the Celts, had submitted to the new Chief who was also the new Proprietor. Under these gentlemen came the families of the

---

[1] This is the Celtic name of probably the oldest place of burial still used in the British Islands—that surrounding the walls of St. Oran's Chapel, near the Cathedral of Iona. It dates from the Columban age, the 7th century. "Oran" was one of Columba's followers.

native population, who were called Tenants, but who were only Subtenants, holding at the will of the Leaseholders or Tacksmen, and complaining bitterly of the oppressions under which they laboured. It was the first business of the Sheriff to inquire into the truth of these complaints; and though he indicates that they were exaggerated, yet, in the most practical of all ways, he supports them by suggesting the only remedy. The old Celtic exactions levied by the Chiefs and Chieftains upon their Subtenants, rested and could only rest upon the ultimate power of removal. The Subtenants were not protected in respect to rent or services by any definite covenant or bargain, nor were they protected in respect to tenure by holding for any definite time. Very often the Tacksmen had brought them in upon the lands when these Tacksmen themselves obtained their Lease, just as we have seen that this was the actual case when the De Hays took a farm from the Abbot of Scone in 1312. Moreover, as in that case so in many others, there was an express stipulation in the Lease that the Tacksman should remove these men when he himself removed. In all cases of "Tacks" during all the intervening centuries the Leaseholding Clansman and Tenant held the complete power of the Owner over all his Subtenants, unless this power was restrained by the terms of his own Lease on behalf of the Proprietor. But any such restriction does not appear to have been common, and in the Western Isles, where the powers of Celtic Feudalism had been widest and most unchecked, it was probably unknown. There the dependence of the Subtenant upon the Tacksman, who alone represented the power and position of the Proprietary Chief and the authority of the Clan, was complete and absolute. The proper remedy then was clear,—now that men were giving up the life and the habits of the Clans, and were beginning to look steadily to the improvement of the country, and to the increase of its value, founded upon the increased produce of settled industry. The remedy was to give to the Subtenants the same kind and degree of security which had long been given to the relatives of the Chief—that is, the security of a Covenant or Lease. This accordingly was the policy recommended by Sheriff Campbell. The Leases of certain Tacksmen were about to expire. He advised that they should not be renewed except upon new conditions. Their Subtenants should have the same kind of protection which they themselves enjoyed. The rents and services of these men should be fixed and definite, and their tenure should, in like manner, be of a specified duration. Nay more, the larger Tenants should be bound in their Leases to cause better houses to be built for the smaller class of holders, where these men continued to be Subtenants at all. Many of them, however, were to be lifted out of this category altogether. They were to have Leases directly from the Proprietor, and to become themselves "Tacksmen," with the full status and security of that class.

It is important to observe that this proposed reform rested entirely on the possession and on the exercise of the fullest powers of Ownership on the part of the Proprietor. Moreover, it rested on these powers as exercised over the very pick of those who represented and indeed constituted the Clan. It was the old class of Tacksmen, who held whatever rights belonged by Celtic usages to the blood and personal following of the Chief. Yet, we see here that when these Leases came to an end, the Proprietor of the lands they held could tell them that unless they agreed to entirely new conditions, they must make way for other men. This was the only power of enforcement which the Proprietor could hold or could exert in modifying, reforming, or extirpating the oppressive usages which had become established among the Celts. Nor was this power of removing Clansmen from Farms at the end of their Leases a power which was used as a threat only, without being actually exerted. It was used, as we see, from the Report of Sheriff Campbell, in a great number of cases where the lands were re-let directly to the old Subtenants, or to new men who were more likely than their predecessors to work the new system with intelligence and fidelity. Although this Report was written thirteen years before "The Forty-Five," which is popularly supposed to represent an epoch of change in tenures, and although it goes back to a previous condition of things which implies an unbroken history of many centuries, there is not even a hint or an expression which implies that any doubt existed in the minds of any of the various classes concerned, that the Proprietor was exercising any other powers than those which were not only known to the law but were also familiar to the people.

And as this power was the only engine which could be used to redeem the poorer classes from the oppression of others, so also was it the only engine which could be used to redeem them from the consequences of their own ignorant and barbarous customs. Just as the prohibition and abandonment of some usages, traditional among them, was imposed upon the Tacksmen under the penalty of removal, so the prohibition and abandonment of other usages, as old and as firmly established, was imposed upon the class of Subtenants—under the same penalty of having to leave the estate if they were unwilling to accept the new conditions. In both cases, equally, the first steps towards a civilised condition, and towards agricultural improvement, were taken, and could only be taken, on the strength of the fullest powers and rights of Ownership. Nothing short of those powers could have overcome the desperate tenacity of the people in resisting every change and clinging to habits which, originally bad, had gone from bad to worse through that great law which determines the development of corruption. It is proved by the whole tenor of Sheriff Campbell's Report that the domestic economy of the people in this part of Scotland had remained worse than stationary for more than a thousand years. Although they lived in a country where rock and

stone was abundant, and in general easily accessible
—although a whole Island[1] of the finest limestone
lay off both Mull and Morven, and was separated
from them only by a narrow strait—although the
people had before their eyes for more than six
hundred years the rough but massive and splendid
masonry of the Cathedral of Iona and of St. Oran's
Chapel,—yet they continued to live in hovels composed
of nothing more solid than turf lined, and
perhaps propped on the inside, by wattled branches
of birch, oak, and hazel. These were the lineal
descendants of the houses, dating from prehistoric
times, which sheltered Columba and his brethren
in the Sixth Century, and on which it seems that
no step of advance had been made near the middle
of the Eighteenth, or during an interval of about
eleven hundred years. The rapid decay of such
structures, the constant necessity of removal, was
leading to the destruction of the scanty and shaggy
brushwoods which alone represented the ancient
Caledonian forests. This, however, was by no
means the worst feature of the case. Huts of turf
and wattled twigs may be quite as warm and comfortable
as many of the hovels which in Ireland and
in some of the Hebrides are now always built of
loose stones without cement.

But in a much more important and vital matter,
namely, the husbandry of the people, there is clear
evidence of a ruinous decline. It is impossible
to read the details given in Adamnan's *Life of*

---

[1] The Island of Lismore.

Columba of the agricultural operations of his Monks in Iona, and to compare them with the facts given in Sheriff Campbell's Report, without seeing that there had been a terrible and a truly barbarous decline. It had become the universal custom of the people to cut their corn crops of oats, or an inferior barley, high above the ground. The considerable portion of straw which remained attached to the ear was then destroyed by fire, the ear itself being much wasted in the process. This was the only process by which they knew how to get at the grain free from husks, the half-roasted grain falling out during the combustion, and being afterwards roughly ground by the hand between two stones, a primitive form of Mill, called Querns, which has survived to our own day in some of the remoter Hebrides. The remaining straw which had been left upon the ground, instead of being used for the food of cattle, or for manure, was used for thatch —the whole of this valuable product being thus practically lost—because fern and heath, which was in "great plenty" all over the country, would have made better thatch, and was useless for other purposes. All these barbarous and wasteful usages had been the natural and inevitable result of the insecure life which all classes had led in these countries under the system of the Clans. Men will not even think of building substantial houses, nor barns with threshing-floors, nor mills, when such erections, together with their owners, were constantly exposed to destruction by fire and sword. It was a positive advantage, under such conditions, to have no buildings except such as could be raised in a couple of days out of materials delved with the spade and cut by the hatchet. As usual, men being such creatures of habit, very soon lost all sense of the want of better things. In 1723 the gradual settlement of the country had so far proceeded that one or two of the Tacksmen had built Corn Mills. But the people persisted in using the old Querns. So it was with everything. No improvement could gain even a momentary footing, except when imposed upon the people by the authority of those from whom alone their tenure came. Accordingly throughout Sheriff Campbell's Report every proposal he makes is founded on the unquestioned right of the Owner of an estate to let it to whomsoever he liked, and on whatever terms he could get Tenants to accept possession. Moreover, we see that this power was used not only sometimes and in a few cases, but systematically over large areas of land. It involved very often no less than the old immemorial work of "planting" the country with selected men.

In making this selection political ends were inseparably blended with economic considerations. The Clans of the mainland had been longer in contact with the advancing civilisation of the Low Country. They were both the most loyal men and the men best acquainted with such improved methods of agriculture as were known in that day. Accordingly when a Clansman secured a Lease of some large tract of land in the Western

Islands, it was often his first care to plant it with Campbells, or others of his own dependants brought from the mainland of Argyllshire. Thus the Sheriff reports of three well-known such tracts in the Island of Mull, that having been formerly let on Lease to gentlemen of the name of Campbell, these Tacksmen "had gone a good length to plant there several districts with people of the same name, or their friends, and that it must be acknowledged the Tenants were beginning to manage those lands better than the rest of the country." In marked contrast with this result, he reported in respect to another district, that it had been let to one of the old Clan of M'Lean, and that he, in true Celtic fashion, "kept a swarm of poor people of his own name around him who had neither the skill nor the substance (capital) to manage the land to any purpose." The "keeping" of those people on the farm is not ascribed by the Sheriff to any difficulty in removing them arising out of Tenure, but expressly to the "lenity" of the Tacksman. The truth probably was that he followed the traditions of his class, which encouraged a crowd of dependants, who performed for the Tacksmen all the services they required, and were content themselves with a bare subsistence. This, with occasional plenty, could generally be obtained in former times by plunder, and in 1723 it was only beginning to be felt by these poor people that even a bare subsistence could not be secured when plunder had been stopped, and before industry had begun.

There is no indication, however, in the Sheriff's Report that he saw or even thought of any excess of population over the resources of the country. On the contrary, one of the stipulations he recommends for the new Leases was that the Tenant should be bound to bring into the country, and plant a certain number of men as Subtenants, who should cultivate what was then practically waste. These men, thus introduced and planted by the power and care of the Proprietors, together with those other Subtenants to whom he gave Leases, and redeemed from the exactions of the larger Tacksmen, are the progenitors of the men now known as " Crofters." They have been mythically represented as a native population inheriting for centuries a certain fixity of tenure, independent of the Owner, whereas the historical fact is that the process by which they were " planted " is in many cases, as we shall see further on, later even than 1737 by more than half a century.

There is, moreover, another part of the Sheriff's Report which shows the unquestioned power then exercised by the Landlord in the disposal of his property. This part relates to the question of rents. It was no easy question under the circumstances of the case. The money rents previously paid by the Subtenants to the Tacksmen were ascertained by an examination on oath. The services exacted, too, as well as any fines or feudal dues, were found out as nearly as possible by the same method. But as it was one great object to put an end to Services, and to all dues or exactions merely arbitrary, the difficulty remained as to the additional rent which the commutation of these Services would be fairly worth. All these points resolved themselves at last into the value of the produce of land under the existing conditions of agriculture, but taking into account such of the new conditions as would tell at once on the profit of the Tenant. But here again the Sheriff was met with the difficulty that he was accustomed to consider land values only on the mainland, and did not know enough of the local circumstances to estimate such values in the Islands. This problem could only be solved by taking the values set upon the land by the people themselves. In other words, it could only be solved by putting the lands up to local competition. As soon as the people were assured that they would be protected by Leases and by the authority of the Proprietor, from the resentment and vengeance of their old masters, the Tacksmen, it was found that they came forward and offered freely for their small possessions.

Here we have an example—not of conduct being governed by abstract theories, but—of an abstract principle emerging out of the practical necessities of conduct, and seeking expression in a "rugged maxim hewn from life." The worthy Sheriff was not thinking of any science of Political Economy when he said that until the Subtenants could be persuaded to offer frankly "he could have no tolerable information of the value of the country, since it is by the competition of tenants that the value of land can be known." Political Economy, as a science, had not risen above the horizon in Scotland in 1732. Adam Smith was then a weakly, but a studious and absent little boy, nine years of age, doing his lessons in the grammar-school of Kirkcaldy, and forty-four years were yet to elapse before the epoch of his immortal *Inquiry into the Wealth of Nations*. The Sheriff's aphorism on the only method of ascertaining values was nothing more than the half-conscious expression of a general rule drawn directly from observation and experience. None the less is this sentence an emphatic, because an unconscious, testimony to the doctrine and the practice of the time : and none the less was the conduct of the people in those Insular Estates a testimony equally emphatic to their own recognition of the practice, not as an oppression but as a privilege. It implied of course that the Owner of the Estate had the right of freely disposing of his lands, as an inseparable part of the right of Ownership. It implied also that they themselves had no other right of tenure than that of agreement, and that failing such agreement they were liable to removal. But no doubt or question as to either of these facts had ever entered their heads. Nothing in their own past history or traditions could have raised it. Some of them probably knew that their fathers had moved from the lands of one Chief who could not protect them, to the lands of another who could. Others of them perhaps knew that their progenitors had at no very distant date enlisted under the Chief of the Macleans as soldiers enlist under a famous Captain, and had been allowed to settle on his lands as his "men" and retainers. Others again, doubtless, had themselves been removed at the end of a Lease from the farm of one Tacksman Tenant to the farm of another. All of them knew by daily experience that upon these Tenants they themselves were absolutely dependent, and could and would be removed if they failed in dues or services. Lastly, they all knew that those who were above them—the Tacksmen, their masters, and often their oppressors —who were the very aristocracy of the Clan,—themselves held their lands by no independent right, but by Leases terminating at certain dates, and freely granted by the Proprietor. It was not a loss, but an immense gain to them to be raised from tenancy-at-will to tenancy under Lease. For the first time in their history they were free to bargain for their farms. For the first time they could be sure that nothing would be exacted from them beyond the terms of that bargain, and that their removal could not take place except for breach of covenant, or until the expiry of a certain time. Accordingly the Sheriff reported that when they were fully assured of protection they came in and offered for these new and great advantages a considerable augmentation of rent.

We have here the clearest evidence of the perfect continuity of law and of practice in respect to the Ownership and Occupation of land which has marked the progress of Scotland over the whole of its area and from the earliest centuries. We see the fullest powers of Ownership assumed and recognised as undoubted and unquestioned, and we see its functions in promoting the civilisation of the country as clearly as we have already seen it at earlier periods when Parliament appealed to it for the suppression of intolerable evils. Lest, however, this evidence of Sheriff Campbell should be in any way subject to detraction from his relations with his Chief, by a fortunate accident we have, a few years later, the same evidence confirmed and amplified on the authority of an independent and a very celebrated man.

Among the names of illustrious Scotchmen at this critical period of our history, there is no name, perhaps, which shines with a purer lustre than that of Duncan Forbes of Culloden. Himself a Highlander of Highlanders, with an intimate knowledge of their character and habits, he was able to sympathise, so far as mere feeling was concerned, with the personal attachments which made them Jacobite. But his religion, and his culture, and the noble profession of the Law—of which he was a distinguished ornament, and of which he rose to be the head in his native country—kept him true to the historical developments of the Scottish people. He used all his influence, and strained every nerve to prevent the Rebellion; and when it was suppressed, by the bloody battle fought upon his own Estate, he exerted himself with equal energy to mitigate the vengeance of the Government against the vanquished. As a Statesman, as a Lawyer, and as a Highlander belonging to another and a distant Clan, he had pre-eminent qualifications for giving wise advice on the difficult questions—partly political and partly economic—which were involved in the management of such Estates as those which had come into the hands of the Argyll family in the Islands. The possessor of them at that time was John, the Second Duke (1678-1743), who as a Soldier played an illustrious part in the wars of Marlborough, and at home as a Statesman took a share not less illustrious in the Councils which, at the death of Queen Anne in 1714, secured the Protestant Succession.[1] These two men were intimate friends. Their sympathies were the same in the great Constitutional questions of their day, and they were not less alike in those dispositions of character on which so much depends in the management of affairs. Difficulties had evidently arisen in carrying into effect all the recommendations of Sheriff Campbell. He had said in his Report that the people seemed "bewitched"

---

[1] Lecky's *History of England*, vol. i. p. 164. It is a curious illustration of the power of genius in Sir Walter Scott's immortal works, that this Duke—the companion in arms of Marlborough and Eugene—the friend of Pope and Thomson, and sung by both—is nevertheless now commonly identified as "Jeanie Deans' Duke" from the beautiful and touching story in the *Heart of Midlothian*. The additional Dukedom of Greenwich was granted to him by Queen Anne for his public services. As this Duke had no sons, the Title of Greenwich lapsed with his life. The present Duke of Buccleuch is his only direct descendant, through a daughter.

in the tenacity of their adherence to their wasteful customs. The Tacksmen had opposed a passive but combined resistance to changes which affected so much their own power; and they had easily succeeded in persuading the simple and ignorant people under them that old customs were better than new conditions. Under these circumstances, and in view of the expiry of a number of existing Leases, Forbes of Culloden, in the same year in which he attained the dignity of Lord President of the Supreme Court of Law in Scotland, 1737, undertook for his friend a mission to his Island Estates in Mull, Morven, and Tyree.

The account of his journey, and the Report of what he saw and encountered, is one of the most interesting and authentic documents we possess in respect to the condition of the people of the Western Coast and Islands at that time.[1] It confirms the previous account of Sheriff Campbell in every particular. The Lord President is emphatic in his testimony, and severe in his language as to the use made by the Tacksmen of the absolute power they held over the subordinate tenants. He speaks of their "tyranny" and "oppression." He speaks of their "unmerciful exactions." He speaks of the land even lying waste by reason of these exactions, and declares that "if the system had continued but a few years longer, the Islands would have been

---

[1] It has been now published in Appendix A to the "Crofter Report," 1884, vol. i. p. 387. It was recovered among the papers of Lady Mary Coke, daughter of John Duke of Argyll and Greenwich, by the present Earl of Home, who most kindly presented it to me.

entirely unpeopled." He reports that within the previous seven years "above one hundred families had been reduced to beggary and driven out of the Island." Yet these Tacksmen were the genuine representatives of the Clan system. They constituted, in fact, what was called the Clan—for those below them had long ceased to be treated or regarded as more than "the men" under them; it is plain, that both by law and by continuous usage, the Leaseholding Clansmen ruled with absolute power—that is to say, so far as the possession of the land was concerned.

Historically speaking, the existence of this power —more than the use made of it—is the important point. The use made of it must have varied in different districts, and still more in the hands of different men. But the fact is all-important that this absolute power is referred to as universally existing in the hands of the Tacksmen over all who held land under them. No doubt on this fact is even thought of. Throughout the narrative there is not one single indication of any limitations or obstacles in the way of this power, arising out of any independent or customary rights of subordinate tenure. The Tacksman held over the whole of his Farm, and, during the term of his Tack, the whole powers of Ownership, in so far as they were delegated by the Lease. Amongst these powers there was of necessity the power of removing those who would not, or could not, pay the rents or perform the services which the Tacksman might demand as the condition of possession. But since that demand was indefinite, and variable from year to year, the condition of the Subtenants was necessarily precarious. For such evils there could be only one remedy. They arose from the powers of Ownership being separated from its special interests, and therefore from its natural motives. They were delegated to men whose own possession was not permanent, and whose interests were therefore not identified with the growing wealth and permanent prosperity of the people. The remedy clearly was to go back to a connection founded on the nature of things—to keep in the hands of the Proprietor, and in his alone, the power of removal—to deal directly with the Subtenants— to give to them the same measure of security which the Tacksmen had themselves enjoyed. It was, as Culloden[1] expressed it, " to deliver them from the tyranny of Tacksmen, to free them from the oppression of Services and Herezelds, and to encourage them to improve their farms by giving them a sort of property in their grounds for nineteen years by Leases, if they showed themselves worthy of the intended favour by offering frankly for their farms such rent as fairly and honestly they could bear." If farms with Subtenants on them were to be let at all to the old class of Tacksmen, these Subtenants were to get a separate tenure, subsisting for the same period as the Lease.

[1] I adopt here the Highland custom of calling Forbes by the name of his estate.

Such, accordingly, was the policy adopted by Culloden, as it had been already recommended by the Sheriff. Culloden, however, came not only to recommend, but also armed with authority to act upon his opinion. Accordingly, he announced to the Subtenants that he was prepared to let their lands to them upon Leases, and he invited them to offer. To the Tacksmen he made the like proposal, under the stipulated restrictions and conditions. To his surprise he found himself met by an organised combination not to offer at all, or to offer only very inadequate rents. The Tacksmen had persuaded the Subtenants to regard with fear and with suspicion the proposals made to them. The first thing to be done was to break up a combination which rested on the cunning and selfishness of a few, and on the ignorance and prejudice of the many. And this Culloden was prepared to do at any cost. During some days of explanation and persuasion, he found the most effectual argument to be a warning that he would leave them in their former subjection to the Tacksmen. At last the truth dawned on the minds of some of them, and he induced a certain number of the small Tenants to make tolerably fair offers for their holdings. These offers he immediately accepted, and concluded a bargain with those who made them. Dealing with the Tacksmen, he was more peremptory and severe. He had in his own suite some gentlemen of the same Highland class, but who, from living on the mainland, were better acquainted with the essential conditions of agricultural progress. Some of these were induced to make fair offers for the larger farms, whose former Tenants were manœuvring so unscrupulously to thwart the most necessary reforms. Suddenly several of these men found that their farms were re-let to others, and that they themselves were dispossessed. Such examples speedily had the desired effect. The Subtenants, when they found that any reasonable offer of their own was at once accepted, and that they ran no risk of being relegated to the dominion of the Tacksmen because of a higher offer, came in readily, and became themselves regular Tacksmen—relieved from all but a few stipulated services, and possessed for the first time of a definite tenure of their small possessions. The remaining Tacksmen also became more reasonable, and in the final result Culloden had the satisfaction of reporting that those large Insular Estates had been re-let, with some little immediate increase of rent, and under such new conditions as would lay the foundations of indefinite improvement for the future.

The Leases which were given at this time carried fully into effect the great reform which it was their object to attain. Many of them were given directly to men who had been Subtenants. Amidst the almost universal neglect and destruction which have overtaken old Leases, a fortunate accident has preserved some few specimens of those which were drawn up by Culloden, and signed by him as Com-

missioner over the Duke's Estate, at a time when
he himself had become Lord President of the Court
of Session. They are of considerable interest on
more points than one. The application to Subtenants, who had always been Tenants-at-will, of
the old law and practice of Scotland in respect to
Leases of Farms, was not without some difficulties.
Not only in the Highlands, but all over Scotland,
this class of Occupier lived in clusters, groups,
villages, or "Clachans." Some parts of the Farm
they generally held in common. Other parts they
held in various shares, generally divided on the
"runrig" system by yearly lots. Partly, no doubt,
for facilities of defence, partly as a traditional
survival of mere habit from the far distant day
of Village Communities, this method of occupation was nearly universal. But never in historic
times had these Townships any corporate existence
either in law or in usage. For centuries the
Proprietors had been moving some, and planting
others, whilst individuals were brought in from
time to time by the same authority, with the
grant of "rooms," or of shares or portions of the
Farm. To whom then, were the new Leases to be
given? To the group, or to the individual Tenants
of whom the group actually consisted at the time?
Culloden was not a man to be foiled by speculative
difficulties, nor was he a man to make any changes
not really needed for his purpose. He solved the
difficulty by taking things as they actually stood,
by changing as little as possible, and by applying

the principle of the Lease to the actual Occupiers, and according to their actual methods of occupation. Thus in the case of one Farm occupied by six Tenants, but unequally divided, a Lease of 1739 was granted by name to each of them, but with a specification of the share belonging to each man or woman. The whole Farm as known by its name, with all its pertinents as known by use and wont, is let to the six Tenants, for the term of nineteen years, in the proportions specified—one-half to Hugh M'Lean, one-sixth to Rachel MacArthur, one-twelfth to Donald Macdonald, and so on. Thus far, the Tenants were dealt with separately, and the Lease was given to each in his individual capacity. That which the Lease assured to each of them was the "peaceable possession" of the Farm, in the specified shares, "during the space (of time) aforesaid." Subletting, or assigning, was excluded, but each Tenant could leave his share to his natural heirs. On the other hand, there was a clause which recognised all the Tenants as in some sense, and for some purposes, a Community, because in some practices they were so of necessity, from living so close together, and from possessing more or less grazing land in common. This clause was a special provision, that in case of the failure of any one of the Tenants, the others were bound either to take up his share themselves, or else to find another fit Tenant who could do so on the same conditions. The rent was a fixed sum for the Farm as a whole, for which all the Tenants were bound as a Community, jointly and severally. Failure in the payment of rent voided the Lease, and the Proprietor was then free to re-let the Farm to others. The share payable by each was left apparently to their own arrangement, but the arrangement would naturally follow the proportions specified in the Lease. Then, after the clause fixing the rent, comes the new clause which constituted the great reform in favour of this class of Tenant— the clause in respect to Services. The words are these (following the sum of rent) :—" and that (sum) in full satisfaction of all Herezelds and other prestations (obligations) and services whatsoever, which are hereby discharged,—except the services of Tenants for repairing harbours, mending highways, or making or repairing Mill Leads (conduits) for the general benefit of the Island." [1]

In these words we see the symbol and consummation of a change which amounted to a revolution. In the abolition of all Services, except a few strictly limited and defined, which were for purposes directly connected with the benefit of a whole district and of a large community, we see the last step, or almost the last, from the mediæval to modern conditions of society. In the admission of a class to the benefit of Leases who had hitherto been always merely Tenants-at-will, and had in practice been often compelled to move from the necessity either of seeking protection or of rendering service, we see the elevation of a large portion of the people from a

[1] This Lease, with explanatory notes, is given in Appendix I. p. 323.

state of complete uncertainty and dependence, to a state in which they could themselves rely, and could make others rely, upon definite engagements.

Nor is the significance of these Leases given to Subtenants some years before "The Forty-Five" exhausted, when we have noted the clauses which they do contain. Hardly less remarkable than the insertion of some of these clauses, is the omission of other clauses which in such Instruments had been almost universal. Services of a military kind had for many hundred years been among the fundamental obligations of those to whom the occupation of land had been lent or given. Even in the Kintyre Leases, which we have seen were granted about one hundred years before the Leases framed by Culloden, there were at least some surviving echoes of the Military Ages. In the full stream of those Ages, when we put our ear to the language of such Instruments, we hear, as it were, always the sound of fighting—the atmosphere of war. If it was not always being actually waged, it was at least always in habitual contemplation. In the Leases of about 1639 there are only a few customary phrases, coming from the old days—phrases, which were even then little more than survivals of a time drawing to its close. Under the influence of the alarm which was occasioned by the first Jacobite Rebellion of 1715, Parliament had in that year[1] prohibited, as contrary to public policy, all clauses in Charters or Leases which imposed the ancient

---

[1] First of Geo. I. cap. 54.

obligations of "Personal Attendance, Hunting, Hosting, Watching, and Warding." These had been the last survivals, but they had long been practically obsolete. They now became illegal. Accordingly in the Leases of Culloden in 1739, there is not even a whisper of the kind. We have entered finally on the times of peaceful industry.

But there is another feature of these Leases which is remarkable. Just as some old customary clauses were dropped, both as obsolete and as no longer lawful, so also some other clauses which were soon to become universal, had not yet come to be introduced. I refer to what are called the "cropping clauses"—stipulations to secure good husbandry, and to prevent the deterioration of the land by gross violations of its rules. In those Leases of 1739, there is not a word upon the subject. Doubtless this was due to the fact that the attention of Culloden was concentrated on the one great fundamental reform of establishing in the class of Subtenants the principle of tenure by Lease and at a fixed rent, instead of tenure at Will, and subject to services vague, indefinite, and unlimited. One step at a time—seems to have been his motto and his method of proceeding.

But curious and instructive as these facts are, in respect to the first steps then taken for improving the condition of the Western Highlands, they would be incomplete without giving some account of the evidence we derive from the same distinguished man as to the depths of ignorance and of barbarism into which the people had actually fallen, and on the necessity for further steps of remedy and reform. Culloden was not content with visiting Mull and Morven—districts which were near to the mainland and comparatively accessible. He determined to inspect personally the Island of Tyree, which lies from twenty to thirty miles farther out into the Western Ocean. Unlike the nearer Hebrides, this Island is not mountainous but low and flat, with large areas of very fine land, capable of raising excellent crops of corn. Its very name is said to be derived from its agricultural richness—the Iona Monks having called it "Terra Ethica," the land of corn;[1] and its Celtic name still retaining the letters of this derivation in the form of Thirithe. The climate is better than on the mainland, because the heavy rain clouds which shed their torrents on Ben More and the other hills of Mull, pass over without notice the unobtrusive levels of Tyree. An old Gaelic poem calls the Island "the Low-lying Land of Barley." Even without any culture the natural grasses and pastures of the Island are exceptionally green and rich, so that cattle can live and thrive upon it with less help than is generally required in the Highlands from food prepared and stored by human foresight. Yet on this Island, so favoured by nature, Culloden found the people far poorer than in the Isle of Mull, where soil and climate were all greatly inferior. The conditions of agricultural knowledge and prac-

---

[1] The word "ech" or "ich" signifies corn or barley, and the name of the Island passed through several stages of decay during the Fourteenth and Fifteenth Centuries. See Reeves's *Adamnan*, p. 48.

tice which he found prevailing may well seem incredible in a country where, undoubtedly, a far higher civilisation had given lessons to the people more than a thousand years before. Barley was the staple produce of Tyree, but the land, from never being allowed to rest and from being never manured, was so overrun with rank strong weeds that it was an absolute impossibility to drive a sickle through it. Culloden never saw fields covered with a greater load of herbage than the corn-fields in Tyree, but when this herbage was examined not one-tenth part was corn, the rest being all wild carrot, mustard, and other weeds. The poor creatures who depended on these crops did not know how to clear the land of this vegetation, into which all the natural fertility of the soil was allowed to pass. As they could not cut their corn they knew no other mode of gathering it than by pulling it up by the roots. Then they sacrificed the straw by burning, whilst the grain, from being half roasted, became unsaleable. Even this operation could not be performed until the noxious seeds had ripened before the corn, and had time to be shed upon the land to the still more complete suffocation of each succeeding crop. These were but samples of innumerable other practices, equally barbarous, which Culloden had not time to specify or describe, but which he dismisses with the significant general description, "all the other ridiculous processes of husbandry which almost utterly destroy the Island." He traces all these evils to the ignorance and poverty of the people, consequent on the exactions of the Tacksmen. He found himself encountered by the same kind of combination as in Mull. The remedy he recommended was also the same, and the measures he took to break down an interested and ignorant oppostion, were identical in both cases. With equal difficulty he at last persuaded some of the small Tenants to accept the security of Leases, and several of the larger Farms he re-let to gentlemen from the mainland, who came under the new reformed conditions.

The graphic and authentic picture thus drawn of the condition of a Hebridean Estate in the second quarter of the Eighteenth Century, is a picture of the whole of the Highland area, with such local modifications as were due to the comparative nearness of each district to the old centres of civilisation and of law. It is the picture of Celtic Feudalism dying hard. But it was dying—and it had been dying for a long time from causes with which the Jacobite rebellions had nothing whatever to do. In principle it was already dead when Culloden wrote, eight years before " The Forty-Five." Everything he says implies that nothing of it was left except a few traditions. Some of its worst evils had already been put an end to, even in the Hebrides, where it had attained its most rank development. The ferocious feuds and fightings of the Clans had ceased for more than a hundred years. Reiving and thieving had not been ended, for this was carried on systematically to a somewhat later period, and was still indeed the habitual resource of the Clans wherever they were in proximity to richer lands which could be plundered. But the same resource was not open to the poor people of the distant Hebrides. Nothing of the Clan system remained to them except the old power of unlimited exactions, in the hands of Tacksmen who had come to represent the Chiefs and Chieftains of other days. In the ages of intertribal war and plunder this power had its compensations, of a kind, to those who lived under it. But in the dawning age of peace and industry, it was a practice of the Clan system which presented an insuperable obstacle to progress. The transformation of this power for evil into a power for good, had been the great work of reformation all over Scotland. For this purpose nothing was required except to carry back the power to the only legal foundation on which it had ever rested, namely, the power of Ownership, and so to evoke the higher motives which must inevitably give to it a wise direction. Accordingly, nothing is more remarkable in the Report of Culloden, as it had been in the Report of the Sheriff, than the undoubting certainty with which he assumed, and everybody else assumed, that, even in those distant centres of Celtic Feudalism, the Proprietors of the land had the fullest right to let it to all comers. Without this right, Culloden could have done nothing and advised nothing. If the Occupiers could have insisted on remaining, they could have insisted on continuing all the barbarous customs to which they were ignorantly but passionately attached. To this day they might have been living on crops of which one-tenth was corn and nine-tenths were weeds. They might have been pulling them up by the roots, consuming all the valuable straw, and damaging by fire the little residue of grain. The improvement of the country would certainly have been postponed for generations. Those only who know the desperate and almost superstitious tenacity with which they clung, and in some places do even now cling, to customs and usages of the most injurious kind, can estimate what the West Highlands would have been if, in the last century, they had been separated in law, as they had long been separated in lawlessness, from the redeeming agencies at work in the hands of Ownership for the improvement and civilisation of the Scottish Kingdom.

On one point I have repeated the language of Culloden almost with a feeling of compunction. His Report is expressed with great severity as respects the conduct and the habits of a class which was then, and had long been, one of the most essential elements of society in the Highlands—the class of gentlemen Tenants who held farms under Leases or Tacks from the Proprietor. The remnants of this class survived down to our own times. I have a personal recollection of some of them, all of whom were excellent, and some of them even distinguished, men. Not a few were old soldiers, and many were descendants from collateral branches of the family of their Chief. None of them were Farmers in the modern sense of the word, although some of them acquired a taste for, and knowledge of, the breeding of cattle, by which they made an adequate profit and lived mainly on the produce of the farm. Beyond this, and perhaps the making of some fences, very few of them were agricultural improvers, and I know of no case in which any great step was taken by men of this class in introducing into the Highlands those reforms in the cultivation of land of which the country stood so much in need. On the other hand, all those whom I have known or heard of as belonging to this class, were gentlemen in the best meaning of the term—men incapable of a dishonourable action, and disposed to deal as justly and humanely with their inferiors as was consistent with the standard of obligation universally recognised in their day and generation. It is possible that Culloden, though himself a Highlander, may not have kept fully in mind what that standard of obligation was in the remoter parts of the country where the progress of law and of legally defined rights had not yet broken down the vague customs and usages which had come down to them through many generations. It is well, however, that the glamour which fiction and romance have cast around these usages should be dispelled by the broad daylight of Culloden's evidence, and that the incompatibility of those customs with the first elements of our modern civilisation should be seen now as it was seen, not after, but before the "Forty-Five," by a great Lawyer and a great Statesman, brought into personal contact with the whole conditions of society which had been moulded by them.

Culloden does not explain the nature of the "services" or "exactions" which were imposed on the Subtenants by the Tacksmen or Leaseholders. But this omission can be supplied from other sources. They were doubtless the same as those usually paid to Proprietors where there were no Tacksmen, or where such Proprietors were of the smaller class, living on the spot as the Tacksmen did. They are to be found given in detail in a very instructive paper, drawn up in 1795 by Sir John Sinclair, for the Board of Agriculture. That paper refers especially to the northern counties of Cromarty, Ross, Sutherland, and Caithness, with the Islands of Orkney and Shetland. But the same customs prevailed everywhere in the Highlands, and, indeed, at a still older date, over the whole British Islands. Specie or money being very rare, the rents of the small Tenants were principally paid in grain—that is, in Bear or Oats. "In addition to the rent," says Sir John, "the Tenants of that description were bound to pay the following services, namely, tilling, dunging, sowing, and harrowing a part of an extensive farm in the Proprietor's (or Tacksman's) possession, providing a certain quantity of peats for his fuel, thatching a part of his houses, furnishing straw-ropes, or ropes of heath for that purpose, and for securing his corn in the barnyard, weeding the land, leading a certain quantity of turf from the common for manuring, mowing, making, and ingathering the hay, the spontaneous produce of the meadow and marshy ground, cutting down, harvesting, threshing out, manufacturing, and carrying to market or seaport a part of the produce of the farm." Besides these services, the Tenants paid in kind the following articles under the name of customs, namely, straw bags, ropes made of hair for drawing the plough, reeds used for similar purposes, tethers, which, being fixed in the ground by a peg or small stake, and the cattle tied to them, prevented them from wandering over the open country, straw for thatching, etc. The Tenants also, according to the extent of their possessions, kept a certain number of cattle during the winter season—paid vicarage on the smaller tythes; as of lamb, wool, etc., a certain number of fowls and eggs, veal, kid, butter, and cheese; and on the sea-coast the tythe of their fish and oil, besides assisting in carrying sea-ware for manure. Sometimes, also, a certain quantity of lint was spun for the lady of the house, and a certain quantity of woollen yarn annually exacted. Sir J. Sinclair tells us that such were the "services" "which almost universally prevailed" in the county of Caithness, so late as thirty or forty years before he wrote—that is, so late as (say) 1760, or twenty-four years later than the Report of Culloden.[1]

It is needless to say that payments and services so numerous, so various, and so indefinite in amount, might be so worked, and, indeed, could not fail to

[1] *Agricultural Reports,* Scotland, vol. iv., part iv., County Caithness.

be so worked as to leave the small Tenant no certain time for the cultivation of his own land on any improved system.

Now, it is important to observe, that most of these services and exactions, even when due, never could have been actually imposed by the great Landowners, because they had no farms in their own hands scattered all over the country upon which alone such labour could be of any value. But the smaller Proprietors could, and did, exact them, at least near their own residences; and when Tacksmen were allowed to sub-let without restrictions, these services must have become widely oppressive and destructive to industry.

The reform, therefore, which consisted in the double operation of letting farms directly to those who had been Subtenants, and of limiting or abolishing the power of imposing services in the hands of individual Tacksmen, was a reform of the first order of importance.

As I am in possession of some of the Leases which were granted nineteen and twenty years later by Archibald, third Duke of Argyll, I am able to explain the general nature of the further steps then taken in pursuance of the same principles. This is an interval which overleaps the famous "Forty-Five," and at the end of it we find nothing but the quiet, continuous progress of a change which had been commenced before. As the Lord President Forbes was quite as intimate a friend of this Duke as he had been of his more illustrious brother, it is probable that Duke Archibald's Leases embodied the latest recommendations of Culloden. In the first place, the "Tacks" or Leases given in, and subsequent to, 1755, to the larger class of Tenants, that is, to the old class of Tacksmen, prohibited all subletting upon "precarious tenures," that is, tenures at Will, with dues as uncertain as the tenure. In the second place, the smaller Leaseholder himself, although still bound to perform for the Proprietor certain services as part of his rent, had these services not only strictly defined and limited, but also made redeemable at a fixed and specified rate of commutation. So many days' service each year—twelve or twenty-four days—was the usual stipulation, and it is a curious illustration of the enormous change in the value of labour, as well as in the value of money, that one day's labour was commutable at the rate of one penny, so that twelve days' service in the year was redeemable by the addition of one shilling sterling to the rent. It was, moreover, a special part of the stipulation that the labour or service could not be exacted either at seed-time or at harvest. In this modified form, the rendering of a certain fixed amount of service or of day's labour each year has been a stipulation surviving in some cases down to the present day.

Between the Report of Culloden and the potato failure and consequent famine of 1846-7, I am in possession of a continuous series of documents showing the progress of affairs in the Island of Tyree. They prove in the greatest detail that every single step towards improvement which has been taken during the last 150 years has been taken by the Proprietor, and not by the people. Not only so, but every one of these steps, without exception, has been taken against the prevailing opinions and feelings of the people at the time. "All in this farm very poor, and against any change"—such is the description repeated over and over again in a detailed Report on each Farm sent to my grandfather, John, sixth Duke, in 1803, when he was contemplating certain changes to which I shall afterwards refer. Great poverty and great ignorance are always "against any change." They are invariably associated with a languor of mind which is incompatible with the possibility of improvement. The very desire of better things is absent, and even if the desire existed the means would still be wanting. Under such conditions every reform must begin outside the people, and absolutely requires to be pressed upon them. I am not speaking merely of the outlays of money, which come from capital. I am speaking of those exercises of mind—of foresight, and of authority—which come from Ownership, and cannot be enforced without the possession of its fullest rights. The abolition of the Run-rig system was always most unpopular in the Highlands. In Tyree, as elsewhere, it was abolished, and could only be abolished by the authority of Ownership. Again—illicit distillation, with the worse than waste of an immense quantity of grain,—was another inveterate habit, suppressed with the greatest difficulty by the same power. Every subsequent measure of improvement—the regular division of individual holdings—the fencing of them—the selection of the best candidates for the occupation of them—the prohibition of cultivation on land liable to destructive sand-blowing—the building of a better class of houses—the introduction of ploughs in substitution for the primitive " crooked spade "—the introduction of carts—of grain of a better kind—of superior stock—of dairy farming; in short, every single item of progress in agriculture has been the work, and often the arduous and expensive work, of the Proprietor. Moreover, even all these would have been useless without the arrest laid upon reckless sub-division, and the steady progress made towards the establishment of more adequate and comfortable possessions.

The legislative measures which followed the suppression of the Rebellion of 1745—the disarming of the people, and the prohibition of the native dress,[1] except as a uniform in the Forces of the Crown—were blows struck at Celtic Feudalism with a special view to extinguish its political danger, along with its spirit and its military power. These measures were needless, and if they had stood alone, would probably have had nothing but a bad effect. Causes, however, far deeper seated than any legislative measures of this kind, had long been operating in the right direction, and these had already almost completed what no mere statute could effect. There

[1] 20 Geo. II. cap. 51.

was, however, one Act of Parliament passed at this time which marks the consummation of a great change, and which raised a hot discussion closely connected with the subject of the present work. This was the abolition of the Heritable Jurisdictions. Accidental events had given this question an importance which it did not really possess. The Rebellion of 1745 had made a deep impression on the public mind both in England and in the Lowlands of Scotland. Englishmen had seen a Highland army invading their country, and marching in triumph through Preston and Manchester as far south as Derby. London for a time had been in a state of panic. Scotchmen had seen their Capital taken, and a Popish Pretender holding his court at Holyrood. Both England and Scotland could not but take serious note of the fact that the Jacobite forces had twice defeated the Royal army in pitched battles in the open field—first, on the 20th September 1745 at Prestonpans, near Edinburgh, where Sir John Cope was badly beaten, with the loss of his artillery and stores; a second time at Falkirk on the 17th January 1746, where General Hawley was routed not less completely. And this was the second of these Jacobite Rebellions within 30 years. The victory at Culloden, therefore, although it seemed to be for the time complete, did not, and could not set men's minds at rest. They were disposed to look with anger and alarm into the causes and the system which enabled a few great Nobles to raise armies of ten and twelve thousand men, and at such frequent intervals, to contend on almost equal terms with the armies of the Kingdom. In this state of mind they confounded together, as men are very apt to do under such conditions, two, or more than two, very different things. They confounded, amongst others, the power of Clanship or of Chiefship with the power of Heritable Jurisdictions. In this they were not only completely mistaken, but altogether wide of the truth. The power of the Chiefs of Clans was wholly independent of Charters or of Law. The Heritable Jurisdictions, on the contrary, were entirely founded on Charters and on Law. They were grants by the Crown of Judicial power given to individual men, not because they were Chiefs of Clans, but because they were the chartered Owners of great territorial Estates. These powers were given to Ownership, and not to "Chiefery." Many of the most powerful Rebels were men who had no Heritable Jurisdiction; many of the great Landowners who did possess extensive legal Jurisdictions, were the most loyal and the most energetic supporters of the Government. On the other hand, not a few Rebel Lords who had chartered Jurisdictions found in them no help at all. The Parliament of Scotland had for centuries been attacking and denouncing the power of Chiefs; whilst, on the contrary, in the Treaty of Union with England in 1707, the Scottish Parliament had inserted two special articles[1] saving the Heritable Jurisdictions of the Barons, and the analogous privi-

---

[1] Articles xx. and xxi., *Act. Parl. Scot.*, vol. xi. Append. p. 204.

leges of Royal Burghs, as Chartered rights of Property.

When, therefore, the British Parliament in 1746 and 1747 came to consider what they were to do against Celtic Feudalism, they soon found that the Heritable Jurisdictions formed no part of it, and had nothing to do with the political dangers which had so alarmed the Kingdom. Yet feeling that these Jurisdictions were for other reasons open to objection, and had long been abolished in England, they followed the judicious course of taking the opinion of a learned, wise, and patriotic man—applying to his knowledge for the facts, and to his wisdom and patriotism for advice. In January and August 1746, the House of Lords, in two Orders, applied to the Court of Session in Scotland for a Report on the different kinds of Heritable Jurisdiction, and for the draft of such a Bill as they would recommend to the adoption of Parliament.[1] The Lord President of that Court was then the same Duncan Forbes of Culloden of whom we have seen so much acting in another character. His Report is dated January 9, 1747. Like everything he wrote it was clear, concise, and eminently judicial in its tone. He explained and defended the Heritable Jurisdictions in the light of the times in which they had been introduced. He recommended the abolition of them (with a few important reservations) in the light of the new conditions of society which had now arisen. "One of

---

[1] A most admirable precedent, which might perhaps still be followed with advantage on some occasions.

the principal causes," he says, "of lodging High Jurisdictions in powerful Families heretofore was the great difficulty the Government was under, of bringing offenders to justice, and executing the laws, when the country was yet uncivilised, and the necessity of committing that charge to such as were able to execute the same; and as that part of the United Kingdom commonly called the Highlands of Scotland has at all times been, and is at this day, in a state so unsettled, that offenders are not from thence easily amenable to justice, nor can Process of Law have free course through it, due care must be taken to bring that part of the country under subjection to the law, and to secure the Execution of Process of all kinds within it, before any hopes can be entertained of seeing a regular administration of Justice by the King's Courts and Judges there." Assuming, however, that the essential preliminary would be otherwise secured, he sent up to the Lords the draft of a Bill for the desired purpose, and on this draft the Act which abolished the Heritable Jurisdictions was drawn and passed in the same year.[1] To a very large extent it was a mere statutory acknowledgment of changes which had already been practically established. In the preamble to the 17th clause the Act narrated as a matter of fact that Heritable Jurisdiction affecting the higher criminal offences, and the penalty of death, had "long been discontinued, or had fallen into disuse as to the exercise thereof." In general and sweep-

[1] 20 Geo. II. cap. 43.

ing terms all Heritable Jurisdictions, both civil and criminal, were now "abrogated, taken away, totally dissolved, and extinguished." They were resumed and re-annexed to their original source— the Crown.

And yet some valuable and significant reservations were made by subsequent clauses in accordance with the recommendation of the Lord President—in accordance, not less, with important usages at that time still in full activity, and with the traditional policy of the native Parliaments of Scotland. These reservations affected only the lower jurisdiction of the Baronial Courts, or, as they were called, the "Baron Baillie Courts," for the framing and enforcement of Estate regulations, and for the recovery of rents due by contract. The view taken by the Lord President of the Heritable Jurisdictions as a whole evidently was, that so far from having been one of the strengths of Celtic Feudalism, they had been, on the contrary, the only means by which that dangerous power could be restrained and resisted. They had been a strength in the hand of Ownership, for the defence and enforcement of legal obligation. But now the government of the Crown was in a condition to undertake this great duty over the whole Kingdom. The Lord President, however, had seen how much still remained to be done in the cause of civilisation which could be done by no other power whatever than the power of Ownership in the management of landed property. For centuries this power had been exercised to a large extent through the lower jurisdiction of the Baronial Courts, presided over by "Bailies," as representatives of the Proprietor or Lord. It was most desirable to retain an Institution which was still in full working order, which had in it some strong popular elements of unbroken usage and tradition, and without which the progress of agricultural improvement might be seriously impeded.

In accordance, therefore, with the advice of the highest Court in Scotland, and of its distinguished President, the old Baronial Courts were allowed to retain a petty jurisdiction in civil cases affecting values up to Forty shillings, and in all cases whatever for the recovery of "rents, mails, and duties," arising out of Charters, Leases, or other Instruments under which land was occupied.[1] This Act, therefore, made no change in the general practice which had been long established of inserting a clause in all Leases of agricultural land, binding the Tenant to attend and to serve on the Courts of the Barony in which his Farm lay. This was not an onerous but an honourable service, analogous to that of serving as Jurymen in the King's Courts. It associated all the Tenants in the administration both of law and of equitable jurisdiction arising out of the most important relations of the society in which they lived. It was only very gradually that these Courts fell into desuetude. The clause providing for attendance upon them survived in Leases down to our own days. I have myself signed many Leases

[1] Clause 17.

out of which this old clause had not yet dropped.
The changes which gradually extinguished these
Courts were many. The class of men who took
Farms gradually changed. Farms, themselves, became
more and more individual possessions—less
and less associated with that uniformity of customs
and of habits which always dies under an active
spirit of improvement. Then, the King's Courts,
the Sheriffs, and the Sheriff-Substitutes, penetrated
everywhere, and the inevitable tendency of reforms
of every kind was to concentrate all Jurisdiction in
the highest and most responsible administrators of
justice and of law. But none the less were the
Baronial Courts a valuable institution during an
important time, and their value lay especially in the
facilities they lent to Ownership in rendering its
full response to the appeal which had been made to
it by Parliament and the Crown.

Belonging strictly to the same category of
Legislation another Act of the same Session deserves
our notice. Amid the fear and hatred roused by
the Jacobite Rebellions against all that was supposed
to be connected with Celtic Feudalism,
another loud clamour arose against certain incidents
of Feudal Tenure which had been developed in
Scotland. These were the incidents affecting all
Vassals or Feuars connected with Fines, Wardships,
and other occasional dues to their "Superiors,"
which in Scotland were called "Casualties." Some
of these were open to great objection—not as connected
in the slightest degree with the power of

Celtic Chiefs, but on the contrary as hampering and embarrassing the great antagonist power of landed Ownership. It was in the hands of the Vassals, and not of the Superiors, that the real powers and virtues of Ownership lay. It was the Vassals, not the Superiors, who possessed the " Dominium utile "—the dominion which incited men to the improved and more profitable use of land. It was a matter therefore of public interest that they should be able to exercise that power upon conditions which were known and calculable. Upon the narrative, accordingly, that certain specified kinds of Casualties "had been much more burdensome, grievous, and prejudicial to the Vassals, Proprietors of the Lands held by these Tenures, than they had been beneficial to the Superiors," an Act[1] was passed abolishing them for the future, and for the past requiring them to be commuted into a fixed feu-duty, either by agreement between the parties, or by valuation through the Court of Session.

We cannot be mistaken in seeing here the handiwork of the same enlightened Judge and Statesman who drafted the Act abolishing the Heritable Jurisdictions, when we ascribe to him an important clause in this further Statute which extended to Agricultural Tenants under Lease the same principle of certainty in obligations which the other clauses secured for the Proprietors under whom they held. This clause[2] was in strict accordance with the principle he had embodied in the

[1] 20 Geo. II. cap. 50. [2] Clause 21.

new Leases which he had drawn up for the Tenants in the Argyll Estates. It did not abolish Services as a part, or as a concomitant, of rent. He knew that some of them were reasonable and even necessary. Neither did it assume to Parliament the task of specifying the particular services it might be expedient to retain. He knew that local circumstances and mutual interests must determine this. But it did abolish, and render illegal for the future, all Services which were indefinite and unrestricted in nature and amount. The Tenant and the Proprietor might bargain for such Services as they pleased; but these Services must be named, and specified. Uncertainty—vagueness—the want of definition had been the ruin and oppression of the cultivating classes under Celtic Feudalism. The Lord President struck at this feature of the system, and extended by law to those classes that same remedial principle to which a wider range had been just given on behalf of chartered Ownership. And so the new clause declared that no Tenant or Tacksman should in future be obliged or liable to perform any Services whatsoever other than such as shall be expressly and particularly reserved and specified, with the number and kinds thereof enumerated in some written Instrument, signed by both the parties thereto—" any former Law or usage notwithstanding."

This was indeed wise and sound Legislation, and it was only another item in the Response of Ownership to the long-standing appeals of the old Parliaments of Scotland. For it is to be observed that these new Statutes were passed in the united or British Parliament, forty years after the Union, in special consultation with the highest Court of Law in Scotland, and with the full assent of the Scottish Peerage and of the Scottish Proprietors. It is indeed curious to observe that although the privilege of recording Protests by minorities in the House of Lords was exercised on the passing of the Bill for the abolition of the Heritable Jurisdictions, that Protest was not signed by a single Scotch Peer. It was signed by only six Peers—all of them Englishmen. It is true that the Chartered Proprietors of the Heritable Jurisdiction were to receive a compensation. But the amount of this compensation was left absolutely to the decision in each case of the Court of Session—and this was made a point of objection by the Protesting Englishmen.

And now, disembarrassed on the one hand of powers which had outlived their time, and emancipated on the other hand, from liabilities which discouraged the use of capital, the Ownership of Land in Scotland was ready to go forward faster, and with redoubled energy, on a career which indeed was by no means new, but which was now to be pursued under more favourable conditions and with an immense development of industrial results.

Before, however, we can enter upon a review of these results, we must go back for a little upon the

Past, and estimate from authentic sources of information what the condition of Scotland was in the beginning of the second half of the Eighteenth Century, as well as attend to some events which arose during that period, and which exerted an influence upon the people more powerful than either new laws or ancient usages.

CHAPTER II.

BEFORE THE DAWN.

VERY nearly a century and a half—144 years—had now elapsed since the Union of the Crowns, and the condition of Scotland, as compared with its condition at that time, presented at least one curious parallel, and one not less striking contrast. In 1603 the Cateran of the Highland Glens was the fellow and the counterpart of the Moss Trooper of the Border Dales. Both were the children of the Clan system—the product of its degeneration and decay. The men who swarmed from the Hills falling into the sources of the Leven, the Earn, the Tay, the Dee, the Spey, and the Beauly Firth, led substantially the same life as those who mustered in the wider valleys or on the gentler slopes which shed their waters into the Solway and the Tweed. The Scoto-Saxon and the Celtic Clans were then in the same stage of progress. The habits of both races had been equally uncivilised and destructive. But now the armed horseman of the Border had not only disappeared, but had been long almost forgotten. When one only of these facts absorbed attention, and when the other had fallen out of mind—when the Cateran was still a terror, and the Moss Trooper had become a mere tradition—it was only natural that the causes which had been common to both should be popularly confounded and confused. Only the calmer spirits, trained in the knowledge of History and of Law, appreciated those causes, and perceived the remedies which could alone prevail over them, in the one case, as they had already prevailed over them, in the other. But in the midst of the anger which swelled around the last Jacobite Rebellion, there were some writers of the time who saw clearly that as regarded the dangers of Clanship the new Statutes of 1747 could only have an indirect effect. One of these writers pointed out that in all the Border Counties Clanship had once been as powerful and as destructive to industry as it still appeared to be in any part of the Celtic Highlands. He urged that after the Union of the Crowns, without any meddling with the Heritable Jurisdictions of the great Landowners of the Lowlands, and without any modification of the Feudal "casualties," those evils of Clanship had been eradicated in the Southern Highlands so completely "that civility, good order, and industry supervened among them, and Clanship wore off by degrees, and at last totally ceased, so that no such thing has been known in those parts within the memory of man."[1]

Although this phrase, "the memory of man," has not a meaning which is precise, yet it has a

---

[1] An Essay upon Feudal Holdings, etc., in Scotland (anonymous). London, 1747. One of a collection of pamphlets of this date.

meaning which is of measurable scope. It must indicate a period of more than a century, seeing that every generation has inherited the memory of its fathers for at least that period of time. This, then, would take us back to 1647, since which it was asserted as a matter of notoriety that no memory remained of the Border Clans—a date only forty-four years after the Union of the Crowns. Within that short period, then, representing little more than a single generation, the whole system must have been broken up, extinguished, and almost forgotten. How had this great change been so speedily effected? Of the universal prevalence of Clanship in the Southern Counties of Scotland up to the Union, and of all the worst habits of life inseparable from it, there can be no doubt whatever. We have the detailed evidence of the Parliament of Scotland in 1587, only sixteen years before, and of many a Tale and Ballad which illustrates that evidence in forms more picturesque and equally authentic. Sir Walter Scott, the latest and most illustrious Minstrel of the Borders, who himself belonged to one of the most powerful of the Southern Clans, has said of his native districts that "for a long series of centuries the hands of rapine were never folded in inactivity, nor the sword of violence returned to its scabbard."[1] The truth is, that his account represents a condition of society more permanently bad than had prevailed in any portion of the Highlands. All down the Eastern Coasts of

---

[1] *Border Minstrelsy.* Preface by Sir W. Scott (ed. 1802), p. 48.

Scotland, indeed, there had always been a broad belt of low country which was the seat of industry and of peace. But the whole area embraced by the Middle and the Western Marches had been nothing but the strongholds of fighting and marauding Clans. Scott tells us that until after the Union, land in those regions had hardly ever been sufficiently cultivated to afford any rent at all. In one respect only had an advance been made beyond the northern portions of the Kingdom. The great Landowners of the Southern Counties had long ago discovered that sheep could graze upon their mountains as well as cattle upon the lower grounds; and it is recorded of James V. that he had a flock of 10,000 of these animals in the Forest of Ettrick alone. But the bulk of the people raised no crops sufficient to feed themselves, far less to afford a surplus for the purposes of exchange. Yet, as there was a large population, it lived, and could only live on the plunder of its neighbours.

This is the only explanation—and even this is hardly sufficient— of the formidable levies which the Border Chiefs seem always to have been able to command in frays, forays, and sometimes in audacious enterprises against the Crown. Not seldom these levies were made so suddenly and so secretly, that the power of collecting them indicates an abundance of population far greater than the produce of their own country could habitually sustain. James VI. himself, with all his Parliament, had suddenly found himself, when a boy, in the hands of the "Bold Buccleuch," who in the year 1571 made a dash at Stirling with 300 infantry and 200 horsemen.[1] But this was a mere squadron of the great force which could be called forth when occasion required a real "Summoning of the Array." We are told that "at the blaze of their beacon-fires the Borderers could assemble 10,000 horsemen in the course of a single day."[2] How came such long ancestral habits to be so suddenly exchanged for others? How came this great military population to be disposed of in favour of the ploughman and the farmer? It had to be done,—for the old life could be led no longer. He whom the Borderers had called in contempt the King of Fife and of the Lothians, had become King of Great Britain and Ireland. The "Marches" and the "Borders" had disappeared, and now there was only one United Kingdom, with a strong Government surrounding on all sides the Southern Clans.

There were but two ways of meeting such a complete revolution in the facts of life. One remedy was sudden and temporary, but was a necessary preliminary to another remedy which would be gradual and permanent. That portion of the population which could not adapt itself to the new life—and this was a large portion—must go elsewhere. The other remedy—that which must be more slow and more gradual—would spring up of itself, out of the new motives which were inseparable from the new conditions. All other "measures"

[1] *Border Minstrelsy*, Preface, p. 37.   [2] *Ibid.* p. 69.

must be weak or futile. Such measures, however, were tried; for men are slow to recognise or understand what the real influences are which the human Will steadily obeys. Legislative measures similar to those which were tried against the Highlanders in 1747, prohibiting their dress, and the carrying of their arms, had been tried against the Borderers— with this difference only, that as their accoutrements and equipments were different, the things aimed at were not the same. For the most part, the Border Clans were horsemen, and not foot soldiers. With wonderful ingenuity they had trained their horses to go upon morasses by throwing themselves down on their bellies and their houghs, and thus gaining an artificial breadth of support, to cross, by short floundering leaps, ground in which ordinary horses were instantly bogged. Accordingly, one of the measures aimed against the Borderers was a prohibition against the possession of horses above the size of ponies. But the real remedies were begun when the native Chiefs and Landowners recruited a Legion of men who, having known no other life than fighting, were incapable of industry, and were glad to offer the service of their lances to countries which were as glad to have them. This Legion repaired to Holland, and were absorbed in the wars of the Low Country.[1] One whole Clan of Græmes, specially intractable, were deported to Ireland, where they did, and where their descendants are now doubtless doing, well.[2]

[1] *Border Minstrelsy*, Preface, p. 49.   [2] *Ibid*.

But the great remedy—the permanent remedy—was the immediate opening up of the ordinary channels of peaceful industry. This was the final and irresistible response to the old appeal from the power of Chiefs to the power of Ownership. The effect was immediate,—such as might be produced by the sudden rising of a new atmosphere, and of a new climate upon the vegetation of the world. The proper seeds were all there—for these are everywhere stored in the nature of Man, and in the nature of his more civilised desires. From the moment peace and security were established, Landowners began to value their estates as they had never valued them before. They now valued them not for the precipitous ravines,—the impenetrable thickets,—the treacherous morasses,—on the edges of which they could build castles, or in which they could hide cattle, or behind which they could retreat from a pursuing enemy. They valued them for the corn they could produce, and for the share of it which was due to those to whom the cultivator owed his tenure,—this being his only right of exclusive occupation. So immediate was this effect that within three or four years of the Union proprietors began to look closely over their own private "marches," and to claim from each other portions of territory which, before, it had been rather a burden to defend.[1] This was all that was required. No special legislation was needed. Old motives had been killed. New motives had taken possession of

---

[1] *Border Minstrelsy*, Preface, p. 44.

Society. There must have been a great exodus from the Dales of the old fighting classes. And more important still, after this exodus had been accomplished, there was a free current of migration to and from the surrounding districts of the oldest Scottish civilisation. There was no barrier of race. There was no barrier of language. The population came and went as agriculture gradually developed, and as the mutual interests of men led them to bargain with each other for what each could give towards the profitable occupation and cultivation of the soil. Within less than half a century, as we have seen, the Moss Trooper cavalry had been forgotten, and the grazier and the farmer reigned in their stead.[1]

And now let us turn from the parallel to the contrast. The Union of the Crowns was a great epoch in the Celtic Highlands, as well as in the Marches of the Border. It closed almost completely the ages of internal war. One of the last ferocious battles of the Clans, the famous and bloody fight between the Macgregors and Colquhouns in Glen Fruin, was fought in 1603. Thenceforward bloodshed had nearly ceased. But there was no exodus from the Highlands of the fighting classes as there was from the Borders, neither was there any continuous outflow and inflow between the Celtic and the Scottish populations, to and from their respec-

---

[1] Statutes against Moss Troopers on the Border continued to be passed down to a much later date. But the old name had come to be attached to mere robbers and banditti.

tive districts, like to that which had arisen on the Borders. More impassable than the mountain barriers, there still remained between the Highlanders and the Lowlanders the antipathies of race, and the differences of language. From all this the fact arose that the Highland Caterans lived on and multiplied in their glens, leading to a very large extent, as they could only lead, a life of plunder. Instead of becoming a thing of the past within little more than a single generation, as the Clans of the Border had become, they continued, on the contrary, to be a living and a very terrible reality for more than a century and a half. Although, during this time, there was little or no advance in agriculture, there was a cessation of deaths in battle, and it is certain that population within the Highland line was pressing more and more closely upon the limits of subsistence. It could not be otherwise. Many parts of Scotland which are now among the richest, were then miserably poor. Thirty years after the Union, in Charles the First's Parliament of 1633, a Bill was brought in providing " that all impositions for restraining the inbringing of victual may be discharged," and this was desired upon the ground that the " whole Sheriffdoms of Dumbarton, Renfrew, Argyll, Ayr, Wigtown, Nithsdale, Stewartry of Kirkcudbright, and Annandale are not able to entertain themselves in the most plentiful years that ever fell out without supply from foreign parts."[1]

[1] *Act. Parl. Scot.* vol. v. p. 49. My attention was called to this remarkable fact by the late Mr. Cosmo Innes.

If this was true at that time of comparatively fertile districts of the Lowland country, it must have been still more true of all the wilder portions of the Highlands. The land was a land capable of yielding adequate means of support, even to a limited number, only as a return to capital, industry, and skill. The life was a life in which industry was impossible, and in which both capital and agricultural skill were unattainable and unknown. Accordingly one eminent authority has said of the old inhabitants of the Highlands that " they were always on the verge of famine, and every few years suffering the horrors of actual starvation."[1]

It is curious how completely this fact is now forgotten or ignored. In part this forgetfulness arises out of one of the most blessed laws of nature that the memory of pain is transient, whilst the memories of pleasure are enduring. Especially would this be true of a highly imaginative people, feeding on Legend, and having no literature of its own except the literature of Song. There is no poetic or inspiring element in the fight with Famine. Yet the moment we examine in detail the historical documents of greatest value, which are Family Papers and the records of Parliament, we find abundant evidence of the extreme poverty of Scotland and of her people. From century to century the same complaint is repeated, and generally in tones which imply not so much any sudden

[1] *Sketches of Early Scotch History*, p. 134. By Cosmo Innes.

scarcity from adverse seasons, as a standing deficiency of food for the adequate support of the population. In the reign of James III., in 1476, this complaint is so worded as to declare expressly that Scotland was then dependent on the Foreigner for its living. "Because," says this Statute, "Victuals are right scant within the country, and the most supportation that the Realm has is by strangers of diverse nations that bring victuals."[1] Five years later, in 1483, the continued pressure of this condition of things opened the eyes of the Legislature to a truth as affecting the Foreign Importer, to which they continued curiously blind as affecting equally the Home Producer,—the truth, namely, that any attempt to regulate the price of imported victuals by law could only do harm, by driving away the Foreigner on whom so much depended. An Act of that year therefore provided that in order to induce Foreigners to come for the benefit of the King's lieges, they should enjoy the benefit of free bargains, and that "no price be set upon their goods, except by buying and selling with their own consent."[2] The span of a single human life had not yet elapsed, when Parliament returned to the subject in a yet more serious mood. It had in the meantime been doing its best to discourage production by arbitrary limitations on price. But now it did more in the same direction by putting arbitrary limits on consumption. Industry

---

[1] 18 James III. c. 5; *Act. Parl. Scot.*, vol. ii. p. 118.
[2] 22 James III. c. 10; *Act. Parl. Scot.*, vol. ii. p. 144.

is sometimes recouped for a small price, by extensive custom. But this, too, was to be checked. The nation had recourse to a Sumptuary Law. It treated itself as if it were a ship at sea, with only a limited store of food which could not be increased, but which might be made to serve longer by everybody on board being put on rations. The idea was embodied in a law with grotesque inconsistencies. It denounced excess in eating as "voluptuosity." But it did not put all men on equal fare. It established a scale corresponding to men's rank in life. The consequence was, the highest Ministers of the Christian Church were put highest on the scale of eating, and therefore lowest on the scale of self-denial. Archbishops, Bishops, and the highest ranks of the Peerage were allowed a maximum of eight dishes, whilst the scale descended, through the various degrees of station and wealth, to a maximum of three. To avoid evasion it was specified that each "dish" must contain "one kind of meat" only.[1] Illogical and childish as this Statute must appear to us now, I am not sure that it is more childish than many theories prevalent in our own time upon the subject of "luxury." There is no rational, or indeed intelligible definition of this word which does not include within its meaning all that exceeds the bare necessities of life. The food of a convict—the apparel of a convict—the lodging of a convict—is the standard with which

---

[1] *Act. Parl. Scot.*, 1551, vol. ii. p. 488. Of course, "meat" meant all kinds of food, and not animal food exclusively.

we must begin. All the comforts and conveniences of life—all that refines and elevates the course and the enjoyment of it—belongs to the class of luxuries, and the Industries which are employed in the production of them are the profitable employments of the people. These Industries cannot be separated from the consumption of their products. "Voluptuosity" must be marked off by a higher and more spiritual touch than the coarse one of Parliamentary enactments, or even of intellectual definitions. The characteristics of it can only be recognised by those moral faculties which establish contact between the Individual, with all his specialities of circumstance, and the duty he owes to the Giver of every good and every perfect gift. We enter here, however, upon other fields of discussion, from which we must retire again.

The interest of this Statute for our present purpose lies in its remarkable preamble: "Having respect to the great and exorbitant dearth risen in this Realm of victuals and other stuff for the sustentation of mankind, and daily increasing." It is a common but erroneous notion that the Highlanders, like the inhabitants of other wild countries, had at least always an abundant supply of game. But neither was this source extensively available. The country swarmed with Foxes, Eagles, Hawks, and, at an earlier period, as we have seen, with Wolves. These animals effectually prevented any abundance of game. Even the Deer being often wholly unprotected, killed out of season, driven about and allowed no rest, were reduced extremely in number, and in the Seventeenth Century were found only in the highest and least accessible mountains of the country.[1] When we remember that this language was used by men living in the richest portions of the country, in or near which there was free access to the Foreign Merchant, we can form some idea of the much greater dearth which must have prevailed elsewhere. These repeated Statutes during several centuries indicate beyond all doubt the great poverty of the nation, and the deep distress which must have been frequent, if not habitual, among the poorer classes, in districts where no imports could ever penetrate.

This state of things is not astonishing. The only matter of astonishment is how any considerable population could have lived at all. Let us remember, in the first place, that the food which now for several generations has been the principal food of all poor agricultural populations, was not then available. There were no potatoes. Let us remember, in the second place, that the climate is a wet one, and that artificial drainage was absolutely unknown. Let us remember, in the third place, that although potatoes will grow on damp and even wet soils, barley and oats will not grow except on land which is comparatively dry. Let us remember, in the fourth place, that in a mountainous country, with a wet climate and no artificial drainage, the best land in the bottoms of the

---

[1] *Sketches of Early Scotch History*, p. 424, by C. Innes.

valleys must have been very wet, and that even the sides of the hills were often covered with a boggy and spongy soil. It follows from all these considerations that corn could only be raised on those spots and portions of land which were dry by natural drainage. Sometimes these may have been in the bottoms of the valleys where the soil happened to be light and shingly, but more often they were on the steepest sides of the hills, on the banks of streams, and among the naturally dry and even stony knolls. Accordingly nothing is more common in the Highlands than to see old marks of cultivation upon land so high and so steep, that no farmer in his senses would now consider it as arable at all. When these marks catch the eye of the stranger, full of sentiment, but deficient in knowledge, he looks upon them, and quotes them as the melancholy proofs of ancient and abandoned industry, of the decay of agriculture, in short of a stagnant or declining state. Whereas, in truth, these are the most sure and certain indications of the low and rude condition of agriculture in former times. They prove that the better lands which are now drained and cleared and ploughed, must have been then under swamp and tangled wood. When again we remember that such dry spots and patches of land as were then capable of bearing corn, were used for that purpose year after year; when we remember that there was no such a thing known as a rotation of crops, since all the green varieties were wanting; when we consider further, that even the rudiments of a system of manuring land were also unknown, it is impossible to be surprised that the population of the Highlands was exposed to frequent and severe famines, and we may well even wonder how any considerable population was maintained at all.

Sir Walter Scott, in one of the most powerful of his immortal Tales, the novel of *Rob Roy*, has put into the mouth of Bailie Jarvie an accurate description of the over-population of the Highlands, as compared with the actual resources of the country in the time of that noted Cateran, who is the hero of the story: "The military array of this Hieland country, were a' the men-folk between aughteen and fifty-six brought out that could bear arms, couldna come weel short of fifty-seven thousand and five hundred men. Now, sir, it's a sad and awfu' truth, that there is neither wark, nor the very fashion nor appearance of wark, for the tae half of thae puir creatures; that is to say, that the agriculture, the pasturage, the fisheries, and every species of honest industry about the country, cannot employ the one moiety of the population, let them work as lazily as they like, and they do work as if a pleugh or a spade burned their fingers. Aweel, sir, this moiety of unemployed bodies amounting to one hundred and fifteen thousand souls, whereof there may be twenty-eight thousand seven hundred able-bodied gillies fit to bear arms, and that do bear arms, and will touch or look at nae honest means of livelihood even if they could get it

—which, lack-a-day! they cannot.... And mair especially mony hundreds o' them come down to the borders of the low country, where there's gear to grip, and live by stealing, reiving, lifting cows, and the like depredations—a thing deplorable in ony Christian country, the mair especially that they take a pride in it,"[1] etc. In this passage Scott did not speak at random. In an article contributed to the *Quarterly Review* in January 1816,[2] we have his picture of the historical facts embodied in *Rob Roy*. In that paper he pointed out that the most remarkable fact connected with the Highlands about a hundred years before he wrote, was the rapid increase of the population, which, pent up within narrow and unfertile valleys, could neither extend itself towards the mountains, on account of hostile Clans, nor towards the Lowlands, because the civilised country, though unable to prevent occasional depredations, was always too powerful to admit of any permanent settlement being gained upon the plains by the mountaineers. But limited to its own valley, each Clan increased in numbers in a degree far beyond proportion to the means of supporting them. Each little farm was, by the tenant who cultivated it, divided and sub-divided among his children and grandchildren, until the number of human beings to be maintained far exceeded that for whom, by any mode of culture, the space of ground could supply even the poorest nourishment. In illustra-

[1] *Rob Roy*, p. 291: 1870.   [2] Vol. xiv. pp. 283-333.

tion of this general description, Sir Walter particularises the rugged district, now so well known to tourists, between Loch Katrine and Loch Lomond, in the neighbourhood of Inversnaid, where 150 families were living upon ground which did not pay £90 a year of rent, or in other words, where each family on an average rented land at twelve shillings a year as their sole source of livelihood.[1]

It is well to have this prosaic testimony to a memorable economic fact, not from any cold-blooded Statistician, but from the greatest Poet of History that has ever adorned the literature of any country. The only error that can be detected in this picture drawn by Sir Walter Scott is, that in some ways it is probably an under-statement rather than any over-statement of the case. The terrible and then increasing disproportion between the old Celtic population and their legitimate means of subsistence, is as powerfully as it is accurately expressed. But the contrast between these two quantities becomes all the more indicative of the extreme unproductiveness of the country, arising out of the ignorant agriculture and idleness of the people, when we discover that the actual amount of the population which was so poor, and which was driven to such expedients for support, was in all probability a much smaller amount than the figures indicated by Sir Walter. The fighting power exhibited in the short but dashing Rebellions of 1715 and of 1745 has led very generally to an estimate of the

---

[1] *Quarterly Review*, vol. xiv. p. 296-7.

number of fighting men turned out by the Highlanders, which is almost certainly exaggerated. It will surprise many to be told that the greatest number of men in arms against the Government in the Rebellion of 1745, from the beginning to the end of it, did not exceed 11,000 men.[1] In 1715 the Earl of Mar had entered Stirling with only 5000, and the doubling of his force at the Battle of Sheriffmuir was due to Irish reinforcements. Of course it is to be remembered that some of the most powerful Clans were loyal to the Government, so that the Rebel forces never represented the full power of the Highland population. Some of them remained neutral. Robert Macgregor, the famous "Rob Roy," hung upon the outskirts of this battle at Sheriffmuir with a contingent, which took no part in the engagement—its astute leader being a waiter on Providence and a watcher of the tide. This broad fact, however, remains undoubted, that although many great Nobles and Proprietors in the Lowlands joined in the Rebellion of 1745, the whole military force which supported the Pretender was entirely raised by the Highland Proprietors, although at least one-half the value of the whole Estates afterwards forfeited belonged to the Lowland Rebels.[2] The explanation of this is obvious. It was in the Highlands alone that a large surplus

---

[1] I take this from an interesting MS. in the *Brit. Mus.*, No. 104, in the "King's Collection," written by a gentleman who travelled over all the Highland Counties soon after the Rebellion of 1745, and seems to have been employed by the Government to report upon them.

[2] *Observations on the Highlands*, by the Earl of Selkirk, 1805, App. A.

population survived over and above those whose time was occupied with any industrial pursuits, and over and above the number which could be supported by them. In the Lowlands the old military population had disappeared,—having been dispersed from their original seats, and absorbed into the ranks of peaceful industry,—some of them in the country, some of them in connection with the rising commerce of the Towns.

At last one outlet was opened for the Highlanders which had been opened for the Border Clans more than a hundred years before—the outlet, namely, of lawful military service. It is constantly repeated that the idea of enlisting Highland Regiments was due to the genius of the elder Pitt, the Earl of Chatham, when he came into power in December 1756, and undertook the conduct of the war with France in America and in Europe. This, however, is a mistake. That great man has enough of glory without ascribing to him the merit of a suggestion which unquestionably came from two native Scotchmen, who were also native Highlanders. There is conclusive evidence that the policy of enlisting Highlanders, as such, in the regular military service of the Crown, was due to the common counsels of these two intimate and hereditary friends, Archibald, third Duke of Argyll, better known as Earl of Islay,[1] and Duncan Forbes

---

[1] He succeeded his brother John, Duke of Argyll and Greenwich, in 1743, and died in 1761. During the whole of the Ministry of Walpole, and some succeeding Ministries, he was intrusted with the chief conduct of affairs in Scotland.

of Culloden. Indeed, a beginning had been made
at a still earlier date. No less than twenty-seven
years before the famous ministry of Pitt, this policy
had been inaugurated, so far as regarded the purposes of a local Militia for keeping the peace of
the Highlands, by the formation in 1730 of the
six Independent Companies which, from the contrast of their dark clothing with the red uniform
of the Army, came to be known as the Black
Watch.[1] These six separate Companies, numbering
in all 510 men, were constituted as closely as
possible on the same system as that which had long
been the system of the Clans. The officers were
taken from the loyal Clans, the Campbells, Grants,
Munros, etc., but the men were recruited from all
Highlanders who would enlist. The "Broken Men"
of the Highlands were as willing to join these Companies as they had always been to join any powerful
Chief. These bodies of men were in the strictest
sense of the word new Clans, formed precisely as
any other Clan might have been begun, in the
palmy days of Celtic Feudalism.[2] We know the
actual constitution of at least one of the Jacobite
Clans engaged in the Rebellion of 1745, and we
see that essentially it was a mere military body
with only the flavour of family or blood connection
arising out of relationship between the officers. It
was the contingent which represented the Stewarts

---

[1] Stewart's *Sketches of the Highlanders*, vol. i. part iii., pp. 240-248.

[2] Col. Stewart says, "their service seemed merely that of a Clan sanctioned by legal authority" (*Sketches*, vol. ii. p. 254).

of Appin. In this gallant corps, numbering upwards of 300 men, there were only six families who were genuine inheritors of the name and blood of Stewart. Of the killed and wounded in all the battles of the campaign, only 47 belonged to them, whilst 109 belonged to "Macs" of almost every sort and kind existing in the Highlands. Yet nothing could exceed the courage and fidelity of the men to their leaders. They contributed much to the defeat of Sir John Cope at Prestonpans, and to the rout of General Hawley at Falkirk. At Culloden they broke the Royal regiment opposed to them, until it was rallied behind supports.[1]

The Statesmen who in 1730 first enrolled the original Companies of the Black Watch upon exactly the same principle, must have been native Scotchmen, knowing intimately the habits of the people whom these Companies were formed at once to watch, to employ, and to keep in order. Between 1730 and 1738 they seem to have exercised an excellent effect upon the Highlands, and it was perhaps due to them that the Rebellion of 1745 was not far more formidable even than it actually proved to be. In the last of these years—1738—the same year in which Culloden gave such wise advice for the agricultural settlement of the population on his friend's Hebridean estates,—he drew up a paper recommending an extension of the policy

[1] These interesting details are given by Mr. Gregory, editor of *De Rebus Albanicis*, and author of the *History of the Highlands*. They were derived from Charles Stewart (Fasnacloich), who was private secretary to Prince Charles Edward.

of enlisting Highlanders in the regular Army.[1] Through Lord Islay it was laid before Sir Robert Walpole, who approved and sanctioned the idea. Although this scheme was not immediately carried into effect on any great scale, yet a beginning was at once made, for it must have been in consequence of the advice of Islay and Culloden that in the following year, 1739, the Independent Companies of the Black Watch were formed into a Regiment —the famous "Forty-Second."[2] The Letters of Service for the formation of this Regiment, dated October 25, 1739, directed that the corps should be "raised in the Highlands," the men to be natives of that country, and none other to be taken.[3]

The steps by which this famous body of men passed from mere Companies, representing the Clan organisation, into regular Regiments of the British Army are curious, and some of them are painful. The original Companies were raised strictly for local service among the mountains. They were scattered over the Highlands, but principally stationed along the line of the Great Glen from which, on either side, they could keep their watch and maintain the law. When they were "regimented" the men did not clearly understand the change from local to general service, although the "Letters of Service" distinctly stated that the Regiment was to take its place in the Royal Army, "according to the establishment thereof."[4] When

---

[1] *Culloden Papers*, Introd. p. 31.
[2] Originally, and for a few years, numbered the "Forty-Third."
[3] Stewart's *Sketches*, vol. i. p. 244.   [4] *Ibid.*

it was marched to London in 1743, and Jacobite agents told them they might be sent to America, there was—not a mutiny—but a wholesale desertion. Following the frequent example of their ancestors, they retreated in a body from London, about May 16 in that year, and tried to regain the Highlands by marching through the centre of England. Surrounded and obliged to surrender their arms, when they had got as far as Oundle in Northamptonshire, they were soon restored to order, and transferred to Flanders to serve in the never-ending wars waged upon that great battlefield of Europe. There, during the two years 1743 and 1744, they won golden opinions by their civility, trustworthiness, and conduct; and there, in 1745, at the bloody and disastrous fight of Fontenoy, the Highlanders established their renown, first by their dash during the battle, and then by their discipline and courage at the most difficult and dangerous post of honour, that of covering the rear of an army in retreat.[1]

Not indeed even then for the first time had the soldiers of Scotland and of the Highlands become known to the Continental States. For many hundred years they had been honoured in France, and during the Seventeenth Century they had borne a distinguished part in the wars of the Low Country. In the great Civil War at home between Charles I. and the Parliamentary Forces, the Highlanders had been called on for a contingent, and the M'Leods of

---

[1] Stewart's *Sketches*, vol. ii. pp. 269-70; *Culloden Papers*, pp. 200-3.

Skye, whose Chiefs were zealous Royalists, had lost in the war, and especially at Worcester, so many men that, by the general consent of the Northern Clans, it was agreed that they should have a respite from military service till their numbers should increase.[1] Nevertheless the conduct of the Black Watch, as one of the regular Regiments of the British Army at Fontenoy, attracted the universal notice of the world. And this was still twelve years before the measure commonly ascribed to Pitt. So far, indeed, was he from having any merit in this matter, that so late as 1744 he was denouncing on principle any additions to a standing army, and declaring that " the man who solely depends upon arms for bread can never be a good subject, especially in a free country."[2] It is clear, therefore, that the honour of this measure is an honour to be ascribed to the Statesmen who were then at the head of affairs in Scotland. Moreover, in the legislation of 1747, the Act which forbade the use of the Highland dress, specially excepted that use as a regimental uniform. This clearly indicated not a temporary or accidental expedient, but a permanent policy. Accordingly the Forty-Second was employed on all kinds of service, both at home, in Ireland, and abroad, during the eleven years between the battle of Fontenoy and its embarkation for Canada in 1756. Not even the first idea of using Highlanders for the reinforcement of the Army in America can be justly ascribed to

[1] MSS. Brit. Mus.   [2] Thackeray's *Life of Pitt*, vol. i. p. 127.

the initiative of Pitt. The Forty-Second had been under orders for Canada, and had actually embarked in 1748, when they were accidentally driven back by storms. But the Forty-Second formed part of the Force sent out under General Abercromby in 1756, and which landed at New York in June of that year.[1] The Ministry of Pitt was not formed till the following month of December, so that the policy of employing Highland Regiments in the struggle with France for supremacy in the New World, cannot possibly be ascribed to him.

The scheme of adding largely to the Highland element in the regular army by the addition of two new Regiments of 1200 men each, and of sending them out to America, seems to have been renewed by Archibald, Duke of Argyll, on the same principle of Clan enlistment which had been found so successful in the case of the Black Watch.[2] The only merit due to Pitt in this matter, was that when he came into power in December 1756, at a time marked by great national depression and disaster, having himself previously denounced the use of Hanoverian troops, he rose above all his former prejudices about "Standing Armies," and directed the immediate execution of the scheme. The truth is, that the defeat of Fontenoy and the Jacobite Rebellion happening in the same year, had put an end to the nonsense of political tra-

---

[1] Stewart's *Sketches*, vol. i. p. 294.
[2] Beatson's *Military and Naval Memoirs*, vol. ii. (ed. 1804), under date 1757.

dition on this subject. Pitt had now entered upon a great war, and he was almost driven by necessity, in January 1757, to resort still more largely to that recruiting ground of a fighting race in the Highlands, the value of which had been tested on the most famous fields of Europe, and had then already come to be universally recognised.[1] During the rest of the century, and during the next century down to the Battle of Waterloo in 1815, this recruiting ground was more and more largely drawn upon—so that between 1740 and 1815 no less than fifty Battalions had been raised mainly from the Highlands, irrespective of smaller corps, and many "Fencible" or Militia Regiments[2] besides.

The effects of this great opening of military service upon the population of the Highlands was very great, both directly and indirectly. The indirect effects cannot be measured by the mere diminution of numbers from the casualties of war. These were never excessive; indeed they may be said to have been trifling compared with those accompanying the murderous conflicts of our own day, in which arms of precision, and of enormous range, mow down men as the ears of corn fall before the reaping-knives. Fontenoy was reckoned a bloody battle at the time, and the severest fight-

---

[1] Mr. Lecky, one of the most careful and philosophical of our living historians, has recognised the "exaggeration" of the merit commonly ascribed to Pitt; but he still leaves to that Statesman more than is his due (*History of England*, vol. ii. p. 458).

[2] Stewart's *Sketches*, vol. ii p. 293.

ing fell to the lot of the Black Watch; yet they lost in killed only 30 men, with 86 wounded. Fontenoy was described by an officer concerned in both actions as "nothing" to the disastrous fight against the French and Indians at Ticonderoga in 1758, when the Highlanders encountered the brave Montcalm,[1] and when their killed numbered 297, and the wounded 306. This was more than one-half the whole Regiment. During the remaining service of this splendid corps, from its embodiment in 1740 to the Peace of 1815—a period of seventy-five years—in all the wars in which it was engaged, in Flanders, Canada, America, the Peninsula, and Waterloo—its total losses in killed only came to 778 men (rank and file), and 2291 wounded. The proportion of officers killed and wounded was immensely greater.[2] At this rate of loss, taking even the whole of the Regiments which came to be recruited, chiefly but no longer exclusively, from the Highlands, the drain upon the population was not very heavy, and probably much less than would have arisen from such intertribal wars and devastations as those which marked the Fifteenth and Sixteenth Centuries.

But the indirect effect of the Highland Regiments was enormous. Men from every part of the Highlands became acquainted with other regions of the world—with higher standards and modes of living,—with other pursuits than breeding a few

[1] Mante's *History of the War in North America*, 1754-1764, p. 148.
[2] The figures are given in detail in Stewart's *Sketches*, vol. ii., App. No. 1.

half-starved cattle, and raising a few bolls of poor
Oats and Bear. They resumed that foremost rank
in the military annals of their country which they
had not held since the days of Bannockburn and
Byland. In particular, they became familiar, during
the war in Canada and in the American Colonies,
with those "Plantations" which sounded so dreadful
in the ears of the Forty-Second when they first
heard of them, that the men rushed off in a panic to
regain their hills. They had now the opportunity
of seeing the glorious lands which are drained by
the St. Lawrence and the Hudson. Allotments in
the Province of New York to the amount of 2000
acres each were given by the Government to such
officers as had occasion to leave the Service.[1]
Thus so early as 1765 the American Plantations
had become a home both to Highland gentlemen
and to Highland soldiers. Not a few of them retired
from the Army and settled there, and those who
came home recounted round the peat fires of Mull,
Skye, the Lewis, and of all the glens of the mainland, the adventures they had met with in the
Forests of the Mohawk, of Lakes George and Cham-
plain, and beside the broad waters of Ontario. The
love of adventure and the love of fighting all over
the world, were incitements thus brought into competition with the rival love of idleness at home.
And as the possibility of fighting had come to an
end there, whilst the necessity of industry grew
more imperative, even old habits, so powerful with

[1] *Memoir and Correspondence of Mrs. Grant of Laggan*, vol. i. p. 8.

all primitive races, became less and less competent to counteract the attractions of the New World.

Powerful as the external influences were which thus came into operation, their action was rendered still more powerful by some new internal causes which about the same time began to crowd the people inconveniently at home. These new causes did not arise from political events of any kind. They arose especially from the concurrence of some discoveries, very different in kind, but all belonging to that class of agencies which often tell on the progress of the world and on the destiny of nations, far more deeply than the valour of soldiers, or the policy of statesmen. The fields of Nature are very wide fields, and of boundless fertility to those who walk on them with an eye to see, and a mind to question. Every now and then, from one or more of her vast domains, there is a rush of new Products, or of new Inventions. Then, suddenly, within perhaps the space of a few years, the Human Family finds itself "endowed with new mercies," and the whole conditions of life are changed over large areas of the world. Such a time, undoubtedly, was the latter half of the Eighteenth Century. Among many others there were in particular Three discoveries, during those fifty years, two of which told upon the whole of Europe, and one of which told especially upon the poorest population of the Highlands. Let us stop for a moment to look at these discoveries, for a whole volume of philosophy belongs to each.

In the dim and far-distant East,—in centuries as remote from ours as the country or the race,—more than a thousand years before the Christian era,—one of those terrible diseases had arisen which belong to the class of Plagues. So sweeping, so fatal, and at the same time so loathsome was it that we might almost suppose King David must have alluded to it when he sang of deliverance from the "noisome pestilence."[1] Yet there is reason to believe that the mysterious isolation of that curious people the Chinese, amongst whom it originated, kept the great nations of Western Asia uncontaminated for hundreds of years later than the latest days of the Jewish Monarchy. The Jews did indeed profit from the commerce of the East. The imagery of their literature is full of allusion to its products, and to the love they had for the employment of them. But neither the "Ivory Palaces" which "made them glad,"[2] nor the "Apes and Peacocks"[3] which ministered to their amusement, or to their sense of gorgeous colour, indicate any access to countries farther east than Hindostan. It was not, apparently, until the last quarter of the Sixth Century of the Christian era that Persian merchants brought the Smallpox from the far East into Arabian ports.[4] But this was in 572—the very year of the birth of Mahomet. And so it happened that this great scourge was planted in the Arabian Peninsula at the very time

[1] Ps. xci. 3.   [2] Ps. xlv. 8.   [3] 1 Kings x. 22.
[4] See Art. on "Smallpox," *Quarterly Review*, vol. xix. p. 361.

when, in the course of a few years, it could not fail to spread into all the regions which were soon to be penetrated by the great Conqueror who had just been born. The basin of the Mediterranean Sea, girdled as it was by all that remained of the oldest civilisations of the world, could not be a barrier, but became rather a channel and a road. The Moors took this new Pest with them when they crossed into Europe, and established their short but brilliant culture in the Palaces of Seville, Cordova, and Granada. Again, when they passed the Pyrenees, and, invading France, were defeated by Charles Martel, Christian Europe was indeed delivered from an Infidel conquest; but even victorious battles could only spread the contagion of disease. And so, from that date onwards, the Eastern Pestilence was established in the Western World, and at frequent intervals it mowed down its thousands among all the races which had settled there. It penetrated everywhere, and was indiscriminate in its attacks upon Celt and Saxon. No place was too secluded, no shore was too remote. From time to time it decimated even the lonely Hebrides. It is strange how entirely this is forgotten now. But we have the abundant evidence of a generation which remembered it only too well. Of the parish of Kilmuir in Skye the Minister writes in 1792 that up to a time beyond the middle of the century Smallpox prevailed to a very great extent, and almost depopulated the country.[1] Of the parish of Snizort

---

[1] *Old Stat. Acc.*, vol. ii. p. 551.

the Minister records that when this disease did visit the Island it sometimes swept whole families away, or left only one, or two, or three survivors.[1] The same tale is repeated from such secluded parishes as Durness in Sutherland,[2] and Glassary in Argyll, where it is mentioned as having been specially fatal among the children.[3] The effect of such a disease in checking population must have been very great.

Such was the state of things when, in 1716, an Englishwoman of high education and lively wit, going as the wife of the British Ambassador to Constantinople, and spending her holiday among the villages around that city, heard of the strange idea which had long been established among Turkish mothers, that by "grafting" this terrible disease upon their own healthy children they could be made to take the infection in a mild form, and could be practically ensured against its more dangerous attacks in after life. Singularly free from prejudice herself, and having that best gift of genius, the willingness to accept a new idea, Lady Mary Wortley Montagu did not content herself with curiosity and wonder, but carefully examined the evidence, and became convinced of the result.[4] Yielding to this conviction she gave proof of her courage and of her intelligence by "grafting" this terrible disease upon her own child in April 1718.

[1] *Old-Stat. Acc.*, vol. xviii. p. 182.
[2] *Ibid.* vol. iii. p. 582.   [3] *Ibid.* vol. xiii. p. 658.
[4] Her first account of it is given in a letter, April 1, 1718. *Works*, vol. i. p. 391. Ed. 1837.

Returning to England in 1719 she spared no exertion in trying to convince others of the safety of this method of escape from a great scourge, and in 1720 was able to tell a friend that the practice had been generally adopted by the highest classes in London.[1] Through some vicissitudes of fortune it made on the whole steady progress, and in 1754 gained the sanction of a most conservative profession in the verdict of the Royal College of Physicians.[2] It is a signal proof of the terror with which the pestilence of Smallpox must have inspired the people who had suffered from it, that a race so hostile to all novelties as the Highlanders was nevertheless quickly moved to try a remedy not only so new, but in itself so repulsive to feelings the most natural and the most deeply seated. It appears to have been introduced into the Highlands and Islands about 1760, and was almost universally practised by the people "with surprising success" even in the remote island of North Uist,[3] long before the close of the Eighteenth Century. The plague was stayed. This is the universal testimony of all authorities. And it is remarkable that, in a few districts where adverse prejudices could not be overcome, the disease continued to be destructive down to a much later date. In 1777-8 no less than 77 children perished in one Ross-shire parish, and the minister declares that the disease had been

---

[1] Lady M. W. Montagu's Works, vol. ii. p. 129.
[2] *Quarterly Review*, vol. xix. p. 366.
[3] *Old Stat. Acc.*, vol. xiii. p. 312.

wont to revisit the district every seven years, or even oftener.¹ Here we have a striking measure of the great effect on population produced by the general cessation of a check so long established, and so tremendous in its operation.

Thus the First of the Three great discoveries to which I have referred was one which promoted the increase of population by greatly lowering the death-rate. The Second was a discovery which still more powerfully promoted population by raising the supply of food. Our knowledge of the circumstances attending this great change is all the more interesting from its contrast with our profound ignorance as to the origin and development of the older staples of human subsistence. We know absolutely nothing of the first cultivation of the Cereals, although it is certain that this must have had a definite beginning and long stages of development.

The rapidly expanding commerce of the Eighteenth Century added immensely, and, in some cases, very suddenly, to the variety of human food. But in most cases these additions came in the form of products which could only be grown in distant climates, and the use of which had long been established among other nations. Tea was among the first and most remarkable of these, and it is curious to observe that the use of this beverage made such rapid progress in Scotland in the first half of the century, that even a man so enlightened as Culloden regarded it with positive alarm, and

---

[1] *Old Stat. Acc.*, vol. i. pp. 262-3.

actually recommended that the Legislature should take measures to restrain the poorer classes in their addiction to it.[1] From 1730 onwards it was already wholly displacing the native beverage of beer, and this so widely in the Towns of Scotland and in the Low Country as seriously to affect the revenue. To a large extent, however, the other new and varied articles of import were rather condiments and luxuries, than staple articles of food. It is all the more curious, therefore, that until long past the middle of the century we hear little or nothing of one new product of the vegetable world which was destined in a few years to bring about the most prodigious effects upon population that have ever arisen from a like cause. Nor, indeed, is there any wonder that little attention, and no expectation, should have been drawn to the Potato as at all likely to play any important part in adding to the resources of human sustenance. Although coming from the New World, it belonged to a family of plants which was well known in the Old, and which was most familiarly represented in Europe by the beautiful flowers and the tempting berries of the Deadly Nightshade. So well known had been the noxious properties belonging to the *Solanum*, that when the fruit of another member of the group was first introduced into Europe for edible purposes from the African Coast, the story of a miracle arose to account for its innocence or its wholesomeness. To this day when the Peasant of Provence includes the

[1] *Culloden Papers*, p. 190.

Tomato in his vegetable diet, he tells his children that originally it had been introduced by the Infidel Saracens as a means of poisoning the Christians, but that the "Bon Dieu" had interfered, and had converted it into a delicious fruit. Although the American *Solanum* had been brought home from Virginia in connection with one of the immortal names of English History, Sir Walter Raleigh, it had remained for 150 years in comparative neglect, cultivated only by a few botanists or gardeners as an object rather of curiosity than of use. Nobody could well have guessed its extraordinary properties, as, indeed, none of us can ever fully fathom or anticipate the wonderful alchemies of Nature. That a root belonging to a well-known and poisonous order of plants should turn out not only to be nutritious, but to be richer in life-sustaining power than any known substance of like composition, and that it should turn out to be easily cultivated in our own climate and in the least fertile of our own soils, —were results not to be foreseen by any science. But when this discovery was at last made, it was naturally seized upon by the population, which wanted above all things a crop which should be at once abundant, and, at the same time, capable of cultivation with a minimum of labour. The Celts of Ireland very soon began not only to use it as an adjunct to other food, but to live upon it as their main subsistence. From them it passed over to the Celts of the Hebrides, having been introduced into the Island of South Uist so early as 1743 by

Macdonald of Clanranald. Suspicious of all novelties, the Highlanders resisted the use of the Potato for some years, and it did not reach the neighbouring Island of Bernera till 1752. Yet within ten years of that date the Potato crop had come to support the whole inhabitants for at least one quarter of the year. Very soon it was found that it would grow luxuriantly almost everywhere—on land little better than sand and shingle, and in bogs, where it only required to be planted in those patches of ditched-off land which all over the Highlands came to be appropriately known as "lazy beds."

To the two great discoveries just described— one of them eradicating a destructive disease, and the other supplying a new and prolific source of sustenance—there now came to be added yet another—the Third—discovery, one which afforded all along the Western Coasts a new manufacturing industry which was at once lucrative and desultory— an industry which yielded a large return, and yet did not need any steady or continuous labour. This discovery was so curious and so almost unique in its history and results, that we must dwell on it for a little.

The men whom the world calls Thinkers are often curiously thoughtless,—else the attempt would never have been made to distinguish between the additions of value which are "earned" by Owners or Producers, because of some meritorious action of their own, and certain different additions which come to them from the exertions of other men, or from the general conditions of Society.

For the distinction breaks down the moment we look into it, and the moment we grasp the fact that all kinds and degrees of value come largely, and sometimes exclusively, from causes with which the Owners or Producers of valuable things have nothing to do. And most especially is this the case with those who live by the labour of their hands. The value of that which alone they have to sell, depends entirely on the desires, or on the knowledge, or on the powers of other men; and it constantly happens that sudden and great additions accrue to them upon that value, which they have not only done nothing to secure, but which it has been entirely out of their power either to expect or to foresee. There is no phrase so rich in fallacies as the common phrase that Labour is the only source of Wealth. It has no truth in it whatever—except when Labour is understood as including every form and variety of human influence and exertion, and especially the forms which are purely intellectual. Moreover, all these forms and kinds and degrees of influence must be included, not only as operating in our own time, but as they have been exerted continuously in all preceding generations. These generations have been the stages of our own growth, and each of them has contributed something to the store on which we are living now. In the sense in which Labour is commonly understood, which is physical labour, nothing can be more erroneous than the idea that it is the only, or the ultimate source of Wealth. Mind comes before Matter; Brain comes before

Muscle; Head comes before Hands. This is the law of Nature, and this is the order of precedence in her eternal Hierarchy. We have seen how, during the Military Ages, this complete subordination and dependence of the lower upon the higher kinds of human energy was evidenced in the enlisting of whole tribes of men under Chiefs of known capacity and power. In the Industrial Ages on which we have now entered the same great law of Nature was illustrated continually in the unlooked-for benefits which were daily and hourly accruing to the owners of Muscle from the owners of Brain, and from the new desires and demands started by their work in the Community at large.

Never, perhaps, was this order of precedence more signally shown than in the great increase in the value of their labour which came to the poorer classes of the Western Coasts of Scotland from the new industry to which I have referred. We have seen that the Founders of new nations in the reign of Elizabeth,—Botanists, and Gardeners, and Proprietors ever since,—had all been concerned in giving them a new product from the Land. Chemists and Manufacturers were now at work to give them a new product from the Sea. And in this case, too, nothing could have been more unexpected, or less connected with any kind of exertion of their own. The Ocean is fertile beyond all conception in animal life—immensely more fertile than the dry land. But, on the other hand, it holds within its vast domains nothing of the vegetable world, except the lowest of its forms. Moreover its vegetation, such as it is, is almost entirely confined to two narrow areas of shallow depth—one which finds its limit between high and low water mark, called the Littoral Zone, and the other an area close to shores which is known to naturalists as the Laminarian Zone. But in these two Zones between high water mark and a maximum depth of about fifteen fathoms,[1] wherever there are rocks or stones for attachment, sea-weeds grow in beds and masses which are often luxuriant and dense. Some of the smaller species, especially those belonging to the Green and Red series, are among the most beautiful Forms in nature. But the Olive-coloured series are not attractive in appearance, although they are the richest in useful products. Torn, slimy, and unsightly, when out of the water, and fetid in their decay, their multitudinous cells of organic structure are, nevertheless, so many batteries for eliminating and fixing in their own walls many of the inorganic elements of our world, which are held in solution by the Sea. In particular, the salts of Sodium and Potassium are richly concentrated in the stems and fronds of some of them, besides such rarer substances as Iodine and Bromine. Chemists in the service of the rising Industries of the Low Country soon found that from those seaweeds which grew between the tides, a plentiful supply could be extracted of the Carbonate of Soda. In the manufacture of Soap and of Glass established at Whitby and at Newcastle, this product was

---

[1] Balfour's *Botany*—Algæ.

valuable. There are many maritime countries to which this discovery would have brought no great source of wealth, because the Sea Coast is very often but a single border line, and much of it occupied by sandy shores, destitute of sea-weeds. But of all countries, probably, in the world, the Western Coasts of Scotland present the rare physical characteristics which could give to this discovery a maximum value. These coasts are wonderfully indented—the Ocean sending out innumerable arms which extend far among the hills—so far, and into such sheltered reaches, that the hazel-nut and the acorn drop ripe into waters continuous with the poles. The shore lines of the County of Argyll alone, with its Islands, extend to 2289 miles[1]—lines which, if unrolled, would almost reach the shores of the New World. Along the whole extent of the outer Hebrides, sea and land are intermixed through a thousand channels, so that within the space of a few miles they often constitute a labyrinth of creeks, rocks, and islets—generally exposed to a great rise and fall of tide. From this last cause the Littoral Zone was unusually ample for the growth of Fuci. Such was the country of which its barren shores were suddenly converted into a fruitful field, and its natural growths could be turned into money, by a kind of work the most simple, and not very laborious. The weed had only to be cut, gathered, and spread to dry upon the rocks or turf. Then a

[1] I derive this curious fact from an *Abstract of Geographical Statistics of the County*, drawn up by the late Captain Bedford, R.N., who directed the Admiralty Survey.

few stones, arranged somewhat in the manner of a prehistoric grave, forming a low and a loose enclosure, was all that was dignified by the name of a kiln. Within this little enclosure a lighted peat or bit of wood was used to set on fire a few fronds of the half-dried weed, and when it burst into a crackling flame, fresh weed had to be added so as to keep it down. In this way the weed was rather melted than burnt into a hot and pasty mass, which finally cooled and consolidated into a glassy and brittle substance not unlike the resin of commerce which is derived from pine-trees. For this substance so easily prepared, from a natural supply of raw material needing no labour in its cultivation, there arose an active demand during the latter part of the Eighteenth Century. It was first established on the shores of the Firth of Forth, so early as 1720, whence it passed to the Orkneys in 1723. In the Hebrides, it was introduced into the Island of Tyree only in 1746. But the price was then trifling. In 1768 the industry had become general and important,—the produce of the Western Coast being estimated at about 5000 tons. The price was then about £6, 10s. at the Glass manufactory of Newcastle. The price varied much during the rest of the Eighteenth Century. But every rise in price was met by increased production. For a short time during the French war the price is said to have reached the high figure of £20 per ton.[1] Among

---

[1] Macculloch's *Western Islands*, vol. i. p. 120. In 1803 I find that the price obtained for Tyree and Mull kelp was only £8, 8s. per ton.

my family estate accounts I find no record of any such price, and down to 1822 the average was probably less than half that amount.[1] Of this valuable material the Hebrides alone produced, when the trade was at its height, about 6000 tons annually—representing in good years a value which was a great deal more than double the whole of the agricultural rental of some of the estates on which it was produced.

Coming, as this new manufacture did, in addition to the two other causes tending to increase population, the trade in Kelp had a prodigious effect. It employed at various seasons an immense quantity of labour, the calculation being that every 300 tons of Kelp gave employment to 200 men during several months in the year. This is intelligible enough when we understand that for every ton of Kelp not less than 20 tons of wet weed had to be cut, dried, and melted,—so that the total produce of the Hebrides represented the preparation of 120,000 tons of the raw material. It brought in wages which had never been heard of before in the districts where it prevailed. In many places it encouraged families to settle and to multiply where the resources of agriculture were of the poorest; whilst it made both Proprietors and people blind to the

---

[1] This account of the Kelp trade I have taken partly from a MS. Report on the subject drawn up for my grandfather, John, sixth Duke of Argyll, in 1788, and from a paper read before the Society of Arts in 1884 by Mr. Edward Ed. C. C. Stanford, through whose chemical skill and enterprise I succeeded in partially reviving the Trade when almost extinct in 1863, and through whose recent discovery of a new Product, which he has called "Algine," a further development may now be hoped for.

dangers of unlimited subdivision. The price paid to the workers for the Kelp they made amounted very often to a great deal more than the whole rent they paid for their holdings—so that as regarded these they sat practically rent free. Under such conditions, the temptations and inducements to early marriage, and a stationary and dreamy existence, were insuperable—and the characteristics of Highland life which we have seen so graphically described by Sir Walter Scott, as applicable to the disposition and distribution of the people at the close of the Military Ages, were repeated and even exaggerated all along the Western Coasts long after the Industrial Ages had begun.

It would have been astonishing indeed, if under such a combination of causes, all coming more or less together, and all stimulating population in different manners and degrees, the Highlanders, and especially the Islanders, had not rapidly multiplied in number. Never, perhaps, in the history of nations, had such unexpected and bounteous fountains of supply been opened to any people—unless, indeed, to Tribes who by conquest had come into possession of some wealthy land. But in this case the new resources had arisen without any exertion of their own. An arrest laid upon the hand of disease and death—a new and abundant supply of food—and, along all the lines of coast, a new manufacture, bringing money where money was almost unknown before:—such were the additions to the value of life and to the fruits of the simplest manual labour, which were brought to the Highlands from outside themselves—from the genius of some, and the invention of others—and the advancing knowledge of the human family. All these were brought to bear upon a people which had already been increasing rapidly beyond the limits of their subsistence, and the previously known resources of the land they lived in. The result was that they multiplied at a tenfold rate, and any temporary abundance was soon turned to want.

The effect of such gifts as these upon any society of men, must always depend upon its preparation to receive them. Here, again, we come upon the contrast between the Highlands and the country of the Border Clans. In no part of the Lowlands of Scotland did the use of the Potato lead to any undue increase of the population. Here and there, for a little while, it may have prolonged old conditions. But population had already in the Lowlands become almost everywhere redistributed by the great current of industrial interests which first set in after the union of the Crowns in 1603, and which had gathered head and power after the union of the Parliaments in 1707. The military classes had been, or were being, rapidly absorbed into the ranks of commerce, of manufacture, and of an agriculture which was at least beginning to be scientific. The Potato came too late to stop the migrations which were determined by these new conditions. It was a pure gain with no drawbacks or temptations to abuse. The Potato was used as an adjunct and a supplement to higher kinds of food, and not as a staple article of subsistence. Its place in agriculture was a corresponding place. It took rank among the new Root Crops which afforded the means of a profitable rotation with the Cereals. It became an important article of commerce, and sometimes brought higher prices than any other produce of the soil. In all these circumstances the effect of the Potato in the Lowlands was in contrast with its effect in the Highlands. There the old military classes, the "broken men," were still occupying the ground in the manner, to the extent, and with all the effects described by Sir Walter Scott in *Rob Roy*. The raising of the Highland Regiments had indeed opened a door for the entering of new motives. But the mere number of men temporarily removed was but a fraction of the numbers which were steadily tending to swell in every glen, and to swarm on every shore. Among them the Potato was seized upon as a new support for a life of inaction. It gradually grew to be the main food of the people during a great portion of the year. It was but little sold or exported. It induced no rise in the standard of living. It brought no increase of accumulated wealth. It was simply eaten. And not only did it feed the people, but it unquestionably made them more prolific. When to this was added a manufacture such as that of Kelp, of which the raw material lay around their own doors, and in the possession of which they had a practical monopoly as compared with all the Southern and all the inland portions of the Kingdom, the

Highlanders or Hebrideans were naturally encouraged to feel that they could live in increasing numbers in the enjoyment of a rude and a low abundance, derived from a few productions of the soil and of the sea. They were thus caught, so to speak, by powerful causes tending to stereotype and aggravate the poverty of old conditions, before they had time to be brought within the stream of the nation's industrial life, as it had been developed in the Low country, and among the Border Highlands. It was not possible for them to think of or to foresee that the one new industry on which they so much depended was an industry depending absolutely on the continuance of foreign wars, or upon the continued maintenance of special taxes limiting or prohibiting the import of raw materials far richer than seaweed in the products it afforded.

The result was one which has been almost forgotten, and which at first sight may well seem extraordinary. The poorest portion of the Kingdom became by far the most populous in proportion to its resources, and speedily exhibited a rate of increase far greater than that which could be seen in the richest and most advancing rural districts of the country. The latter half of the Eighteenth Century witnessed in the Highlands, more especially in the Islands—districts purely rural—a swelling of population which seems almost incredible, and yet the evidence of it is abundant and detailed.

There are two large Islands and two small Islands lying south of the long promontory of Kintyre, and all closely connected with the Firth of Clyde. These are Arran, Bute, and the two Cumbraes. We do not now think of any of these Islands as belonging to the Hebrides or to the Highlands—although there is no wilder mountain scenery in Scotland than Glen Rosa and Glen Sannox in Arran. But the stream of commerce, and of the industrial life of the Kingdom, has now so long circled round them, and has so penetrated through them, that all the conditions are the settled conditions of the Lowlands. But we must remember that in the last century this was not so. At that time they contained Gaelic-speaking populations whose habits of life were the same as those of the other Western Isles. Counting this southern group, then, among the Hebrides, there were in all ninety-five inhabited Islands and Islets, including the lonely St. Kilda, on the Western Coasts of Scotland. There is good reason to believe that in the year 1755 the total population of these Islands was about 52,200. During the sixteen years between 1755 and 1771 the increase amounted to 10,538. During the next twenty-four years, from 1771 to 1795, the further increase amounted to 12,728—so that taking the forty years between 1755 and 1795 the total increase was 23,266, or not far short of one-half of the original number of inhabitants.[1] Considering that the whole of this Insular area may be said to have been almost purely rural,—since two or three so-called Towns were then nothing but insignificant villages,—this is a rate of

---

[1] Walker's *Hebrides*, 1808, vol. i. pp. 24-6.

increase which was probably unknown in any part of Europe, seeing that it arose from breeding only, and included no element of immigration. Moreover, it is all the more remarkable when we compare it with the rate of increase in the kindred population of the mainland during the same period. In 1755 the Gaelic speaking Parishes on the mainland had a total population of 237,598, yet on this much larger number the increase in 1795 was little more than one-half of the increase on the smaller population of the Islands. Although several causes contributed to keep down the rate of increase on the mainland as compared with the Islands, yet we cannot mistake the one cause which operated most powerfully as an artificial stimulus to population in the Hebrides. Beyond all question, it was the Kelp manufacture. It is true that many Parishes on the mainland were extensively bounded by the sea-shores. But the purity and strength of the water in the open Ocean, and the tumult of its uncontaminated waves, are required to stimulate the growth of the richest seaweeds. Apart, therefore, from their immensely more extended lines of coast there were chemical causes at work to concentrate the Kelp trade in the hands of the Hebrideans; and it was on the strength mainly of this tempting, but dangerous, because precarious, industry that these people multiplied so fast. This conclusion is confirmed when we look into the details. The Insular Parishes in which the population increased fastest between 1755 and 1795 are almost always the Parishes which had the most productive shores for seaweed. Thus the Parish of the Small Isles (Rum, Canna, Eigg, etc.) rose from 858 to 1339; Stornoway, in the Lewis, from 1836 to 2639; Kilmuir (Skye) from 1581 to 2500; Tyree from 1602 to 2416. These are but individual examples of a general fact. On the mainland the largest increase was in the Parishes which had the longest boundary of open sea, whilst in some of the inland Parishes there was no increase at all, and even, in some cases, an actual decline in numbers. Thus the inland Parish of Farr, in Sutherland, diminished by 200, whilst its coast neighbour, Tongue, with a long line of shore, increased by more than 400.[1]

It was impossible that there could be such a rapid and extraordinary increase of population without results specially dangerous among men who were the poorest in the Kingdom, and who were the least qualified to provide against it by the resources of a various and an advancing industry. Under such conditions there could not fail to be a tremendous and frequent pressure upon the limits of a bare subsistence. Accordingly the evidence is abundant which proves the extreme poverty of the country, and the frequency with which its people were exposed to the severest scarcity, and sometimes to the dangers of actual famine. There are ample sources of information which fill up all the time between the date spoken of in Sir Walter Scott's tale of *Rob Roy* and the close of the Eighteenth

[1] Table of population in Walker's *Hebrides*, vol. i. pp. 28-9.

Century. We have the famous Letters of Captain Burt written about 1730 by an Officer who was stationed at Inverness, and travelled often through the Central Highlands on his way to and from the Capital of the North. We have the Tour of Mr. Pennant, who, in 1769 and 1772 visited not only the mainland, but the Hebrides, and saw everything with the eye that belongs to the Naturalist and the Scientific Observer. We have the systematic and admirable work of Professor Walker, the result of successive journeys through every part of the country undertaken at various intervals between the years 1760 and 1790. We have the *Statistical Account of Scotland*, organised by Sir John Sinclair in the last decade of the Century—1792-5—in which we have all the information which occurred to the best educated men in the country,—the Minister of each Parish giving as complete an account as he could of its history and of its actual condition. Lastly, we have the Professional Reports drawn under the direction of the Board of Agriculture about the same time. The great advantage of all these books is, that they were written before many modern controversies had arisen, and when the view taken of facts was unbiassed by the social theories and the political passions of a later day. The burden of their song is uniformly the same, and the earliest of these writers, Captain Burt, illustrates his picture of the condition of the people by details and incidents which are often more instructive than any general statements, however accurate.

"QUEENAIG," RANGE OF MOUNTAINS, SUTHERLAND.

There is, for example, no indication of the condition of industry, and of the standard of living, in any country, more significant and more accessible to observation, than the scene presented by its Marketplaces. If its natives have any produce at all to sell, it must be brought to these places, and the range of variety, of quantity, and of price to be met with there, is an infallible index of plenty or of want. Inverness, though a mere village in 1730, was still not only the most important place in the Highlands, but the only Town existing in the country. Yet Captain Burt's account of its Market-days is an account of almost incredible poverty. One man might bring under his arm a small roll of linen, another a piece of coarse plaiding. Such men were quite considerable Dealers. Others would bring two or three cheeses of about 3 or 4 lb. weight. A kid sold for sixpence, or eightpence at the best. Small quantities of butter, tied up in bladders, were set down in the dirt of the street. Here were a few goat-skins—there a piece of wood for a cart-wheel. The price of such articles when sold was spent by the natives in purchasing a horn, or a few wooden spoons, or a wooden platter, or some such rude plenishing for their huts. One Highlander might be seen near eating a large onion without salt or bread —another gnawing a carrot—or other such vegetable rarities, none of which were then produced in the country.[1] Nor can we encourage the sentimental comfort that although little was sold, yet plenty

---

[1] Burt's *Letters*, vol. i. (ed. 1876) pp. 83-4.

was produced, everything being consumed at home. Poverty in marketable surplus is an infallible indication of a corresponding poverty in home consumption, and in home production. Where there is habitually little or no surplus, not even a bare sufficiency can ever be secure. There may be years of plenty; but there are quite sure to be many years of scarcity, and some of famine. Accordingly, Captain Burt tells an anecdote "of the time of one great scarcity here,"—as if the full record of such times would include a number. And the anecdote he does tell of that one time, brings pathetically before us the tremendous difference between that kind of destitution which affects individuals alone from the want of money, and that other kind of destitution which affects a whole people from the want of food. A woman came to the wife of the Officer in command at Fort-William, imploring her to get for her a single peck of oatmeal from the Military Stores, to save her children from starvation. But even the Military Stores were at a low ebb, from the impossibility of buying meal in the country, and the detention of some expected vessels. The poor woman was therefore offered a shilling as a mark of sympathy. After looking at it for a moment, she burst into tears—laid the useless coin down—and exclaimed, "Madam, what am I to do with this? my children cannot eat it." The peck of meal was given to her, and Captain Burt says he never saw such joy. But what must have been the condition of the people who were not near any Military Stores, and had no importing vessels to look to when storms had passed?

Some forty years had elapsed from that date to the date of Pennant's Tour. There was no change for the better. The use of Potatoes had extended, and the manufacture of Kelp had become universally established wherever the materials existed. But population had pressed hard on the heels of every new resource. During even a portion of that interval—during even one quarter of it—the number of mouths to be fed had in many Parishes increased not by dozens, or by scores, but by hundreds. The consequences were what might have been expected where there had been absolutely no corresponding advance in the knowledge or practice of a higher agriculture. Pennant saw poverty everywhere, with scarcity at the very doors. In the great and fertile Island of Islay he saw "a people worn down with poverty"—raising wretched crops of Bear, and "drinking more of it in the form of whiskey than eating of it in the form of bannocks." In their smoky cabins "pot-hooks hung from the middle of the roofs, with pots pendent over a grateless fire, filled with fare that might rather be called a permission to exist than a support of vigorous life"—the inmates lean, withered, dusky, and smoke-dried. Notwithstanding the excellency of the land, above £1000 worth of meal was annually imported. A famine was threatened at the time of his visit, but was prevented by the seasonable arrival of a meal-ship.[1] Of the Island of Rum he

[1] Pennant's *Tour*, 1771 (ed. 1776), Part I. pp. 261-2.

wrote that the people were a well-made, well-looking race, but carried famine in their aspect."[1] Of Skye he said that the produce of the crops was very rarely "in any degree" proportioned to the wants of the inhabitants. Golden seasons had happened, when they had superfluity. But "the years of famine were as ten to one."[2] It is nearly the same story everywhere. In Sutherland he found the people almost torpid with idleness and most wretched, the whole tract seeming the very "residence of sloth." Until famine pinched, they would not bestir themselves; but crowds were passing when he was there, emaciated with hunger, to the eastern coast, on the report of a ship being there loaded with meal.[3]

In all descriptions written by an English stranger some allowance is to be made on account of the much higher standard of living to which he was accustomed among the agricultural population of the South. As regards certain particulars, this allowance may be large; as, for example, when such strangers speak with horror and disgust of the Highland huts and hovels with no chimneys, the fire made in the middle of the floor; or when, in respect to food, the people are described as repairing to the shores to live on shell-fish. Such houses were not very much poorer than those which the Chiefs themselves had inhabited only a few years before; whilst the habitual use of shell-fish as one

---

[1] Pennant's *Tour*, 1771 (ed. 1776), Part I. p. 319.
[2] *Ibid.* p. 353.   [3] *Ibid.* p. 365.

article of diet was no evil at all, and had certainly descended by unbroken usage from prehistoric times. Shell-fish are now among the luxuries most enjoyed by the most comfortable artisans in our largest Towns. To be driven to live upon shell-fish almost exclusively is, however, a very different condition of things. On the other hand, we must remember that this low standard of dwellings and of food, as compared with the same classes in the South, is part of the case which illustrates and establishes the dangerous position of the Highland people up to the close of the Eighteenth Century, when, in the face of such poverty, they were nevertheless increasing at the rate which has been shown. Moreover, we have such evidence as that of Pennant more than confirmed by men from whose language no deduction whatever can be made on account of their being strangers, or on the ground of unfamiliarity with traditional and poor conditions of habitation, or of food. The truth is, that the language of Pennant, spoken of the years preceding 1772, falls far short of the descriptions—although less eloquent and sensational in form—which are given of some following years by the native Ministers, whose invaluable Reports constitute the First Statistical Account. Only ten years after Pennant's Tour, in 1782-3, there was a great failure of the Oat and Bear crop all over Scotland, and the scarcity told, of course, with double severity in the Highlands. Thus, even in Easter Ross, a district comparatively fertile, the Minister reports that the resources of the sea in fish, and especially in shell-fish, were the main support of the people in his own Parish of Fearn, and in all the neighbouring Parishes ; " so that hundreds of men and women, with their horses, were seen daily coming home with great burdens and loads of the best cockles." But bad as this was, it was better than forty years before, when (in 1740), many people were starved to death.[1] The same Minister, writing in 1791, declares that the terrible year of 1781 was only the beginning of a series of bad seasons, which had then continued ever since, so that nothing like a good crop had been raised among them during the ten intervening years.[2] Another Minister in the same County says that the scarcity of 1782 had impaired the constitution of some of the poor for the rest of their life.[3] From Orkney we hear that in some "late bad years" the people lived very miserably, mostly upon milk and cabbage, although none had actually died.[4] But within the memory of then living men, in 1739-41, the years had been so bad that many had died of want.[5] In Mull the memory had survived of a terrible famine about a hundred years before, in the reign of William III., which had almost depopulated the whole Parish. On one extensive line of shore only two families had survived.[6]

The great interest of these facts lies in this, that they reveal a principle and a law. A people

---

[1] *Old Stat. Acc.*, vol. iv. p. 300.
[2] *Ibid.* p. 299.
[3] *Ibid.* vol. i. p. 262.
[4] *Ibid.* vol. xiv. p. 352.
[5] *Ibid.* p. 319.
[6] *Ibid.* p. 188.

which has little or nothing to sell is quite sure to be a people liable at times to have little or nothing to eat. It is a common sentiment to admire the olden times, and the primitive conditions in which small communities lived for themselves only, consumed all that they produced, and produced only what they could consume. But though this is a common, it is nevertheless an ignorant sentiment. Where there is no surplus, there can be no storage, no saving, no accumulation. And where there is none of these there can be no security against the vicissitudes of the seasons. The production must be without knowledge, and the consumption without foresight. It would be presumptuous, indeed, to say that great civilised communities, in the possession of skill and capital, can never be liable to famines. It is easy to imagine, and even to specify, contingencies under which the richest populations might be overwhelmed. If, for example, any disease comparable in destructiveness with that which in 1846 attacked the Potato, were to attack the Wheat plant, or still more the Cereals in general, nothing could avert a desolating famine. It is well that we should remember such possibilities, and that we should recognise the dependence which they imply. But as a matter of historical fact the prevalence of scarcities and famines has steadily diminished over the world in proportion to the establishment of civilised conditions. And the very first of these conditions is the working of all Producers beyond the mere getting of a subsistence for themselves. In the making of some surplus, and in the storing of it, or of its value, lies the origin of Capital. Both are the direct result of Mind—of Mind in the form of knowledge, or of invention, or of skill in working; and of Mind in the form of intention and foresight in the use to which gains are put. A people that is consuming almost all that it produces, can be contributing nothing to the progress of the world, and is quite sure to be pressing very hard and very dangerously on the limits of its own subsistence. There may be cases in which this is at least comparatively unavoidable, because of the barrenness of the land they live in, and the poverty of its resources. But in the vast majority of cases it arises simply from ignorance, and from mental lethargy.

The Human Species presents in this matter a great enigma. It is the high prerogative of Man to subdue Nature—by knowledge to find out her fruits, and by skill to cultivate and to improve them. But whole generations, and even centuries, may pass over particular portions of the Human Family during which this prerogative seems to fall with them into complete abeyance. In matters purely physical it becomes literally true that seeing, they see, and do not perceive—that hearing, they hear, and do not understand. No suggestion, however obvious, seems ever to occur to them. They tread upon with their feet, and fumble in their hands, many of the most bounteous gifts of the organic world, each one of them with immense possibilities of development—and yet not a single hint is taken—not a single seed is sown—not a single germ is tended. Even the slender inheritances of former ages are hardly preserved, or are actually suffered to fall into ruinous decay. It is the frequency of this phenomenon that gives force to the argument of Archbishop Whately that no race of Man has ever risen from the lowest stages, except by contact with some Intelligence other than, and higher than, their own. Nor is this a question of race. All races have exhibited this condition during long periods of stagnant life, and some of them, too, in combination with high qualities of imaginative and lively wit. Such was the condition of the Highlanders in respect to their knowledge of the agricultural resources of their own country, not only during all the Military Ages, but down close to the times in which we are now living. The detailed accounts of it which we have from the most authentic sources, and that which some of us could give from our own observation, seem really to be hardly credible. And yet it is always to be remembered that the same thing was true of the Lowlands at an earlier date. The Highlanders were from one to two centuries behind in almost everything. Many causes contributed to this—distance, language, the habits and the usages of Celtic Feudalism.

It is, however, a great mistake to count among these causes any natural barrenness of soil. The Highland country is not a poor one as regards some great natural productions. Its climate, though unfavourable for certain fruits of the earth, is pre-eminently fitted for others, and these of a highly valuable kind. The truth is that it yields some such products in a rich abundance with which few other countries can compare. The native crop of the country is its natural Grasses, which are luxuriant beyond description—covering with verdure the steepest mountains, and the loftiest tablelands, insinuating themselves among the barest rocks, and carpeting the sandy levels along the margins of the sea. Some parts of the country, which have been reputed to be the poorest, and in which the inhabitants have been most, and longest poverty-stricken, are now well known to be naturally the richest in the quality of their Grasses. The Hebridean pastures are of the very finest quality. From the earliest times all over the Highlands the people had been possessed of a native breed of Cattle, and of a native breed of Sheep—domestic animals through which these Grasses could be converted into the most coveted forms of human food, the very best of meat, and the very best of cheese and butter. Yet they did not know the methods of breeding or of feeding, which to us now seem the most obvious and elementary. For example, it never occurred to the people that the over-abundant herbage of summer could be cut and dried, so as to furnish provender for the winter. The consequence was that their Cattle died by thousands in every season which was at all severe. All the surplus grass, which might have been made into hay, was allowed to rot in absolute waste. Those which survived the winter were miserably small,—not because the breed was a bad one, or because it was incapable of improvement, for even now it is a favourite in the market,—but simply because the animals were neither bred nor fed with the slightest knowledge of the simplest methods.

But more than this :—strange to say, whilst no natural hints or suggestions in the direction of improvement seem ever to have been taken, even the most accidental causes in the direction of decline, were not only yielded to without resistance, but were accepted and cherished under ridiculous arguments and superstitions. Thus, the pressure of famine had driven the people occasionally to resort to the barbarous and destructive expedient of bleeding their Cattle for the purpose of mixing blood with the produce of their scanty grain, and so making cakes more sustaining than oatmeal and water. They had forgotten the origin of this custom, and they did not know that it must tend to aggravate the feebleness and exhaustion which affected their animals from poverty of winter food. The idea arose that the Cattle were the better of being bled, and the practice was continued when the original necessity had ceased. I have myself spoken with men still alive, and not of extreme age, who recollect having eaten those cakes when they were children, and who seemed to regret the loss of them among other Celtic blessings which a remorseless civilisation has swept away. The miserable size and condition of the Highland Cattle, even when they survived the winter at all, is described by many writers. Captain Burt likened them in size to "Northampton Calves." And yet these Cattle were the only produce of the country which was ever sent to southern markets. They were the staple of the whole area of the Highlands, the only produce on which the people could depend for any surplus, or any means of purchasing the fruits of other lands.

The same story, but with some circumstances of special aggravation, has to be told of the treatment in the Highlands of that other domestic animal which constitutes one of the very chiefest resources of Mankind. The native breed of Sheep, like the native breed of Cattle, was small and degenerate. It is now wholly extinct. But there seems good reason to believe that it might have been improved by the same methods which in later years made the Black Cattle of the Highlands so excellent and so profitable. Sheep were never an article of sale. The people had never discovered that any breed of Sheep could live at large upon the mountains. They were treated as delicate and tender animals—folded and housed at night. In this way, of course, they were kept in small flocks only, and wholly for domestic use. Hence, in the Highland code of honour, they were not generally "lifted," or stolen, like Cattle, which were considered always as lawful prey. The wool of the Sheep was worked up into homespun clothing, and the deficiency of milk from the half-starved Cows was eked out, as it still is in Italy, by the milk of Ewes. Yet, with all the care which such valuable uses did ensure, the care was so little allied with knowledge, that the treatment of the Sheep was even more ruinous and destructive than the treatment of the Cattle. Their pasture was the poorest, and often at a great distance. They were folded in summer and harvest, and housed in winter and spring. No attention was paid to the choice of Rams, and they were left to nature as regarded the breeding season. Consequently the Lambs came before the grass,—all being stinted, and many starved. From the middle of May they were deprived of half their mothers' milk, by separation during the night, so that the Ewes might be milked for human use in the morning. About the end of June the Lambs were weaned—sometimes in a most barbarous manner, by tying a small stick across their mouths, which not only prevented them from sucking, but even from pasturing with any tolerable ease.[1] No wonder that the breed decayed,—that they were considered, perhaps erroneously, as incapable of recovery, and were soon everywhere supplanted by another breed, which, for some centuries, had been more skilfully treated in the Low Country.

These miserable conditions of pastoral economy, in a country by nature pre-eminently pastoral, explain and justify an observation made by those who first came to examine and report upon the Highlands. Generally, they said, the natives of

---

[1] *Agricultural Survey of Argyllshire*, 1798, p. 240. By James Macdonald, A.M., 1811. Drawn up for the Board of Agriculture.

most countries, even the least advanced, have something to teach others,—some local product in which their own land abounds, and in the cultivation of which they show a skill from which strangers can learn something. But in the agriculture of the Highlands nothing of the kind was to be found among the people.[1] They did not know how to utilise, with even tolerable economy, the natural and spontaneous resources of their Hills and Glens. They treated with similar simplicity even that most ancient and immemorial gift—the cultivation of the Cereals. The grey Oat, and the Bear, and the Rye, which they grew, were all of inferior sorts, and bore every mark of having degenerated in their hands. So little did they know that most elementary of all principles in the improvement of the fruits of the earth,—the selection of the best seed for propagation,—that they were actually known to select the worst, on the idea that the best should be used as food, and that the worst was good enough for casting into the ground. There are a few places in the Hebrides where a light sandy soil so drinks in the rays of the sun, and so retains the heat, that they used sometimes to yield a large and an extraordinary early harvest, even from twenty to twenty-five fold. But the general return of arable land in the Grey Oat of the country did not average more than from three and a half to four fold, although neither the soil nor the climate could be blamed for this. Nowhere in Europe was

[1] Walker's *Hebrides*, Introduction, p. 4.

equal labour bestowed on such an inconsiderable crop.[1] And to the scantiness of their harvests in respect to quantity was added the loss constantly arising from the difficulty of securing them. This was almost entirely due to the inveterate habit of sowing so late in the spring that the grain rarely ripened before the early autumnal gales. Furthermore, the people, before the introduction of the Potato, had not a single garden vegetable, or any vegetable product whatever, except their grain.

Yet it was in the face of all this poverty of knowledge, and consequent scantiness of production, that the population was, nevertheless, increasing at the tremendous rate which has been shown. On almost every farm there were double, sometimes treble, or quadruple the number of hands which were required for the labour to be expended. And this too, in spite of implements and methods of handling them, which were as primitive and as wasteful as their customs in respect to the breeding and feeding of Cattle and of Sheep. Their Plough was a rude machine, to which four horses, or sometimes in the Eastern Counties, eight oxen, were yoked abreast, and which were tended by at least three men. One of these had the strange function of walking backwards in front of the animals, and striking them in the face, "to make them proceed forwards."

[1] Walker's *Hebrides*, vol. i. pp. 212-213.
[2] *Ibid.* vol. i. p. 123. The real object of this arrangement seems to have been to enable the man to stop the team at a moment's notice, lest the least check from a stone or a root might carry away the whole rickety gear.

But this was not all. The Plough was often preceded by another archaic machine, called a Reestle, for cutting the fibrous roots which the Plough was incompetent to deal with. One or two more horses were required for this, and two additional men. Thus, from four to six horses, and from three to five men were performing, and performing very ill, the work which could have been better done by two horses and one man.[1] There was thus all over the country a great superfluity of hands, which it was impossible fully to employ, and of mouths which it was quite as difficult adequately to feed. There were few farms in the Highlands which could not be equally well cultivated with one-third, and some with one-half fewer men-servants and horses than were actually used.[2] Two Parishes are mentioned which afforded more than 500 men to the Regiments in the American War of 1755-63, and yet all their cultivation went on as before. In one district of these two Parishes, of which the rent was £700, there were 700 women, all of necessity half idle.

The perfect similarity between many Highland and many Lowland Parishes, as regarded soil, climate, and character of surface, made the contrast all the more striking between their rural economy in these respects. In the South, there was no such waste of labour, no such extravagant superfluity of horses and of hands. There the population had become adjusted to the industry and the known resources of the country.[3] Hence

---

[1] Walker's *Hebrides*, vol. i. p. 125 and p. 83. [2] *Ib.* p. 84. [3] *Ib.* p. 82.

the contrast, too, between the two portions of Scotland, in respect to the activity of the people. The language which Sir Walter Scott puts into the mouth of the Glasgow Bailie respecting the habitual idleness of the Highland people, is language which was perfectly correct as the description of an hereditary habit, but would be wholly incorrect as a description of any peculiarity of race. Thousands of the people who were so industrious in the Lowlands were quite as much of Highland blood as any of those who remained among the mountains. The people in the Highlands were idle simply because they had little or nothing to do, and thus idleness had become with them, as it will become with all men under like conditions, habitual and hereditary. They had long been multiplying beyond the opportunities and the calls for labour which could be afforded by the knowledge and by the habits of the society to which they belonged.

Such was the state of things when some acquaintance with more civilised conditions began to stir the minds, and elevate the desires of the Highlanders. Men returning from the more plenteous lands in which they had fought and bled with unsurpassed courage, discipline, and devotion, could not but feel the nakedness of their own country, and the poverty of their own hereditary modes of life. The same influence arose in numberless districts from men who went to service in the Low Country. Restlessness, and a sense of discomfort arose among them. They did not see any means of improvement in their own country, because its poverty was inseparable from those very habits and institutions to which they themselves had always been most devotedly attached. On the other hand, they had seen the New World. The men of the Forty-Second had been quartered for many months in Albany, the Capital of the Province of New York. There they had been the admired of all admirers, petted and caressed by the old Dutch families who had founded the Colony, as well as by the English settlers; and there, among the still uncleared forests of the Hudson, they had taken part in happy excursions of camp life, which must have recalled the summer Shealings of the Highlands.[1] Along with several other Highland Regiments they had revenged the defeat of Ticonderoga on the Heights of Abraham. New scenes, and with them, new visions, had opened up before them.

The consequences were natural and inevitable. Within a few years of the close of that war in 1763, a steady stream of emigration to the Colonies poured out from many parts of Scotland, but especially from the Highlands. It began, as all important movements must begin, with the most intelligent and educated classes—those who had occupied the position of Tacksmen, and had been, as it were, the officers and non-commissioned officers of the Military Clans. It extended rapidly among all the subordinate classes of the tenantry—

[1] *Memoirs of an American Lady*, by Mrs. Grant of Laggan, p. 57.

embracing, in some places, a large number of those who, by selling their stock, could realise a sum sufficient to cover the expense and to start the family with some little capital in America. This movement began about 1762, and became general and extensive about 1770.[1] Indeed, forty years before, as early as 1722, no difficulty had been found in recruiting a considerable number of Highlanders at Inverness to emigrate to Georgia. These dates are important. Even the latest of them is before the new system had time to operate, by which the wasted and neglected mountains of the country were for the first time turned to account by the grazing of Sheep. The earliest of these dates is long before that immense work of reclamation had been even thought of. The movement was purely spontaneous and instinctive, and it spread steadily among all the most congested populations of the Western Coasts and Islands. From Duirinish, in Skye, between 1771 to 1790, no less than eight large Transport Ships had sailed with Emigrants for American settlements. They carried off at least 2400 souls;[2] yet so tremendous was the multiplying power that, in 1792, the total population of the Parish was as great as in 1772. From Glensheil, on the opposite mainland, the movement had been led, in 1769 and 1773, by men who were substantial farmers.[3] In the latter year it reached the remote parish of Reay in Sutherland,[4] and the far Island of

---

[1] Earl of Selkirk's *Observations on Emigration*, 1805, p. 171.
[2] *Old Statistical Account*, vol. iv. pp. 132-3.
[3] *Ibid.* vol. vii. pp. 131-3.   [4] *Ibid.* p. 574.

South Uist, from which "vast numbers" are said to have followed during the next twenty years.[1] Jura and Colonsay lent their contingent at the same time.[2] The Small Isles followed a little later —the Minister in this case specially reporting that these little fragments of a broken land were "overstocked with people" from the fruit of early marriages, and an area of soil which was "able to supply them but scantily with the necessaries of life."[3] The parents often divided with a newly married son their holdings, already of necessity very small, which "reduced both to poverty and misery." From Appin, one of the oldest seats of the Military Clans, and a Parish with a very small area of arable land as compared with the vast and steep mountain surfaces which were then almost useless, the emigration began in 1775, and, in spite of it, the Minister reports, in 1790, that the inhabitants were then so crowded that "some relief of this sort seemed absolutely necessary."[4]

This was a rush indeed. Some of the Ministers who refer to it call it a "rage." It was purely spontaneous, and in some of its circumstances was marked by the special characteristics of popular waywardness and impulse. The selection made of particular Plantations for the new home, seems curiously capricious, but it was in reality determined by accidents connected with the clannish instincts of the race. Wherever some friends or Clansmen

---

[1] *Old Statistical Account*, vol. xiii. p. 298.   [2] *Ibid.* vol. xii. p. 324.
[3] *Ibid.* vol. xvii. p. 281.   [4] *Ibid.* vol. i. p. 488.

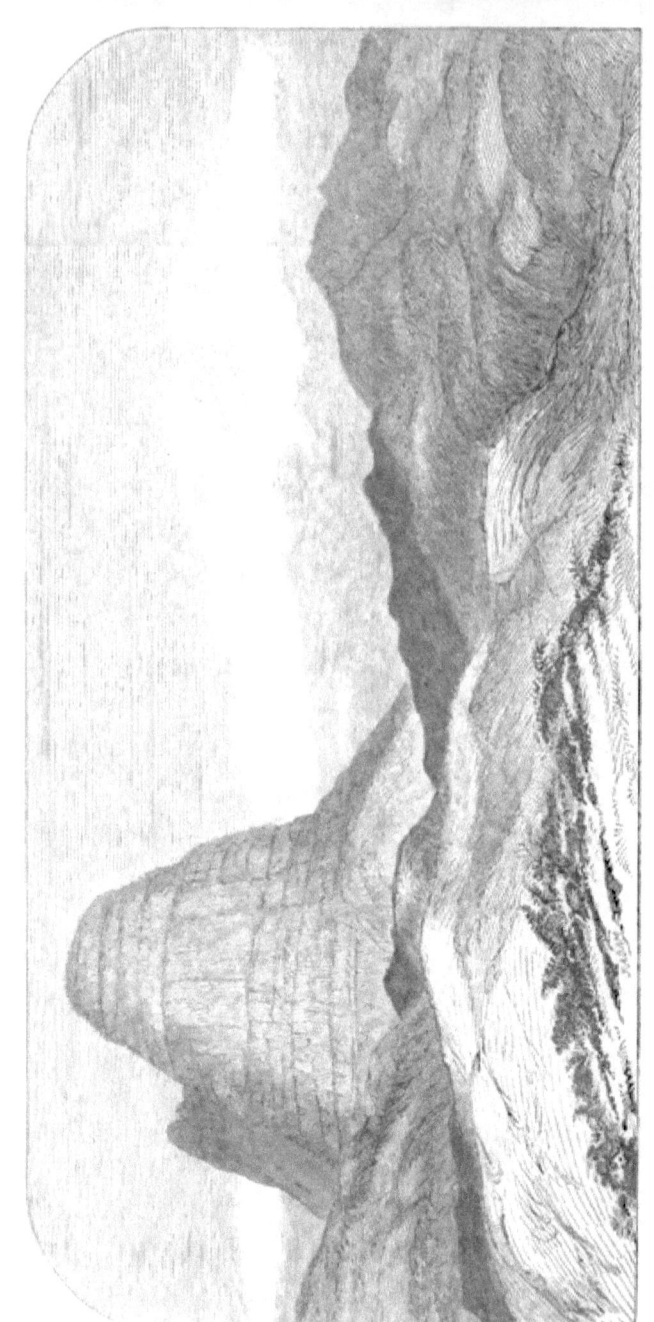

"SOULVEIN," SUTHERLAND.

from the same glens or Islands had happened to precede them, there the rest followed, when they moved at all. Thus almost each separate district of the Highlands had its own preference. The people of Inverness had formed an early connection in Georgia. From Perthshire, Badenoch, and Strathspey the Highland Regiments had been largely recruited for Chatham's war against the French, and the people of those districts of the Central Highlands naturally resorted to the great Province of New York, and formed Settlements on the Delaware, the Mohawk, and the rivers of Connecticut. Argyllshire with its Islands, Skye and the Outer Hebrides, as also Sutherland and Ross, all sent their earlier emigrants to North Carolina, where they formed a Settlement noted in the subsequent American war for its loyalty and misfortunes. The outbreak of that war checked the tide of emigration during the seven years (1776-1783) of its duration, and diverted what remained of it, to Canada, Nova Scotia, and Prince Edward's Island. But there a home was found for those who moved from Lochaber, Glengarry, Moydart and some other parts of the County of Inverness.[1]

The thoroughly popular nature of the movement is curiously illustrated, moreover, by the methods which were taken. When in any part of the country any considerable number of people had determined to emigrate, some leading man circulated a subscription paper, and a regular contract

---

[1] Lord Selkirk's *Observations, etc.*, pp. 166-7.

was entered into between the subscribers, and some one of their own number who acted as agent and contractor for the rest.[1] The emigrants did not generally go to any of the Lowland ports. They did not wish to attract attention. They knew that the movement was not favoured by those above them. Perhaps they themselves had even a strangely surviving feeling of military desertion. Vessels were engaged, which came round to the solitary bays and arms of the sea, which everywhere sent their waters close up to the doors of the overcrowded homes. In these the Transports spread their sails quietly and unobserved, and were soon hull down on the neighbouring and friendly Ocean. On the other side of it, as quietly and as unobserved, they landed their invaluable freight—spreading broadcast the seed of a noble race over immense and fruitful lands.

It is indeed a most curious fact that when this movement of the Highlanders first came to be widely known it excited not only general regret, but even general irritation and alarm. The knowledge of it was spread by the Parochial Reports in the *Statistical Account* organised by Sir John Sinclair in 1790. These began to be published in 1791, and continued to appear in successive volumes during the five following years. The Ministers who drew up those Reports were, of course, men of very various abilities. Some of them regarded the emigration with a passive but

---

[1] Lord Selkirk's *Observations, &c.*, pp. 143-4.

grudging resignation; most of them with regret; some of them with angry denunciation,—a few only with a clear and enlightened estimate of its causes and its probable results. Yet the evidence of these men was in reality uniform and unanimous as to the social conditions of which the emigration was the natural and inevitable result. They all testified to the scanty and decreasing returns of the soil, to the lean and half-starved Cattle, to the frequent returns of scarcity and famine, and in the face of all this, to the steady, general, and, in some cases, enormous increase of the population between 1755 and 1791. On the other hand, in a limited number of Highland Parishes, the new Tables showed a diminution. The panic and the outcry which arose on this discovery is one of the strangest phenomena of our national history. It is all the more remarkable when we observe that the very first volumes of the *Statistical Account* showed in many Lowland Parishes a diminution quite as great, and in some cases very much greater. Moreover, some of the most conspicuous of these cases of "depopulation" were in Parishes close to Edinburgh, such as Yester, Cramond, and Dalmeny,—cases in which the decrease amounted to 18 and 25 per cent.[1] Nay, more—the slightest examination would have shown that great diminution was taking place, as a rule, in all Parishes which were purely rural and agricultural. Hardly anywhere was the population in-

---

[1] *Old Statistical Account*, vol. i. pp. 345, 224, 232.

creasing, except in Parishes with villages, towns, manufactories, or mines. Everywhere the first step in agricultural reform was the division of labour, and the consequent migration of supernumerary hands. An excellent account of this was given by the Minister of Dalmeny, whose Parish had been largely benefited. Subdivided farms with bad husbandry, puny crops, and both men and beasts almost starving, had given place to thriving tenancies and well-fed labourers.[1] Not the slightest outcry or alarm was raised by this contemporaneous depletion of Parishes in the Low Country, nor was the least attempt made to combat the reasoning by which it was so satisfactorily explained.

This difference of feeling would hardly have been rational even if it had been true that the diminution had been the result of mere Migration in one case, as compared with Emigration in the other. It was not very wise or intelligent to think or feel that men moving off to our own Colonies were less happy, or less useful to the world than men moving off to our own Towns. But, as a matter of fact, even this distinction was by no means an universal characteristic of the movement as between the Highlands and the Lowlands. The Lowland Counties during the same years sent many Emigrants to the Colonies, whilst the Highland Counties sent many thousand Migrants to the great centres of industry in the south.

[1] *Old Statistical Account*, vol. i. pp. 232-233.

The Highlanders were undoubtedly more attracted than others by the possession of land, and they were notoriously less accustomed than others to continuous labour. Nevertheless, Highlanders as well as other Scotchmen had long been induced by the high wages of the Low Country to settle in great numbers there. The excitement and agitation, therefore, which arose when men discovered that some Highland Parishes were less crowded than they had once been, and the complete indifference with which the same result in Lowland Parishes was regarded, are an indication of one of the most rapid changes of sentiment that has ever perhaps been exhibited by any people. Forty years earlier the Highlanders were universally regarded in the Lowlands with mingled feelings of hatred and of fear. Now they seemed to be as universally valued as the main defence and the principal ornament of the nation. Beyond all doubt this great change of feeling had a just and an honourable cause. It arose out of the memories of Fontenoy, Ticonderoga, and Quebec. It had been confirmed by the known opinion of General Washington, who having served first with the Highlanders and then against them, carefully acted on the principle that the Highland Regiments must be confronted with special caution as the strongest point of the British line.[1]

But amidst all that was natural and praiseworthy in the outcry against Highland Emigra-

[1] Marshall's *Life of Washington*, vol. iv. p. 84. (Ed. 1805.)

tion there was also an element of selfishness. It was not right to think of the Highlands as nothing but a recruiting-ground for soldiers, or to think of its people as fit for no other function than that of fighting. It was not rational to expect that the Highland population would be long contented to live without any share in the growing wealth and comfort of their countrymen in the Lowlands. If the public had looked carefully into the reports of the Parish Ministers, they would have seen that, even as regarded the love of military service, a great change had already set in. During the war with France in Canada and America, the Highland Regiments had been true Clans—military bodies exclusively Highland, alike in men and officers. Many of the rank and file were gentlemen by birth and by position, and all the officers had personal and local connection with the men whom they commanded. But no such Corps had ever been, or ever could be formed again. Even so soon as in the subsequent war of American Independence, the character of the Highland Regiments had begun to change. They were no longer exclusively recruited in the Highlands; and in some Parishes the Ministers now reported, in 1791, that few recruits for foreign service could be got. This was a change which went on increasing. Just as in the Military Ages, now departing, it had been " broken men " out of whom many of the old Clans had been formed, so henceforth it was chiefly among those Highlanders who had already left their own country, that enlistment continued to be successful. Notwithstanding the frequency of great wars, the Military Ages were coming to a close. The new institution of Standing Armies were completely changing the nature of Military service. It was no longer a pastime. It had become a profession. Highlanders could no longer rush off to short campaigns with old friends and old companions; and then rush back again to live as before on the milk of Ewes, on the blood of Cattle, and on cakes of oatmeal. If they were to move away from home permanently, or for long and indefinite periods of time, they might as well try for something better than the pay of a soldier, and the monotony of a barrack. They had seen and heard enough of higher conditions of life to make them desirous of sharing in them.

The American War of Independence had arrested Emigration. But the last year of that war, and the first of peace—1783—was coincident, as we have seen, with a terrible time of scarcity and almost of famine. What had been called the "rage" for Emigration naturally revived, and in 1801-2-3 a whole fleet of Transports had been carrying off loads of Highlanders from the Western Coasts. The ignorant jealousy and alarm with which the movement was regarded, swelled apace. It affected, almost as much as any other class, the Proprietors of land in the Highlands. It is a vulgar error very commonly entertained that these early Emigrations were incited, or even encouraged by Landowners. They had just formed a Society,[1] of which my grandfather, John, fifth Duke of Argyll, was the first President, full of Celtic enthusiasms: one of whose aims it was to watch over every interest connected with the Highlands. In 1801 this Society appointed a Committee to consider the wonderful phenomenon of the emigration of a half-starving people. They spoke of it not only with sorrow, but with positive bitterness, and suggested every kind of theoretical scheme, by which it might be discouraged and prevented. So keen was the sentimental and benevolent spirit displayed, that Landowners were unjustly accused of a desire to keep up their supply of cheap labour for the manufacture of Kelp, or of indulging their old pride in a multitude of idle retainers. False, and indeed absurd, as such an accusation was, it is at least worth remembering as an antidote to the opposite accusation, that they were driving off the people from their Estates. It is an unquestionable fact, that at this early period the Landowners of the Highlands and Islands disliked the Emigrations, and did not fully comprehend the meaning or the causes of them. That meaning lay deeper than anything of which they were conscious. Sheep-farming had indeed begun, but it had not reached many of the Highland Parishes from which the Emigration was most copious and persistent. Neither had it reached, nor did it ever

---

[1] The Highland and Agricultural Society, an admirable body, which has ever since exercised a salutary influence on the progress of Agriculture, not only in the Highlands, but all over Scotland.

reach, many of the Lowland Parishes which Migration had depopulated with even greater sweep.

And yet, however unconsciously, the Proprietors of land had long been contributing gradually and steadily to the great change which led irresistibly to these movements of the people. They had made this contribution in every step they had taken towards a higher civilisation—when they began to think of increasing the produce of the soil—when they ceased to give farms to men who knew nothing of farming—when they sent forth their own sons and kinsmen to officer the Army and the Navy, or to serve the Crown as Governors and Founders of the Colonies—when they abolished or commuted Services at home—when they granted Improvement Leases—when they persuaded their Tenants no longer to cast lots every year, each man for patches of arable ground no bigger than a tablecloth—when they built enclosures—when they showed their people how to make hay, and how to improve their Cattle, and how to manure their land, and how to alternate their crops. There is such a deep-seated and searching Unity in Nature, which includes the Mind of Man and the habits of Society—that not one single new idea, or one single new desire, can be introduced or followed without carrying with it a host of consequences. Every one of these steps in the path of new duties and of new inclinations, tended to break up an old world, and to usher in another which was different in everything. One Highland Minister pathetically epitomised it all. He complained that the people in his Parish, round their peat fires, instead of discussing, as of old, feuds and deeds of war, were now tamely discussing how they could better tend their Sheep, and improve their wool.[1] But as yet the Proprietors did not see the inevitableness of the results which were typified by the lessening sails of Transport Ships, as their topmasts disappeared behind the waves into the splendours of the West. And so their Committee talked of the "malignant" spirit of Emigration as if it were hardly less wicked than Military Desertion. They even succeeded in persuading the Government of the day to pass an Act which, under the guise of sanitary regulations as to food and ventilation in ships, was strongly, though perhaps unjustly, suspected of an intention to prevent it. Lord Selkirk, who favoured emigration, speaks in his Work upon the subject, of the "jealous antipathy" against it which he found "in the minds of the more considerable Proprietors of the Highlands."[2] It was in this spirit that the Committee of the Highland Society drew up their Reports in 1802 and 1803. And yet in that very document they showed their complete knowledge of the fundamental fact on which everything depended. The first cause to which they attribute the Emigration is "such an increase of population as the country in its present situation, and with a total want of openings for the

---

[1] *Old Statistical Account*, vol. iv. p. 576.
[2] *Observations, etc.*, 1805, p. 130.

exertion of industry, cannot support."[1] Every other cause was a mere consequence of this one cause—which was in itself all-embracing and all-sufficient. It was not peculiar to the Highlands, but was operating quite as powerfully in every Lowland Parish under like conditions. Only, in the Islands and Western Highlands the stream had been pent up longer, and was overflowing with a rush. One simple explanation—one great natural analogy—would have spared the Committee all their sorrow. A great Hive was swarming. Chiefs and Landowners, Field Marshals, Poets, and Philosophers were standing round the "Skep," gaping, staring, wondering, and scolding, at the naughty instinct of the Bees.

[1] *Observations, etc.*, p. 137.

CHAPTER III.

THE BURST OF INDUSTRY.

There is one scene in Scotland which, more than any other, groups within a single landscape so many features identified with the history of the Country and of the Nation, that there is hardly an age in all its Past, which has not some striking memorial in sight. It is the scene lying all around that reach of the Firth of Clyde which not very many years ago was the site of a small fishing village, and is now occupied by the Quays, the Harbour, and Roadstead of Greenock. Splendid as the view is on a clear day, it is not less remarkable on account of the immense variety of interests which belong to all its features. The hills that sweep round from West to North, falling steeply into the Firth along its opposite shores, are the southern extremity, or escarpment, of the Highland mountains. From these shores they stretch without a break, except their own glens and fissures, to the boundary line between Sutherland and Caithness. There is good reason to believe that these mountains, although very far from being among the highest, are among the oldest in the world—older than the Alps, or the Pyrenees, or the Apennines in Europe,—older than the great range of the Himalayah in the Asiatic Continent. The Geologist must ever regard them with curiosity, as suggesting many hard questions in his science, which have not yet been solved. The sudden depression in this line of Hills, which is a conspicuous feature in the landscape immediately opposite to Greenock, marks the boundary line of the Grampian ranges towards the East,—a line which runs almost straight from that depression on the Clyde to the North-East Coast of Scotland at Stonehaven. These are interests which concern not the Nation but the Land, and carry us back to times before the birth even of the " everlasting hills."

Turning our eyes now up the course of the River Clyde every feature in the landscape is crowded with human memories. In the farther perspective we see the point at the foot of the Kilpatrick Hills, where the soldiers of Agricola terminated the line of Forts which then was, and long continued to be, the northern boundary of the Roman Empire. Fifty-six years later the same line was occupied by the continuous Wall of Antoninus Pius.[1] In all history there is perhaps no more striking contrast than the blaze of light which shines upon that Wall and on those who built it, as compared with the profound darkness that encompasses the Tribes against whom it was erected. We know, indeed, that our ancestors were brave, and that they were formidable even

[1] Irving's *History of Dumbartonshire*, ch. i.

in the eyes of Rome. We know that they were defeated, but by no means easily defeated, in open battle with the Mistress of the World, against whom they fought with Chariots and with Horsemen; nay, more—we know that although they lost in the battle, they won in the campaign. Agricola retired from their country into the Province he had gained and fortified. Yet some of them seem to have been so savage that Gibbon sees no reason to doubt the story that they were cannibals.[1] This, however, is a story of events later by about 280 years than the battles of Agricola. It is the story of a mercenary Tribe in the pay of Rome and transported into Gaul. Time does not always mellow or improve. Sometimes it develops Savagery. It certainly did so among the Cæsars during the same time. The brutal cruelty of Valentinian is not a greater contrast with the virtue and wisdom of Marcus Aurelius and of Antoninus Pius, than the alleged cannibalism of the Attacotti, with the noble eloquence ascribed to Galgacus. The condition of the Tribes he led, remains a mystery. Of their habits, of their manners, of their polity, of their habitations, and of their dress, we know practically nothing, or so little, that it all seems equally perplexing and inconsistent. We cannot believe that the Caledonian Chief really addressed his army before the battle of the Mons Grampius in a speech the least like that which is put into his mouth by Tacitus.[2]

[1] Irving's *History of Dumbartonshire*, ch. i. p. 6; and Gibbon's *Decline and Fall*, ch. xxv. [2] Tacitus's *Life of Agricola*.

It bristles with epigram, and with the results of philosophic reflection. It expresses these results in words so vigorous and terse that one of its sentences has, through all later ages, become proverbial.[1] In short it is a speech breathing the most cultivated eloquence of Rome. Yet neither, on the other hand, can we believe that Tacitus would have put such a speech into the mouth of Galgacus, if that Chief had been known to be a Savage. We are left, therefore, in darkness that can be felt. On the other hand, of the people who built that Wall from the Clyde to the Forth, and whose dominion extended southwards to the Pillars of Hercules, we may be said to know everything in the most minute detail. Such is the power of Literature. The contrast is all the more striking when we remember that this was the epoch when the Roman Empire was at its best. The well-known and splendid panegyric of Gibbon represents the age of the Antonines as the Golden Age of the whole Roman world. Remembering these things, this landscape on the Clyde acquires a special interest. Looking at the Kilpatrick Hills we can see, in imagination at least, the Standards of the Sixth and of the Second Legions covering the men who worked at that famous Rampart. Nor are surviving monuments wanting to fill up the picture. The artificers and the artists of Rome have everywhere left some lasting records of their sense and feeling for the Empire which they served.

[1] "Omne ignotum pro magnifico."

When the Engineers of our own day were set to join the Clyde and Forth by a Canal, they found that they could do no better than follow the Wall of Antonine. At frequent intervals the pick and the spade struck upon its foundation stones. Here and there some massive Tablet told how many thousand paces had been accomplished by each laborious Legion. Occasionally, too, some sculpture more elaborate and more beautiful than the rest, embodied the natural feelings of satisfaction and of pride with which the Roman Generals regarded every extension of the Imperial dominion. Such were the Tablets found at Kilpatrick, representing Winged Victories in majestic attitudes of triumph and of repose.[1]

A very little nearer to us than the foot of the Kilpatrick Hills, and seen against them—at the junction of the Leven with the Clyde—rises another feature in the landscape inseparable from the history of Scotland—the great Rock Fortress of Dumbarton. There could not be a more striking symbol of the passage from Roman to Mediæval times. It is not certain whether it was or was not included within the Wall of Antonine. This uncertainty is itself significant. It arises from the fact that Rock Fortresses were despised by Rome. They did not enter into her military system. Roving tribes and rude barbarians had need of natural Strengths. But

---

[1] Three Sculptured Stones, one of great beauty, are engraved in Irving's *History of Dumbartonshire*, p. 14, and are preserved in the Museum of Glasgow.

Rome had none. If a Roman General wished for some sudden hollow for the purpose of fortification, he did not hunt for a ravine; he dug it with the spade; he made a Fossa. If he wished for some Steep around his position, he did not go out of his way to find a precipice. He threw up a Vallum, or he built a Wall. The lofty rock, therefore, which the southern Celts or Britons of Strathclyde made the capital of their territory,—which they called " Alcluid," and which, in another Celtic dialect, has since been called after them, " Dun-briton,"—does not seem to have been valued or thought of by Agricola or by Antonine. If they included it at all in their lines, it was for the purpose of covering a ford across the Clyde, which at that time would have given easy access to the Imperial Province on the southern bank. But when the Romans retired, the great "Dun" of the Strathclyde Britons resumed its military importance. Its very name reminds us of the mixture of races from which we spring. For centuries it was one of the Strengths of the Scottish Kingdom—captured and recaptured —used alternately as a retreat, as a palace, and as a prison. More than once it was both of these in the pathetic career of Mary Queen of Scots. It was to gain its friendly shelter that in May 1568 she set out from Hamilton to the fatal battle of Langside; and it had been from the short grassy slope which dips into the river on the western face, that twenty years before, in her early childhood (1548), with her attendant " Four Maries," she had been carried into

the Barge which bore her off to be the Bride of
France. It is not easy for us now to realise the
importance which in those days was set on the Rock
Fortress of Dumbarton. Another revolution in military science, quite recent, has brought us back to
the sentiment of the Romans. In the face of our
new Artillery, Hill Forts have lost their value. But
in the Seventeenth Century the dearest interests of
the future were concerned in the possession of that
precipitous mass of volcanic rock. Scotland was
a special scene of contest between the Catholic
Reaction and the interests of the Reformed all over
Europe. It was through Scotland that the attack
could best be made on "Great Elizabeth." The
House of Guise was encouraged when they heard
that Dumbarton was held for Mary. The English
Queen wrote personal letters of congratulation when
she heard it was captured for James VI.[1] John Knox,
in the last year of his life and in physical decay,
which left untouched his indomitable spirit, heard
with joy of the daring escalade of Crawford of Jordanhill, by which it fell to the Protestant cause in 1571.

This, however, is not by any means the only or
even greatest historic memory which is recalled by
the same prospect up the Valley of the Clyde. There
is another time, much earlier and much more noble
in all the influences it has left. Again, a little
nearer to us than Dumbarton, on the declivity of
the hills of Cardross, which here form the right bank
of the Leven, King Robert the Bruce chose his place

[1] Irving's *History of Dumbartonshire*, p. 132.

of residence during the last years of his glorious reign. There he spent his time governing his Kingdom, now and again hunting and hawking, or sailing and rowing in his royal Galley on the two beautiful and then unsullied rivers which flowed—one on each side—beneath his Castle walls. The high but flat-topped ridges of the Kilpatrick Hills, the rocky precipices of Dumbarton, and the far-off blue summit of Benlomond, formed the scene on which King Robert looked when he sickened prematurely under the weight of a memorable life, and when dying he bequeathed his heart to be carried to the Holy Land, in the pathetic scene recorded in verse by Barbour, and by Froissart in prose not less poetic.[1]

The long and troubled Centuries which followed the death of Bruce—the relapse of a large part of the Kingdom into comparative barbarism—the ferocious Epoch of the Clans—have each and all their memorials in the scene before us. The whole length of shores opposite to Greenock are those of the old Province of the Lennox, half Highland, half Lowland, full of the sites on which Celtic Feudalism yielded, slowly but steadily, to the higher Feudalism of Civilisation and of Law. It so happens that immediately fronting Greenock there is one feature in the physical geography of the country which stands in sad connection with the close of that struggle. The high ridge which slopes somewhat steeply into the Firth of Clyde is backed by another ridge, in some lights hardly separate, but

---

[1] Froissart's *Chronicles*, chap. xx.

which on a clear day is seen to be higher and steeper than the nearer summit. This division between two parallel ranges marks the hollow in which lies Glenfruin. Although so close to one of the great centres of our modern life, few wilder or more solitary Glens are to be found in all the Highlands. It was in this Glen that on the 7th February 1603 was fought the last of the savage and bloody battles of the Clans.[1] The Colquhouns of Luss were beaten and decimated in resisting a blood-feud raid of the Clan Gregor. The horror of the scene was brought home to the rising civilisation of the Lowlands not only by the death of several gentlemen of distinction from the valley of the Leven, near Dumbarton, amongst whom was Tobias Smollet, ancestor of the novelist, but also by the butchery in cold blood of some student lads and boys of that Burgh who had been induced from curiosity to watch the fight.[2] There can be no more curious contrast than that between the prospect from the nearer summit, then, and the prospect from it, now. On the northern side lie the deep shadows and the wild but peaceful pasturages of Glenfruin. On the southern side lie the reclaimed fields of modern agriculture, and all the various and busy industries of the Clyde.

And yet even this contrast is less striking and less instructive than the change—the transformation—which was wrought as if by magic, in the character of the celebrated Clan which on that and on many

---

[1] Irving's *History of Dumbartonshire*, pp. 147-50.

[2] The doubt which has been cast on this ghastly story seems to me to be dispelled by the evidence. *Ibid.* p. 150.

previous occasions had been pre-eminent in ferocity. Sentiment is an excellent thing. It is indeed the salt of the world—the cheap defence of nations. But Sentiment may be bad as well as good; and then if the light that is in us be darkness, that darkness is intense! It is a bad sentiment, and not a good one, that can make any man look back with sympathy to the Epoch of the Clans. Sentiment—deep and even enthusiastic—may well be felt for those changes in our national history which broke down that Epoch, and which brought back the character and the genius of Highlanders within the advancing influences of our national civilisation. They soon showed that there they had a part—and a great part—to play. And perhaps never was there a case of it more signal than the case of the Clan Gregor. James VI. was shocked and scandalised, as well he might be, by this massacre in Glenfruin, occurring as it did in a part of his native Kingdom where it could not be concealed, and just at the moment when he was mounting the throne of England.[1] The Clan Gregor were proscribed and pursued as a Blood and as a Race, in a manner hardly less savage than their own slaughter of the Colquhouns.

Yet it was not their race nor their blood, but the system under which they lived, which had made them savage. The Savage is close under the skin with all of us. Our humanity and our civilisation depend entirely on our inherited ideas—on our loyal accept-

---

[1] Queen Elizabeth's death took place on the 24th of March 1603—or forty-five days after the massacre of Glenfruin.

ance of them—and on these ideas being themselves consistent with the historical developments of an advancing Commonwealth. The Clan Gregor, like other Clans, had been taught to believe that the robbery of Cattle was not immoral. The Robber Clans, when they condescended to reason or to think at all on such matters, had a theory of their own. Cattle in Scotland had originally been an indigenous animal. They said that God made the Cattle—that He also made the grass upon the hills, and therefore their conclusion was that Cattle—the very earliest form of human property—could not be considered as rightful property at all.[1] The strongest might always take it, and those who defended it could only hold it by success in battle. This theory is not perhaps quite so incoherent as the modern form of it which applies the same reasoning to property in land, but shrinks from applying it to property in the produce. The old Highland Reivers, on the contrary, applied it only to the produce, and did not think of applying it to the soil from which the produce came. Anarchical doctrines and slovenly reasonings—when not translated into deeds—were little regarded in those days. But the doings of the Clan Gregor in Glenfruin were a little too tangible to be suffered. Their own methods were the only methods which Society could take to confound their doctrines. And so, however cruelly, yet with the universal consent of all, they were proscribed, and their very name forbidden. But their dispersion,

---

[1] MS. Brit. Mus. 1748.

and the transplantation of many of them into another country and another atmosphere of custom and opinion, proved but the beginning of a nobler reputation. In the Church, in the Army, and in the Civil Professions, Macgregor has long been, and is now, a familiar and an honoured name. But there is one branch of the old Clan Alpine which more than any other has exhibited the qualities of a reclaimed and ennobled Race. Here, again, the rights of legal Ownership proved to be the successful remedy for the illegal powers, and the dangerous influences of "Chiefery." The Earl of Murray transplanted three hundred of the proscribed Macgregors from Menteith, and settled them as a barrier against another turbulent Clan, the Mackintoshes, in Aberdeenshire.[1] There, under the name of Gregory, these descendants of the Clan Alpine gave birth not only to some, but to a whole galaxy of the most distinguished men that Scotland has produced. One of them was the friend of Sir Isaac Newton, and among the earliest teachers of his Philosophy. Another of them was the Patriarch of a whole dynasty of Professors of the highest scientific and literary distinction in several of the Universities, both of Scotland and of England. One of them was the inventor of the Reflecting Telescope. Another was at the head of the Medical Profession in Edinburgh, when Society there was at its best, and where, from the combination of many charms of genius and of virtue, he reigned supreme

---

[1] Sir Walter Scott's Introduction to *Rob Roy*.

as the " Beloved Physician." With one of the last of this distinguished family I had the honour of being intimate in early life—the late Dr. William Gregory, Professor of Chemistry in the University of Edinburgh—a man of the utmost refinement of character, and of the most liberal and cultivated mind.

The continuity of our national history is not less remarkable than its changes, and this characteristic is not less visibly represented in the scene before us. In looking at the mountains which enclose Glenfruin, we are looking at a district which is still the property of the Colquhouns of Luss. There they have been—traceable without a break—for some 700 years,[1] and there they are at the present day. The thriving Town of Helensburgh, which stretches its gardened Villas up the slope of the hill leading to Glenfruin, is built upon land acquired and held from the Colquhouns by feudal Charters, granted under the rights and powers on which property has rested in Scotland since before the days of Malcolm Canmore.

And now letting our eyes fall from the hills in front of us, to rest upon the broad water at our feet, there can be no doubt of the multitude of objects which are representative of the latest developments of our national life. We are standing in the birthplace of James Watt, and we have before us, in all their amplitude, the triumphs of his genius, and of the genius of his successor, Henry Bell. There is

---

[1] See *The Chiefs of Colquhoun and their Country*, by William Fraser, C.B., LL.D. Edinburgh, 1869.

not a sight or a sound among the many which fill the eye and the ear from one of the greatest commercial centres of the world, which is not a monument, direct or indirect, to the memory of these two men—of Watt, who, in 1765, by the inspiration of one new idea, which flashed upon him on the Green of Glasgow, that of the "Separate Condenser,"[1] started the Steam-engine on the path of its immense, and yet unfulfilled developments; and of Bell, who on these waters, in 1812, was the first in Europe to apply it to the purposes of Locomotion. It does indeed seem almost incredible, when we remember that there are men not only now living, but keeping a front place in the contests of active life, who were born several years before a single steam-vessel had moved in British Waters. It is but seventy-four years ago since the "Comet" was launched by Bell upon the Clyde, whilst now its harbours and its bays are crowded with Liners who keep up communication with America more frequently—more regularly—and with more safety—than sailing ferry-boats then kept up communication with the neighbouring Sea-lochs of Dumbarton and Argyll.

But the shipping and the harbour of Greenock are the standing memorials of another epoch in our national history which preceded the epoch of Watt and Bell, and in which the way was prepared before them. That was the epoch of the Legislative Union in 1707. The Union of the Crowns in 1603 had put an end to such horrors as the massacre of

---

[1] Smiles's *Lives of Boulton and Watt*, 1865, pp. 127-8.

Glenfruin. But it was not until after the Union of the Legislatures in 1707, that such sights of commercial enterprise as that presented by the Clyde were, or could be seen. I have already observed upon the greatly exaggerated importance often ascribed to the defeat of the Jacobite Rebellion of 1745. On the other hand, as an Epoch, the Legislative Union with England, accomplished in 1707, is almost as immensely undervalued. It was not only the beginning, but it was the one indispensable foundation, of all the later progress of Scotland in industry and in wealth.

The Clyde bears witness to this truth with a loud voice. The only foreign commerce which Scotland enjoyed before the Union was some traditional and old-standing trade with France and Flanders. A stringent Navigation Law had been passed by the Scottish Parliament just after the Restoration, in 1661, which proceeded on a preamble that trade and navigation had terribly declined during the Civil Wars, and it is remarkable that one of the clauses of this Act confesses that Scotland had then no shipping to protect in any Trade with any part of Asia, Africa, or America, nor, in Europe, with Russia or Italy.[1] Not very much of the world was left to us after these subtractions. All the vast and growing Dominions and Plantations of the British race in India and in the New World were under the Government of the English Parliament.

[1] *Act. Parl. Scot.*, vol. vii. p. 258 (1 Carol. II. c. 277).

Commerce at that time was universally regulated by the accepted doctrines of restriction and monopoly. Scotland was as jealously excluded from the privileges of English merchants and of English shipowners, as if she were, as in deed she was, a foreign country. In her own protecting Navigation Law of 1661 she had, indeed, offered free trade with England and with Ireland, provided the privilege were made reciprocal.[1] But her comparative poverty, and the smallness of her demand, did not commend this to the English as an equal bargain. On the other hand, Scotchmen had an aptitude, and even a genius for commercial pursuits which had begun to appear in every direction. The Bank of England was founded by a Scotchman—William Paterson ;—and it was in the desperate efforts of Scotland to get some outlet for her rising spirit of enterprise that her Parliament and people were led, in 1695, by the same remarkable man, to throw themselves with enthusiasm into the famous Darien scheme. Founded on the most enlightened commercial principles, and intended to open and to establish a new Trade Route to the Indies which will be one of the triumphs of our own day, this great scheme of a Scotchman, who was far in advance of his time, was thwarted and ruined—as it seemed, entirely by the jealousy of England. Her Parliament and her commercial Companies opposed it with passionate resentment, and pointed with horror to the prospect of Scotland becoming a Free Port for

[1] *Act. Parl. Scot.*, vol. vii. p. 258 (1 Carol. II. c. 277).

half the commerce of the world. Yet only one-half of the Capital Stock was to be held by Scotchmen. The other half was open to Englishmen, and a large amount of it was actually subscribed, and held by them. This, however, did not conciliate the English Parliament. Narrow and odious as its spirit seems to us now, it is impossible to read the Scotch Act of Parliament[1] establishing this great new East India Company, and especially the liberal and enlightened regulations for free trade with all nations promulgated at the Settlement,[2] without seeing that Scotland and England could no longer work together without either a more complete union, or a more complete separation. Two immense Monopolies trading by opposite routes with the same markets,—contending with each other on every Ocean,—jealously separate in destinations which were nevertheless geographically united—and both these Monopolies entitled to the protection of common forces under a common Crown,—could not possibly have been worked together. The thing was impracticable. Every detail was as full of difficulties and incongruities as the principle of the whole. The drawing of strict fiscal lines between Scotchmen born and living in Scotland and Scotchmen born or living in England, when every day made the passage and the intercourse of the two populations more easy and continual, was like drawing straight lines in water.

[1] *Act. Parl. Scot.*, vol. ix. p. 277 (1 Will. III., c. 10).
[2] See Life of Paterson in Chambers's *Eminent Scotsmen*, vol. iv. p. 108.

A complete union or a complete quarrel were the only alternatives. Scotland would have to return to her old historic alliance with France, hostile to England, or the two nations must admit themselves to be one.

It is well to remember how narrowly we escaped from the wrong alternative. The passionate jealousy in England of any rivalry in trade,—the supreme power exercised by the spirit of monopoly over the English government,—the ruinous losses inflicted on Scotland by the failure of the Darien Settlement,—all so exasperated the national feeling in Scotland, that at last in 1703-4 the two Parliaments were actually taking measures for arming against each other.[1] The Scottish Legislature went the length of passing an Act providing that on the death of the reigning Sovereign, Queen Anne, the next Sovereign of Scotland must not be the successor to the English Crown, unless previous to that event some more satisfactory security had been obtained for the liberties and interests of the Scottish nation.[2] To this they were driven by the logic of necessity. The bond of Union, through the Crown alone, was proving under trial to be no bond at all. Or, if it was a bond at all, it was a bond which tied their hands in fight for the interests of their country. Their King, surrounded by English Ministers, and swayed by the feelings of the English Capital, had responded cor-

---

[1] De Lolme's *Essay on the Union*, 1787, p. 19.
[2] *Act. Parl. Scot.*, vol. xi. p. 136 (2 Qu. Anne, cap. 3).

dially to the most outrageous expressions of hostility against the Scotch on the part of the English House of Commons;[1] nay more, he had used his Prerogative in Scotland in the same sense. He dismissed his Scotch Ministers, who had the confidence of the Nation, because they promoted the Trade and Commerce of their country.[2] William's part had been, no doubt, a difficult one to play. His relations with the Dutch, as well as his position in England, embarrassed him in dealing with the bold attempt of his Scottish subjects to rival both in the commerce of the Indies.[3] Chiefly, however, it was international jealousy, fast rising into international hatred, between his Southern and his Northern Subjects in Britain, which determined his conduct. The nearer, the wealthier, and the more powerful of the two carried the day. Yet nothing can justify the vindictive and almost savage orders which had been issued by the English Government to all the Governors of Plantations in America and in the West India Islands, that they were not, on any account, to succour or support the emigrants from Scotland to the Darien Settlement. This order might have endangered, and in the sequel did actually endanger, the lives of many of the most loyal of William's subjects, as a penalty upon them for undertaking, not only a lawful, but a most meritorious enterprise. It was also a direct invitation to foreign enemies, and

---

[1] *Life of William Carstares*, p. 250. By Rev. R. H. Story, 1874.

[2] *Dalrymple's Memoirs*, vol. iii. p. 132.

[3] See the explanation given in a Paper, purporting to be written by King William, in Story's *Life of Carstares*, p. 251.

particularly to the Spaniards, to attack the Settlement.

Such an exhibition of the spirit of international jealousy between subjects of the same Crown, and contiguous inhabitants of the same Island, is all the more shocking, and all the more instructive, when we remember that some of the leading men against whom the order was directed were the same men who had lately been intimately associated as fellow-countrymen with the merchants and financiers of London in another scheme of great national importance, and from whose aptitudes for Commercial Business, England had derived manifest advantage. But such are the inevitable results of encouraging the passions of separate Nationalities, under the nominal unity of one Crown. Antagonism becomes only the more fierce and ungovernable in proportion to the number of jealousies which are aroused, and of contradictory interests and aspirations which cannot be satisfied. At last— not one moment too soon—the English Government became thoroughly alarmed by the bitter animosity which had been roused in Scotland. In June 1704 the Queen addressed an almost imploring letter to the Parliament sitting in Edinburgh, pointing out the dangers to the Protestant Succession, and the encouragement of common enemies, which must arise from the increasing estrangement between the two Kingdoms. She intimated, too, the repentance of England in respect to the Darien affair by a promise to agree to conditions by which such injuries should cease. This Letter or Message was read on the 11th of July 1704, but the only reply was an angry Resolution voted on the 17th that Parliament would not settle the Succession "until we have a previous Treaty with England regulating our commerce and other concerns with that Nation." And this was followed on the 4th of August by the Act providing that the Successor to the Crown of Scotland "be not the Successor to the Crown of England," unless under the protection of a Treaty securing the interests of "this Crown and Kingdom from English or any Foreign influence."[1] Clearly the Spirit of Separation was taking fast— it might be fatal—hold. There is nothing so easy as to fan such flames, and few things more reckless. Scotland had been, and indeed still was, exhibiting consequences not dissimilar in her own dealings with Ireland. Recent acts of the Scottish Parliament had forbidden Trade with Ireland, one of them (1686), in language, and under penalties, which seemed to breathe a special hatred. Not only was any vessel to be confiscated which brought victual from Ireland, but the victual itself was to be "sunk and destroyed."[2] Scotland, no doubt, had her old causes, and causes only too recent, of grudge against that Dependency of the English Crown. For centuries there had hardly been any attempt against the liberties or the nationality of Scotland, which had not been supported by armed men recruited

---

[1] *Act. Parl. Scot.*, vol. viii. pp. 128-137.
[2] *Ibid.* vol. viii. p. 598 (2 Jac. VII. cap. 26).

from among the Celts of Ireland. Nothing can ever be forgotten or forgiven where the amalgamating influences of Time are neutralised and defied, by Institutions which dissociate and repel.

The truth is that the affection, which men call Patriotism, must not be idolised. It may be among the highest, and it may be among the lowest of human virtues. It may be generous and fruitful, or it may be narrow and barbarous, according to the worthiness or the unworthiness—the dignity or the meanness—the amplitude or the narrowness—of the object of it. If our "Country" be a Glen, or a Parish, or a Province,—if our compatriots be a Clan, or a Kindred, or a group of military comrades—our Patriotism will be of a corresponding character. If the idea and the sentiment, by which we feel ourselves to be associated with, and bound to, any group of men, be an idea which has in it any germ of growth and greatness—however small that germ may be—then our love of the country, and of the people by which it is represented, is a noble love. But like all our passions it is liable to degradation. It may cease to expand with expanding growths—it may fail to rise with ennobling opportunities. The love of a great Country may go back to the passions of a petty Province, or to the almost forgotten hatreds and antipathies of the Tribal and Barbarous ages of the world.

This was the danger from which Scotland and England happily, but narrowly, escaped in the years immediately preceding the Union.

When even a man so enlightened as Fletcher of Saltoun was carried away by the narrower view of patriotism, and wrote, spoke, and acted in the interest of Separation, we are better able to estimate all we owe to those wiser Patriots who saw that the larger hopes, and the wider interests of their Country were identified with the cause of Union. Fletcher, we are told, "disliked England merely because he loved Scotland to excess."[1] It was a dangerous moment. The centrifugal forces had begun to work with great momentum. They were arrested just in time. It is pleasant to remember that not a few of those who made this resistance effectual, and directed the national feeling into the true channel of Imperial greatness,—my own ancestors being among the number,[2]—were descendants of the men who had seen the great work of Union begun in the old alliance of Malcolm and of Margaret; of those who in a later time had fought for, and with, the Bruce; and of those who in generations yet more recent had stood by the Scottish Monarchy for three hundred years, against the disintegrating anarchy of the Clans. And now in happier times they saw that the interests of their country, and its glory, lay in assuming its full share of imperial duties under one Imperial Crown. All they asked was that Scotland should retain everything that

---

[1] *Dalrymple's Memoirs*, vol. iii. p. 129.
[2] John, Duke of Argyll and Greenwich, was Queen Anne's Commissioner in the Parliament of 1705, which passed the Act authorising the Treaty of Union; whilst his brother, Lord Islay, was one of the Commissioners who framed the Treaty.

she cared to keep of her own domestic Institutions in Religion and in Law.

The patriotic men who effected the Union of the two Nations wisely insisted too, as an indispensable condition, on a perfect equality between them in all the privileges of Trade. England also consented to refund to Scotland the losses she had occasioned by her violent conduct in the Darien enterprise. The whole Capital Stock of the Company was to be repaid, with interest.[1] This, however, was a small matter compared with the removal of all impediments to Enterprise. The effect was immediate and enormous. Scotchmen not only gained a full share of the expanding commerce of the world, but shot ahead of all rivals and competitors in the race of industry and of maritime activity. Before the Union, Greenock consisted of two straggling Villages, each of them with a single row of cottages, most of them thatched, fronting the natural beach. Only one of them had even the accommodation of a wooden pier along which any vessel could lie. Everywhere else along the shore the boats could only be drawn up upon the shingle.[2] The first ship that ever sailed from Greenock for the American Continent had sailed in 1695, and that solitary ship was destined for the Darien Settlement. The moment the Union was accomplished a new life was opened, and a new career begun.

---

[1] Article xv. of Treaty of Union. *Act. Parl. Scot.*, vol. viii., Append. p. 203.

[2] Smiles's *Lives of Boulton and Watt.*

But Trade and Navigation were not the only industries which received a new impetus at the Union. There was another, older and of necessity slower in its growth, which began at the same time to feel the new blood that was stirring the national life, and penetrating all its members. The scene before us, as we look from the Southern Shores of the Firth of Clyde, is one specially representative and characteristic of all the peculiar conditions of Agriculture in Scotland, then, and ever since. There are many large parts of England which have been cultivated land since before the Conquest. Local memories do not go back to the time when these areas were first cleared and settled. In Scotland, too, there are some areas of land, comparatively small, which are in the same position. But by far the largest part of the country, not only in the Highlands, but also in the Lowlands, were "brown heath and shaggy wood"—forest, bog, morass, and stony waste—down to the time of our grandfathers—sometimes down to the time of our fathers—not seldom down even to our own recent years.

No such transformation has taken place in any country within so short a space—unless, indeed, in the case of new and savage lands, suddenly brought under the dominion of civilised Man. And of this great change the whole country which encircles the harbour of Greenock is a typical example. There is hardly an acre of level arable land visible to the eye. The few that exist are so foreshortened, and so dominated by mountains or hilly surfaces that they form no feature in the landscape. Early in the present Century, during the war with France, some French prisoners were sent in a frigate to the Clyde. One of them, on looking round him from the deck, exclaimed, with almost a shudder at the prospect, "Ah! quelle Terre aride!" This may have been a natural impression for a Frenchman who perhaps came from beautiful Provence, and who had no idea of any fertility except in abundance of Corn, and Oil, and Wine. It was nevertheless a most erroneous impression, because in no part of the South of Europe are the mountains so well clothed with grasses as in the West of Scotland. The naked limestone Ranges of the Maritime Alps, of Italy, and of Greece, are barrenness itself compared with the schistose Hills of Dumbarton and Argyll. But the Frenchman's impression was at least so far well founded, that the land around him on every side, whether on the Lowland and Southern, or on the Highland and Northern Shore, was a land which gave no indications of an ancient and settled agriculture. It was a land which yielded nothing except to laborious Reclamation, and when he spoke, that Reclamation had not proceeded very far. Even now when fields, and enclosures of every kind, have climbed the hills, and spread along all the shores, there is little that can convey to us through the eye any adequate impression of the Work which has been done,—of the Capital which has been invested—of the Enterprise which has been shown—of the prodigious change which has been effected. In this respect Agriculture is at a disadvantage as compared with other kinds of industry. It is peaceful, quiet, unostentatious. The great buildings,—the tall chimneys,—the crowded quays,—the gallant ships,—the forest of masts, which all catch the eye and impose on the imagination when we look at any of the great Hives of manufacturing or maritime activity,—are all in singular contrast with the unobtrusive instruments, and the equally unobtrusive results of Husbandry. No man can see the tangled woods which have been cleared, the bogs which have been drained, the stones and boulders which have been blasted, broken, and removed. Still less can we see the ignorance which had to be encountered, the stiff resistances of prejudice which had to be overborne. It has come to pass that the results of forethought, and of skill, and of faith in principles, are all now represented by nothing but the silent growths of Nature. Agriculture hides her laborious works under the verdure, or under the golden radiance, of her fruits.

Some personal recollections of the second quarter of this Century will give an excellent illustration of this prominent distinction, and of the kind of work which had been going on during the life of men who were then still in the vigour of their years.

All round the shores of Scotland, but specially conspicuous along the shores of the Firth of Clyde, there are the marks of an Old Coast Line, which is from 30 to 40 feet above the present line of tide.

At some date which we do not know, and by some agency which is not thoroughly understood, but which, geologically speaking, has been very recent, the whole of Scotland seems to have been hitched up out of the surrounding seas to that extent. If it be possible for the Ocean to change its level, and suddenly to sink or retreat below the line at which it has stood for centuries, without any corresponding change in particular areas of the land itself, the effect may be due to such a change. This is a geological and a physical problem which must be left to speculation and to science. Whatever may be the explanation, the fact is certain. The old level of the sea is indicated by a line, more or less continuous, of steep banks or low rocky precipices, which present in many places the distinctive features of cove and cave, and of under-cut shelves of rock. These are the well-known work of water gnawing at the land. The sea must have washed our Island at this higher level for long and uncounted ages. The horizontal distance between that Old Coast Line and our present Coast Line varies greatly, of course, according to the conformation of the land, and the consequent shallowness or depth of the water at different portions of the shore. In some places where the shore was, and still is steep, the Old Coast Line is close to the existing line—only lifted higher up. In other places where the old shores were shallow, the space which has been left dry by the retreat of the sea is very wide—sometimes one or two hundred yards.

There is no physical feature of our country more distinctive than this difference between two portions of the old sea-margin—the sudden bank and the flats below. Nor is there any more intimately associated with separate historic times. The precipitous rock or bank was the home of the Military Ages. Upon it they built their "Towers along the Steep." The level lands between it and the sea were left for the Industrial Ages to occupy and reclaim. In this historical separation there were, no doubt, some exceptions. Where the old sea-bottom had been sandy or muddy, it was speedily covered with sward. In such places it often became the site of such agriculture as was known and practised by the earliest human inhabitants. But generally along our exposed and rocky shores the spaces thus added to the land had a very different character. They had been swept for Centuries by the ice rafts of the Glacial Age. They had been covered with the boulders and stony rubbish which these rafts bore away from fretted and disintegrating shores. Upon such surfaces, when upraised, nothing but the rough forests of ancient Caledonia could find a footing. When these had been destroyed by fire or flood, peat mosses had been formed, or the land remained as hard and stony as when first it had been elevated above the sea. These old wastes and woods are now generally reclaimed. Very often they are the best fields upon the best farms. Very often they are the sites of comfortable Villas, or of thriving Towns.

Yet the processes by which this great change has been effected are out of sight and out of mind. The very peacefulness of the scene takes away all sense of Work, and all memory of the Workers. I speak from experience. I was born and brought up in a Castle which, somewhere about the Twelfth Century, had been built upon the top of the Old Coast Line, where the last of the Highland mountains slopes into the basin of the Clyde. It was the stronghold of the Clan Macaulay. They were descended from a younger branch of the old Earls of Lennox, and all through the Military Ages they had kept their ground in their Strong House of Ardencaple. From improvidence in expenditure—probably from joining in the new habits of civilised life before new values of produce had enabled them to afford it — their extensive possessions had been gradually alienated, and the last portion of them had been acquired by Lord Frederick Campbell in the latter half of the last Century. Not until after they were dispersed had they produced any very distinguished man. It was reserved for them in our own time to give birth to the most brilliant Essayist, and one of the most interesting Historians in the English tongue. The Macaulays had lost their lands just before the Age of Industry had begun. They had not been improvers. Yet from the high Tower which in later times had been raised upon the massive foundations, and the dungeon-like apartments of the old Castle of the Clan, I used to look down in childhood upon a broad field of level and fertile land, between the Castle and the sea, grazed by "deep uddered kine"—sometimes loaded with golden sheaves—and sometimes rich in the untainted foliage, with its purple and yellow flowers, which used to make the Potato crop one of the most beautiful of all. Those were still the early days of steam navigation in the West of Scotland, and I recollect one river boat, which could be held in the cabin of some of the great Liners now yearly launched, which was called the "Pride of the Clyde." All the talk I heard was of the opening triumphs of the Engineer—of the future of navigation on the Ocean, and of the yet unsolved problem of the navigation of the Air. The two brothers Hart, from whom Mr. Smiles has borrowed some pleasant anecdotes of James Watt,[1] were favourite guests—simple, and self-made men from Glasgow, full of knowledge and of suggestion on every problem of science applied to use. My Father[2] was a mechanic, and not an agriculturist. He was himself an accomplished workman, making, with exquisite finish, various implements and articles in wood, and in ivory, and in metal. Nothing was ever said of the older, slower, and less exciting conquests over Nature, and over the waste condition in which her great natural Engines had left the encumbered soil.

And yet there was one tool-mark of the Reclaimer which might have recalled his work. Running straight from the foot of the old Coast Line

[1] *Lives of Boulton and Watt*, pp. 499, etc.
[2] John, seventh Duke of Argyll, then Lord John Campbell.

down to the sea, through the middle of the cultivated flats, there was one deep and open cutting, called by the country people the "Red Drain." It had been excavated out of the solid Old Red Sandstone rock, which there overlies the flanks of the Highland Schists. I had often been attracted to its edges by the wild strawberries, which nowhere else grew so large; and by the thickets of bramble in which the Whitethroat skulked and sang. But a chasm—in some places between seven and eight feet deep—with smooth sides of rock, not easily climbed, seemed to a child rather a formidable trap. Of its history and of its purpose I knew nothing —till old documents, in faded ink, have in later years revealed the story. It was the great Outfall by which the fruitful fields, I had so often looked over from the Tower of the Macaulays, had been redeemed from the condition in which they had been left by the Glacial Age, and by the tangled thickets of "Woody Caledon." The operation at the time had been the talk and the wonder of the neighbourhood, in a generation not long preceding that in which my childhood was spent. The Red Drain had been cut at a cost which was considered fabulous at the time—a time when money was as yet scarce in Scotland. The surrounding areas on both sides had been sub-drained and trenched at a further outlay, not less new and astonishing to the natives. Great roots and prostrate trunks of Oak and Fir had been uncovered in the operations. Loads of stones had been dug up, carted away, and built into dikes, whilst boggy holes and quagmires had been filled up and levelled. Without any mention of details, significant allusions to the change effected by Lord Frederick are to be found in writings published before the close of the Century. Thus we hear that land on which Cattle could not walk with safety, had, in 1794, been converted into land firm enough to bear their weight.[1] Before this operation we are further told that not even a Dog could have run over it without sinking to the belly. This account, meagre as it is, testifies to a further and a later change almost as great as that which had already been accomplished in 1794. To speak of any one of the fields on the Estate of Ardencaple as sound enough to bear the weight of Cattle, would, in my earliest years, have been as absurd as to speak in the same language of the oldest wheat lands of Essex or of the Lothians. Over some 700 acres, every foot of which I knew, it is hardly conceivable to me, even now, where any marsh or bog can possibly have existed. Long before 1823 not a trace, and strange to say, hardly a memory had remained of their unreclaimed condition. The very perfection and completeness of the work had rendered it impossible to think of it as a work at all. It was another country, and in all its surroundings it may almost be said to have been another world.

This story of a particular case is the story of a movement which soon became general and simul-

---

[1] Ure's *Agriculture of Dumbartonshire*, p. 27 ; Reports to Board of Agriculture, 1794.

taneous over the whole of Scotland. It is a vignette from a great Picture. It presents to us the starting-point,—the position and the character of those who began the race,—the triumphs they achieved, and the causes also which have led in our day to a very inadequate appreciation of them. Everywhere in Scotland, not only on the shores of the Old Coast Line, but on all the slopes of all the hills—on many of the great plains which were swamps and peat-mosses,—on every variety of surface which was covered with tangled thickets of Alder and Birch and Oak,—over large areas which had before been cultivated in spots and patches—the work of agriculture in Scotland has been the work of laborious and costly reclamation. That work was begun by the Owners as a pleasure and a pursuit, when as yet its economical results were doubtful, and when the outlay was as far beyond the means of the cultivating class, as the effects of it were beyond their comprehension and belief. It was objected at the time to such improvements that they cost many times more than the price of the "fee-simple" of the land;—that other land of much greater extent, and of better quality, might be bought for less than quarter—often for less than a tenth part—of the enormous outlay thus incurred. And all this was true. Such land was really made, not merely inherited or bought. It was redeemed from absolute waste, and rendered contributory for the first time to the sustenance of Man. Where the Snipe probed in quagmires, and the Badger burrowed under roots of trees, and under cairns of stone, very soon new ploughs were turning the furrow, and Cows of a newly created breed were filling the pails with milk.

The Pioneers in this immense work of reclamation were invariably the larger Landowners, both because generally they were the only men who, by intercourse with an older civilisation in the South, had acquired the spirit, and the knowledge, which are the moving influences of the world, but also because they were the only men who had any command at all over the capital necessary for the work. The last Macaulays seem to have been a perfect type of the true old Celtic school of men who thought much of their Chiefery, of their old connection with the Clan Gregor, and of the retainers whom they could send out to fight or reive in alliance with them,[1] but who thought nothing of the acres under their own power which could be made to bear the fruits of industry and of peace. And so when, after the Union, first of the Crowns, and then of the Parliaments, the possibility of living came to depend not on swords and dirks, but on ploughshares and the spade, their resources were dried up, and they sank into irremediable decay. The roof of the old Castle of the Macaulays was falling in, and their once extensive territory had dwindled to a few farms, when the last of them, somewhere about 1765, had to sell the remnant.[2] The old coast lines, over which they had looked for

[1] Irving's *History of Dumbartonshire*, p. 124. [2] *Ibid.*

centuries, and the wastes and morasses which they had valued only for purposes of defence, came into the possession first of my grandfather, and subsequently of his brother, Lord Frederick Campbell. This was the very year, more perhaps than any other definite date that can be named, when the first streaks of the Industrial Dawn were breaking into Day. Both in manufactures and in agriculture this was about the birthday of the new life in the West of Scotland. Fortunately, the place of such Chiefs as the Macaulays was very often taken—not by strangers, but by other Highlanders as Celtic as themselves, but who had kept in the stream of advancing civilisation—had enlisted in the Regiments of Industry,—and had opened their eyes to a wider horizon than the mountain battlements of Glenfruin. They were men who had carried on those best traditions of Scotland which had been embodied in the appeal from Chiefs to Owners, and who now, in the morning of a new day, devoted all the power, and influence, and wealth which had come from a wise rule over Tribe and Sept, and Clan, to the strengthening of an Imperial Crown, and to increasing the resources of a united People.

If such men had not thrown themselves into the new work, it would have been postponed indefinitely. But they did throw themselves into the work with an admirable spirit, and a high intelligence. Across a narrow strait of water belonging to the Firth of Clyde, the elder brother of Lord Frederick, John Fifth

Duke of Argyll, was carrying on similar reclamations on a much larger scale upon his Estate of Rosneath. There, on the same old Coast Line, Edward I. of England had held a Strength when he was attempting the subjugation of Scotland, and there, in the capture and burning of the Castle, one of the traditional exploits of Sir William Wallace had been achieved. There the Glacial Sea had wound round the whole Peninsula—insinuating itself into intricate creeks and coves, where dead valves of the great Clam[1] are frequent—a shell fish now living in Arctic regions, where it is the favourite food of the Walrus, but which has finally disappeared from the shores of Clyde, along with the icy temperature in which it flourished. All the flats and ancient shores, corresponding with those of the old Macaulay lands, are now covered with fine timber, or converted into good arable soil, every acre of it planted and reclaimed during the same years. Men with whom I have myself spoken recollected the time when a favourite horse had been lost in a bog-hole which is now the most fertile corner of a spacious field.

Such operations were no matters of routine then. They were the beginning of a new era. They were the fruit of a new impulse set up by men whose minds had been awakened by contact with wide movements and Imperial interests. Lord Frederick was the first public man who brought the influence

[1] The *Pecten Islandicus*, a very handsome shell common in the glacial days.

of Government to bear upon the systematic preservation of our neglected National Muniments. He was the first head of the newly founded Register House of Edinburgh; and in that great national Institution the benignant wisdom of his countenance is still preserved by Gainsborough's incomparable brush. Another brother, Lord William Campbell, was Governor of South Carolina, where so many Scotchmen and Highlanders had gone, or were going before the revolt of the Colonies. He was afterwards Governor of Nova Scotia, where he founded the Town of Campbeltown on the southern shore of the Bay of Chaleur, where that great Inlet is joined by the beautiful river, the Restigouche, which divides the Provinces of New Brunswick and Quebec. The eldest of the brothers, John, Fifth Duke, had begun life in the army, had fought at Dettingen, had learnt affairs under his two cousins, his most eminent predecessors, and from their friend Culloden. He was the second Lieutenant-Colonel of the Black Watch, and had done much to discipline them before their departure for Canada in 1757. He succeeded in 1770, and spent the rest of his life in devoted attention to agricultural improvement, dying in 1806 the oldest Field-Marshal in the British army.

Such were the men and such was the class of men who all over Scotland carried on and began and established the work of Rural Reform. It needed all their mental activity, all their enlightenment, all their influence, and all their wealth to make even a beginning. In almost every County it is the same story. In looking over the detailed Reports to the Board of Agriculture in 1794-95, it is impossible not to be struck by the great part played by the principal Landowners all over Scotland, in stirring up into a new life the dead and inert elements with which they had to deal. In the North the family of the Dukes of Gordon is remembered as the beginners of the work,[1] stimulated, as it is said, so early as 1706, by an Englishwoman, daughter of the Earl of Peterborough, who was himself a great improver in the South. In Ayrshire the Earl of Eglinton takes a high rank among the most energetic improvers of the country.[2] In East Lothian the Haddington family were eminent, whilst the Tweeddales also remind us of those earlier Hays who were the improving Tacksmen under the Abbots of Scone in 1312. In Fife the very ancient title of Rothes acquired a new eminence in the arts of peace. In Banff an Earl of Findlater receives especial honour from all contemporary accounts[3] for his exertions both in agricultural and manufacturing industry. From the great County of Aberdeen, which had been terribly desolated by the years of famine at the close of the previous century, and a large area of which had actually been abandoned and thrown out of cultivation, we are told that to enumerate all those to whom its recovery, and

---

[1] *Northern Rural Life*, p. 24 (D. Douglas, Edinburgh, 1877).

[2] Reports, vol. i., *Agriculture of Ayr*, p. 16.

[3] *Ibid, Agriculture of Banff*, p. 13. The Findlater family is now merged in the Earldom of Seafield.

subsequent advance were due, it would be necessary to give a complete list of all the gentlemen in the County.[1]

The class of capitalist Tenant Farmers had not yet arisen, or were only beginning to appear in the South and East. The introduction of one of this class from East Lothian into Ayrshire by the Earl of Eglinton, is specially mentioned as an epoch in the West. There also some of the smaller Proprietors had more means, and they early joined the race. But all over the West Country, and all over the Highlands, this class had little or no command of money. The extreme poverty of the country in the middle, and during the whole of the latter half of the last Century, seems almost incredible. Some of the oldest families in the Lennox, and some of the most considerable Landowners, were obliged to have recourse to loans when they were called upon to pay sums of the most trifling amount. The Dennistouns of Dennistoun, a Knightly family, so old, that their boast was that Kings had come from them, not they from Kings, in borrowing £33, 6s. 8d. from the Minister of Cardross, somewhere about 1720-5, had to grant a bond backed by two Glasgow merchants. The Napiers of Kilmahew, the most ancient representatives of an illustrious name, in the same Parish, were, in 1732, in much trouble about a bill amounting to £6, 5s. $3\tfrac{1}{2}$d.[2] Illustrations without number

---

[1] *Agriculture of Aberdeenshire*, p. 75, Reports, vol. i.
[2] *Old Cardross*: a Lecture by David Murray, M.A., 1880.

could be given of the same kind. The whole circulating medium in all Scotland, at the time of the Darien scheme, was supposed to be not more than £800,000, and of this one-half was risked and lost in that unfortunate speculation.[1]

But although Scotland, at this time, was a country singularly poor in realised Capital, it was a country rich in everything that is the source and the fountain out of which Capital can be made. Scotland had an immense "Wages-Fund." For here we come upon distinctions of the very highest interest and importance. The "Wages-Fund" is a formal and scholastic phrase belonging to antiquated theories of Political Economy. The doctrine it expressed has been fiercely and successfully assailed in the interests of Muscle, and the opponents of the doctrine have made good a portion of their case. It is not true that the wages of Muscular Labour come only from realised Capital. That kind of Labour has a good right to vindicate its own inherent contribution to Value. Without its help no Value can be embodied, and no Capital can be gathered. Wages may be advanced for a time out of the savings of the past, but only in the confident expectation that they will be more than repaid out of the gains of the future. Wages therefore come out of Work, and Muscular Labour is a rightful sharer, to the stipulated extent, in the ultimate Value to which it contributes. It may fairly be said that, whilst standing in some aspects

[1] *Life of W. Paterson*; Chambers's *Biographical Dictionary*.

pretty nearly abreast in the fighting lines of Industry, Muscular Labour comes rather before than behind its comrade, Capital. It certainly can find, and has often found, employment where there has been little or no Capital—little or no money—whether accumulated in Banks, or in Shares, or in the more primitive investments of silver and gold hidden in holes, or kept in stockings. Money must be made before it can be saved or stored; and in the getting of money or of money's worth some kind of Muscular Labour is always of necessity concerned. But the truth is that both these sources of Wealth, whilst nearly equal in rank as between themselves, stand a long way behind and below another, which is nearer than both to the fountain-head. Capital is the product and representative of a prior and a deeper source. Men who have no Capital—no hoarded or accumulated money—will, nevertheless, employ Muscle, if they have a reasonable expectation that it can be hired for a stipulated Wage, and that the value conferred on mere physical work by the higher agencies of Enterprise and Forethought, will belong securely to those who wield them. But this reasonable expectation can only be entertained where the laws of Covenant and of Ownership are firmly settled. Such a system of Law therefore is the richest inheritance of any people. It is the true Wages-Fund. Like all other things of the highest rank in Nature, it is intellectual and moral—not physical or material. Here, as elsewhere, it is true that the things which are seen are temporal, but the things which are not seen are eternal.

Scotland was then poor, not only in money, but in money's worth, so far as actual productions were concerned. The habits and usages of her people were rude and ignorant. Like many other customs, their usages were tending more and more to mischief. Their miserable agriculture had been getting worse and worse. The small area of soil which alone had been cultivated was getting more and more exhausted from over-cropping. Their desperate local attachment was leading to reckless sub-division. In the Highlands ancient predatory habits had grown into such settled and almost acknowledged customs of robbery by violence, that regular Blackmail rents were paid to the Robber Clans, as the price of exemption. But these usages — and others less conspicuous, but hardly less destructive — had never been allowed by the Parliaments of Scotland, or by her Judges, to corrupt her Law. Rooted in an ancient and noble civilisation, that Law had been not only kept pure, but, without departure from fundamental principles, had been adapted from time to time to new requirements of Society. Her poverty was thus, as it were, accidental, temporary, and superficial—arising only from ignorance of some natural laws, and of some natural products. The moment these became known, and in proportion as they came to be generally understood, Enterprise sprang up as if by magic. But Enterprise entirely rested, and could only rest on that confidence in the results of action, and in the fruits of Work, which itself again can have no other foundation than a complete system of acknowledged Rights and of sanctioned Obligations in all the relations of Industry.

Nothing, indeed, can be more misleading than the ordinary definition of the sources of Wealth, and no wonder—because before we can make clear to ourselves the sources of anything, we must begin with some clear idea as to what that thing is in itself. Wealth must be defined before its sources can be traced. Yet the common definitions of Wealth by the Political Economists very generally omit, or slur over, the one most essential element in the whole group of ideas which are represented in the word. I know of only one definition which goes straight to the point, and leaves a complete and satisfying impression upon the mind. It is the definition given in the searching words, " A man's life consisteth not in the abundance of the things which he possesseth."[1] Here the whole strength of the definition is concentrated in the last word—" possesseth." No mere enumeration, or description of the kind of things possessed, however elaborate and ingenious, can ever convey the idea of Wealth, unless stress is laid, before all others, upon the one fundamental idea of Possession. Wealth may be defined to be—the Possession, in comparative abundance, of things which are objects of human desire, and which cannot be obtained without some sacrifice, or some

[1] St. Luke xii. 15.

exertion. There may be infinite variation in the kind of things which men desire. There may be infinite variation in the strength of that desire. There may be infinite variation in the quantities which constitute abundance in the eyes of a poor or of a rich community. But there can be no variation in the one fundamental conception of Possession as the root idea of Wealth.

The sources of Wealth must therefore be inseparable from the sources of Possession. We all know what these sources are. In early and rude societies the mental and physical qualities which make men Chiefs and Leaders, are the powers which enable them to take, and to give, Possession. As society advances these powers are translated into Law. This, then, becomes the source and the guarantee of all Possession. It is in this august name that we find the ultimate source of Wealth. It is a source, like all other ultimate sources, which lies in Mind—in the settled Jurisprudence of a well-ordered Commonwealth. Compared with this, nothing can be more poor and meagre—nothing indeed can be more confounding and confusing than the stereotyped definitions of the sources of Wealth. Land, Labour, and Capital, are the orthodox Three. In this enumeration the deepest source of all—Possession—is either omitted altogether, or else it is hid under a word which does not suggest it. Labour of the Brain is confounded with Labour of the Hands. Capital is treated as something separate from both, which it certainly is not. Capital is the purest representative of Mind, because our very conception of it turns on special acts of Purpose and of Intention in the disposal or use of Income. Land is a most confusing word if it be intended to designate the whole external world. The definition, therefore, altogether is scholastic and artificial in the highest degree—teaching nothing, suggesting nothing,—because none of its distinctions correspond with such great dividing lines as exist in Nature. One of these lines runs along the seeming gulf between Mind and Matter, and another between our own share in both of these, and the boundless volume of them which is external to ourselves, but with which, nevertheless, we have close relations. These dividing lines are familiar to us all—in our thoughts, in our actions, and in our language. They seem to point to a better Three than Land, Labour, and Capital. Mind, Matter, and Opportunity, would be the amended list. Mind is that which we know—as we know nothing else. Matter is that which is ours also in Muscle, and in all that it acts upon, or that re-acts on it. Opportunity is a convenient term for every kind, degree, and variety of condition, and of circumstance which helps to stimulate our desires, to clear our aims, or to facilitate the attainment of them.

These being the Three great sources of Wealth, Scotland was, by nature, rich in two of them, and was every day becoming richer and richer in the Third. In Mind there was no better fibre in the world than the fibre which had been spun out of her old amalgamated races. Mind among them might be mis-directed and wasted, or it might be sleeping. But it was there—with an immense and unknown Potential Energy. It had been shown for generations in all the special faculties appropriate to the Military Ages. It had now caught the fire which burns in mechanical genius, and in peaceful enterprise. So, in like manner, Scotland was rich in the raw materials of Nature, which it is the function of Mind to work with, to work upon, and to subdue. Her country was soon found to be full of the savings hoarded in the depths of Time, the great accumulations of Energy which had been laid up in her stores of Coal and Iron. Her agricultural and pastoral surfaces were rough and unreclaimed, but they were not poor. Even the Glacial Ages had done Scotland enormous good—for their great Planing Engines, though they had left, here and there, tough and tenacious clays, had also scattered everywhere the materials of a better soil. Nor were these two sources of Wealth all that had been prepared for Scotland in starting her in the race of Industry. The Third, and the last of the Three great sources of Wealth, Opportunity, had been secured and opened up for her in that one fundamental condition on which all the possibilities of Opportunity depend. This was the condition without which no opportunity can be seized—no design can be formed, no enterprise can be undertaken—the condition, namely, of an ancient, accepted, and well-defined system of Law and of Jurisprudence. Men knew their own rights and their own obligations, because these rested on written and recorded Instruments, and because the exact force of all of them had been settled and applied through centuries of Judicial interpretation. As in the Kingdom of Nature the invariableness and certainty of her Laws are the necessary Implements of Purpose and Design, so in Human Society there can be no other foundation for Industry and for Enterprise, than Laws accurately defining, and Courts impartially enforcing, all the rights and all the obligations of men. There is no place in Science for the Slattern or the Sloven. In dealing with Nature the loose reasoner, and the inaccurate observer, soon find their level. So it must be in every Political Society which desires to preserve the germs of life, and to keep open to men the infinite opportunities of knowledge.

If, in the purchase or inheritance of land from old Owners of the type of the Macaulays, such new Proprietors as Lord Frederick Campbell had not been able to trust in the validity of the Titles by which Property had been conveyed for seven or eight hundred years—if the words of Charters, which carried the full rights and powers of Ownership over Moors, and Marshes, and Woods, and Peateries, and over all the other enumerated varieties of surface, had not, during all these Centuries, been uniformly sustained as living and truthful words, not only in all the decisions of law, but also in all the acknowledged obligations and practical transactions of life—then, such reclamations as those of the old Coast Line on the Firth of Clyde, would never have been undertaken, and Scotland would have remained even more waste and wild than she had been in the days of Malcolm Canmore.

But direct, rapid, and costly reclamations of this kind were not the only, nor perhaps the most important, application of that great Wages Fund which consists in the confidence of men in the security of all legal rights, and in the enforcement of all legal obligations. Land in Scotland had for centuries been almost universally let on "Tacks" or Leases. These varied more or less in their conditions and in the period of their duration. But one essential fundamental principle was expressed and embodied in them all, viz., that the Owner lent his land to the Occupant for a time, and for a time only. At the end of it the right of disposing of the land on new conditions reverted to the Owner. This principle extended as a matter of course to Sub-tenants, if there were any such. They could not have any higher or larger right of possession than those under whom they held. As water can rise no higher than its fountain, so derivative tenures cannot rise above the tenures from which they are derived. We have seen how, under the advice of Culloden, many of these Sub-tenants had in the Hebrides been raised from the condition of Tenants at Will to the higher condition of Tacksmen, more than thirty years before the operations of Lord Frederick and of his brother in Dumbartonshire.

But this was before the new practices of Agriculture had begun, and before its new resources had been placed at the disposal either of Owner or of Tenant. All that these Leases therefore did, in this direction, was to encourage definite lengths of tenure for such industry as was then understood, leaving the Tenants to pick up any new methods which might arise. But this is precisely what men of that class, in that stage of society, never do. They run on from generation to generation in the ruts of custom—hating every novelty and blind to every suggestion. One thing, nevertheless, the system of Leases did which was in itself invaluable. It established definite breaks in the continuity of occupation, and therefore saved the country from a perpetuity of ignorance. That feature in Leases which is often made an objection to them by the ignorant, was the very feature that gave saving entrance to the new life, and to the new knowledge, which would otherwise have been excluded for generations. As Leases had been given during 400 years at an immense variety of dates, it followed that everywhere, all over Scotland, at all times, a crop of Leases was coming to an end; and the necessity of making new arrangements for a new Tack gave precisely that kind of opportunity which Mind requires for the discharge of its special functions in directing Muscle. As Longfellow says of the awakening Song of Birds all round the Globe, " 'Tis always morning somewhere," so it may be said of Scotland as regards

these opportunities of improvement, that all through
her Counties and Parishes they were arising everywhere. Thus, for example, the Leases given by
the advice of Culloden on the Argyll estates,
between 1739 and 1750, were expiring during
the very years between 1759 and 1770, when the
enthusiasm of new discoveries and of new aspirations was at its height, and when it was beginning
to transform the whole conditions of the National
Industry in all its branches.

Among these transformations there was one
affecting Agriculture, the value of which is now
confused under an ignorant form of sentiment. It
consisted in the steady but gradual disappearance
of Township farms. These were farms tenanted by
small groups of men, using their pastures in common,
and cultivating their arable lands in Run-rig. I designate the sentiment in favour of these old Townships as an ignorant sentiment, because it is mainly
founded on a misunderstanding as to their real
nature. They were not farms under a common
management for the equal benefit of a community.
The flavour of communism, which makes the memory
of them popular with some theorists now, is a flavour
which comes from nothing but mistaken analogies.
The Township farms were not what we should now
call Club-farms. They were not held nor managed
by the representatives of a community on behalf of
the whole. They were mere groups of individual
men, each man having his own individual property in
the Cattle, and his own exclusive share in the arable

areas of land. The principle of occupation was the principle of pure Individualism—only, under such conditions that none of its benefits could arise. The common grazing might contain the very best land of the farm, if only it could be reclaimed. But no one of the Tenants could exert his mind or his muscles in reclaiming a single morsel, because it would have limited by so much the grazing of the others. Neither could any one Tenant, more intelligent than the rest, and seeing that the common grazing was overstocked, gain anything by limiting the number of his own beasts, because all his more ignorant neighbours would at once add a corresponding number, and so keep down the whole herd to the old starvation point. Neither, again, could any of the Tenants, even if they had the capital and the knowledge, begin to establish a better breed, because the good breed could not be kept separate from the bad. Thus all were kept down, even as regarded the Cattle and the grazing, to one level, and that was the level of the stupidest.

The case was if possible worse as regarded the arable land. Each Tenant had indeed his own scattered patches exclusively to himself, so long as he had them at all. He got no help, if his crop failed, out of any share in the comparative abundance of others, nor on the other did he share with others in any fortunate excess. In all these ways, and in others, he was an individual farmer, and nothing else. But he was not allowed to benefit by any individual wit, if by chance he had it, as regarded the possibility of improvement. He had no inducement to dig deeper, or to manure better his little patches, because all the benefit of his labour would probably go next year by lot to some less intelligent or less industrious neighbour. Then, with other kinds of improvement even more important, the whole system was absolutely incompatible. If one man, seeing the starved condition of the Cattle, wished to make and store a little hay for winter feeding, he had no means of doing so. The moment the harvest was over, the whole area of the arable land was turned into a common pasture field for all the Township. No man could enclose a morsel of ground to save a bite of hay. No man could drain, lime, or otherwise improve any portion of the farm, because, although it was exclusively his own to-day, it would be as exclusively another's to-morrow.

Such was the stupid and ruinous system on which land was tenanted not only in the Highlands, but all over the Lowlands of Scotland during a great part of the Eighteenth Century, and in some cases down to our own time. It was the same in England only a little earlier, and Lady Verney has disinterred the curious fact that one Parish in the County of Buckingham, within a few hours' journey of London, continued to be occupied in Runrig for more than 400 years— from 1444 to 1845, when it was divided into individual holdings by the external authority of the Enclosure Commission.[1]

---

[1] Article on "Allotments," by Lady Verney, in *Nineteenth Century*, June 1886.

Although now banished from every part of Scotland, except where it yet lingers in the most distant and poorest Hebrides, I have myself had to interpose for the abolition of it on the mainland of Argyllshire about forty years ago. As late as the middle of the last century it was as general on farms within sight of the great Lowland Towns of Edinburgh, Glasgow, Paisley, and Greenock as it was round the more Highland Towns of Perth, Dundee, and Inverness. Nothing but an unquestioning and unquestioned adherence to the rights of Ownership, operating steadily but gradually through the opportunities afforded to awakened Mind by the termination of Leases, could have redeemed the country from this system. The people themselves generally clung to it with a dull and blind tenacity. Nor is this surprising. It was a system of which all the parts so hung together, and which as a whole was so rooted in all the routine habits of daily and yearly life, that not one stone of it could be touched without the whole structure tumbling. Any change involved a total change in the prospects and in the life of every family concerned.

Under such circumstances the initiative never is, and never can be taken by those who live under such a yoke of custom. It is so with all of us. Our eyes and our lips can be opened only by the touch of a live coal from some altar other than our own. There was a race of Scotch Judges in the last century whose witty sayings, expressed in the broadest native Doric, were long the amusement of the legal profession in Edinburgh. One of them, on hearing a Counsel plead on behalf of his Client that he had acted in ignorance of the Law, interrupted the pleader at once, saying, "Mr. ———, the Law taks nae cogneesance o' stupeedity." But if Judges can take no cognisance of stupidity, Historians are compelled to do so, because mental blindness is a perpetual wonder from generation to generation as we trace the movements of Mankind, whether in the progress of civilisation or in the backslidings of corruption and decline. There is a profound passage on this subject in the Apocryphal Book called the Wisdom of Solomon, in which the slow progress of our knowledge in Natural Things is set forth as diminishing the wonder, and yet enlarging the estimate, of our ignorance of the Spiritual World:—"For the thoughts of mortal men are miserable, and our devices are but uncertain. For the corruptible body presseth down the soul, and the earthly tabernacle weigheth down the mind that museth upon many things. And hardly do we guess aright at things that are upon earth, and with labour do we find the things that are before us."[1]

It is fortunate, however, for Mankind that very often new truths are borne in upon us by the mere weight of external circumstances, not as the result of any "musing" at all, and when we ourselves may be as blind as ever to "the things that are before us." And so it was with the cultivating classes in Scot-

[1] Wisdom of Solomon, ix. 14-16.

land. Great, and indeed complete, as the change was which came about within a time comparatively short, we must not exaggerate the rapidity of the process. It had begun, as we have seen, in the Border Counties after the Union of the Crowns, more than a century before the time we are now considering, and the displacement of the Military Classes there when the Border Wars ended, had been connected with the poverty and distress which was conspicuous in Scotland before the Union of the Parliaments. It received a great impetus after that event, and about 1760 it went forward at an accelerated pace. But even in the last decade of the century, during the years when the *Statistical Account* was being compiled, and the Reports to the Board of Agriculture were being drawn up, large areas of Scotland were either still occupied in Runrig or were just escaping from it. The causes which at once facilitated the change and forced it on, were all as purely natural as any physical causes, although they operated in and through the Wills of men. In the first place, Englishmen had discovered that the small Black Cattle of Scotland could be fed up to a much greater size, and made the very best of beef. The price of them consequently rose without the smallest exertion on the part of the Runrig Tenants. Moreover, the Dealers who bought them, and the English Farmers who fed them, were known to make a further and a much larger profit upon them. Scotch Tenants and Scotch Landowners very naturally began to think that a much larger share of this profit might be secured to the Producers in Scotland by taking some care to bring them to market in a less starved condition. From this instinctive desire, and this very rudimentary suggestion, everything else that happened necessarily followed. To improve the breed of Cattle there must be the means of separating the good from the bad. To feed them better there must be hay. The same necessity which applied to Cattle as a supply of meat, applied equally to the new management of Cattle as a source of Dairy produce. Cows under the old system, being small and half-starved, gave but little milk, and for a very short time in the season. With better food and, above all, with a continuous supply of it, their Dairy produce in milk rose in quantity by 150 per cent., and could be continued as much longer in point of time. All this depended on better breeding and better feeding. To have hay, even wild hay, there must be enclosures, still more when artificial grasses began to be introduced. Then, along with them came the new Green or Root Crops, and the system of alternating these with Cereals.

Every step in this ascending series of innovations depended on and involved the one essential preliminary of enclosures. Nothing could be done without them. Special and separate areas of land devoted to special and separate purposes, constituted the new source of power. It was the same principle as that which flashed on the genius of Watt when the thought occurred to him of the

"Separate Condenser." In the older Engines one and the same vessel, the Cylinder, was used for more than one mechanical purpose. Expansion and Condensation were effected in one common chamber. Heat was wasted; power was lost. The great principle of the Division of Labour was the principle of Watt's discovery. It is a principle which runs through the whole of Nature. Man in adopting it has been only following her great example. It now penetrated every nook and cranny of the Industrial world; it took possession of the new Rural Economy by the operation of an universal instinct. The grand secret of its success lay in the scope it gave to Brains, which are always personal—individual—and liable to be unequal in infinite degrees. Especially in an age of awakening, the aptitudes of Mind, and the receptiveness of Intellect, and the energies of Enterprise are all pre-eminently individual. It is their function to raise individual men above the common herd, and to enable them to throw off the stupidities of Custom. Common and undivided lands were the Castles and Fortresses of all these stupidities—the strongholds in which they held out the longest. But everywhere their roofs were falling in, and their walls were being undermined—just as about the same time, the old Towers of the Macaulays became uninhabitable.

Enclosures, with all the other works of reclamation which depended on them, became the universal occupation of all the Owners of land as opportunity offered. Like everything else in Scotland which was valuable, it was nowhere absolutely new, because Parliament, even during the Military Ages, had encouraged the fencing and protection of woods and plantations. It had, moreover, recognised afresh, in recent years, the value to be set on the concentration of individual interest and of individual motive upon landed property. In some places, though not generally, the Ownership of land, and not the Occupancy only, had been held on the fashion of Runrig. That is to say, certain areas of land belonged, in small lots, to different Owners, and these were re-divided from time to time. This involved the same evil, and although it did not extensively prevail, yet wherever it existed it affected indirectly all surrounding properties. It did prevail, however, extensively in Annandale, where Border wars had long rendered property valueless. Accordingly, in 1695, it had become sufficiently mischievous to attract the attention of the First Parliament of King William III., and an Act was passed for remedying it—on the significant Preamble that "great disadvantage was arising to the whole Subjects from lands lying in Runrig," and that the same was highly prejudicial to the Policy and Improvement of the Nation by planting and enclosing."[1] Wherefore, power was given to every one having an interest in such property, to call for a separation and final division of it under the authority of the Sheriffs. No such Act was needed for the abandonment of Runrig in respect to Occupation,

[1] *Act. Parl. Scot.*, vol. ix. p. 421 (5 Will. III., ch. 23).

because this could at any time be effected by virtue of the ordinary rights of Ownership. The farms occupied by several Tenants, and grazed or cultivated by them according to the habits and knowledge of the time, were so occupied and cultivated only under the terms of Covenant. The terms of that Covenant might be altered from time to time. There was no legal impediment in the way. No Legislation, therefore, was required. The saving effects of permanent divisions and of individual farming were only just beginning to be understood. Rude and unsubstantial fences had from time immemorial been erected to divide the "Infield" from the "Outfield" land—the area which was under crop from the area which was uncultivated. The same practice had now to be extended to the internal divisions of the arable land, and to the immense areas which were being reclaimed and brought within that description by reclamation from the wastes of common grazings. In the district of the Lennox, typical from its geographical situation bordering on both Highlands and Lowlands, the progress of Enclosure was so rapid and continuous that in 1794 the Report says, "Not a year passes but several thousand acres are surrounded with fences."[1]

In the fine district of Annandale, the old home of the Bruces, the evil of Commons seems to have been specially enduring and obstructive, since owing to them the greatest exertions of individuals could not make the country capable of modern cultiva-

[1] *Agriculture of Dumbartonshire;* Reports, vol. ii. p. 19.

tion.[1] Yet in 1794 scarcely a single Common remained undivided, except in the case of lands belonging to the Royal Burghs. As compared with individual Proprietors, either the intelligence of these Corporate Bodies was less, or their difficulties were greater, since, it was said, "they alone could claim the privilege of keeping waste tracts of the country useless to mankind,—an eyesore to the benevolent passenger, and fit only to indulge the indolent occupier in brooding over his poverty and his turf-fire."[2]

This passage is curious, and directs our attention to a fact of some interest. The Old Royal Burghs in Scotland were in some cases not inconsiderable Landowners. They possessed certain areas of land, fishings, and various other rights of property, as other Landowners did, by Charters from the Sovereigns who had the power and the right to give them along with the Municipal "liberties" and privileges which rested on the same Instruments. Thus the same early Sovereign of Scotland, William the Lion (A.D. 1165-1214), who gave by Charter to the ancestor of Robert Bruce the great Estate of Annandale, also erected the Town of Ayr into a Royal Burgh, and granted it certain lands, which are carefully described by boundary names as purely Celtic as any now used in the heart of the Highlands. It was specified that out of this area belonging to the Town each Burgess might reclaim six acres out of the Wood or Forest "to make their own profit thereby."[3]

[1] *Agriculture of Dumfries;* Reports, App. p. 22. [2] *Ibid.*
[3] *National Manuscripts of Scotland,* Part i. p. 21.

This would seem to point to an unlimited power of individual appropriation corresponding to the number of Burgesses. But practically the use of these Burgh lands was generally the use of pasture for the benefit of the Burgesses as a Community, and for centuries they continued to be so used in common, by all who acquired the position and rights of a Burgess.

It was natural that under these conditions there should be great difficulties in changing the mode of use. But if the Burghs were in 1794 behind in the improvement of their lands, this reproach has been removed long ago. Burgh property in Scotland was called the "Common Good," and the Burghs soon found out by the example of other Landowners around them that the best way of consulting the "Common Good" was to give up common Occupation and resort to individual holdings. Accordingly the landed property of the Burghs has long been managed on the same principle on which it is managed by individual Owners,—except that the public interest of the Community has led to a more rigid and universal system of letting by open competition, so as to secure the highest possible rents. Every tendency to let land on terms below the market rate was very naturally regarded as simply a cover for jobbery. Early Statutes [1] forbade Burghs to grant Leases for a longer term than three years, and the object of this prohibition was to secure to the Burgh the growing value of land, and

[1] Such as 1491, c. 19, *Act. Parl. Scot.*, vol. ii. p. 227.

to prevent the transfer of that growing value from those in whom Ownership resided to those who had no other right than that of temporary Occupation and of special bargain. This principle was finally embodied in stringent legislation by an Act passed in 1832,[1] which prohibited all feuing, alienation, or leasing of any part of Common Good of Burghs except by public roup—that is to say, except at the very highest attainable rent or feu-duty. When, therefore, Burghal Owners discovered, as other Owners did, that lands enclosed, and otherwise reclaimed from slovenly and promiscuous uses, immediately rose in value, and afforded at once double or treble the former rent, they joined in the great industrial race of enclosure and reclamation by which the whole face of Scotland has been transformed from being one of the poorest to being one of the best cultivated countries in the world.

The principle thus laid down by Parliament, that the value of all property belonging to Corporate Bodies must always be tested by competition, and let by public roup at the highest market rent, is obviously the only safe principle in the management of a "Common Good." It is undoubtedly the principle on which all land would be let which falls directly in the hands of the State.[2] Private Owners can and do depart from it with more or less advantage, because the preferences of character and

---

[1] 3 Geo. IV. cap. 91.

[2] Mr. Henry George has repeatedly admitted that the State must let its land by auction.

the considerations of sentiment which lead an individual Owner to let his farms to one man who can give less, rather than to another man who can give more, are preferences which, in his case, must always have their natural limits, and which, whether wise or not, are at least always generous and can never be corrupt. In the case of Public Bodies, on the contrary, such preferences are quite sure to be the result of intrigue and of corruption. Accordingly it is certain that in the centuries when publicity was unknown, and when the government of Burghs was far from pure, the "Common Good" had been often jobbed and wasted. Repeated Acts of Parliament were passed during the Sixteenth and Seventeenth Centuries, recording and vainly endeavouring to check this evil.[1] A strict adherence, therefore, to the principle laid down in the Act of 1832 was the only remedy—the principle, namely, of free and open competition in the hire of land or of other property belonging to all Public Bodies.

It is one of the innumerable benefits of Private over Public Ownership, that it is not bound by such rigid necessities. The free choice of persons in selecting Tenants, is one of the most essential of its powers. The highest offerer is not necessarily the best Tenant, except under an equality of other conditions, which is rare. Yet even in respect to land belonging to private Owners, the larger

[1] *Observations on the Law and Practice in regard to Municipal Elections in Scotland.* By J. D. Marwick, LL.D., pp. 336-71.

interests of the public are at least presumably in favour of the same principle. The rent of agricultural land must ultimately be determined by the produce. The man who can pay the highest rent is presumably the man who can turn out the largest amount of produce. This he can only do by superiority over other competitors in some faculty or aptitude of Mind, or in the possession of Capital which has been stored by the foresight of himself, or by others whom he represents. There are wonderful bits of faculty and of aptitude connected, each of them, with some corresponding bits of Brain, which in Agriculture, as much as in any other pursuit, tell upon the result. It may be a faculty for estimating the "points" in the breeding of domestic animals on which all progress in utility and in value depends. It may be some inborn and instinctive aptitude for the best methods of manufacture in the artificial productions of the Dairy—it may be merely the faculty of thrift in everything, and of turning everything to the best account—it may be any one, or any combination of these, that will enable one man to pay for land a rent much higher than can be afforded by others who have no similar qualifications, and who are the blind followers of routine. Private Owners may, and continually do, prefer some man who is inferior in all these respects, and they may do so wisely on account of personal or hereditary associations. But in general the interests of agricultural production, which on the whole are the interests of the nation, are to some extent sacrificed thereby. It can never be for the public interest that dull men should be preferred to men of ability, or men with no means to men who have adequate capital. It is only when the extreme test of competition for the holding of land is applied to men who are all equally poor, and who seek for it as a means of bare subsistence, that it ceases to have any value in the public interests. Yet even in this case, those who think that the hire of land should be dealt with as a matter of charity, will find it difficult to defend the rejection of several candidates who offer more, on behalf of some favoured one who offers less. It would be a strange exercise of benevolence not to prefer those who, from the very fact of being the most needy, are willing to give the most, because they are satisfied with the smallest residue. Accordingly, the Irish Land Act of 1880 incites and encourages the Cottier Tenantry of Ireland to exact the last farthing they can get for the sale of their interest to any new Tenant. Private Owners had made rules modifying the severity of this principle in favour of incoming Tenants. But the coarse hands of the State, when it intervenes, have nothing to fall back upon except the principle of Competition in its extremest form.

This system when applied to conditions of hungry and necessitous competition which are in themselves disastrous, can end in nothing but the ruin of agriculture and universal pauperism. Under such circumstances there is no presumption in favour of the highest offerer. He is the hungriest, and nothing more. It would be a bad principle of selection applied to a morbid condition of society, and securing further degradation by systematic preference of the most unfit. This was the actual result in some parts of Ireland—not at all as the consequences of English law or of English customs, but, on the contrary, as the natural fruit of the most genuine old Celtic habits and traditions.

The total absence of any elevating guidance, or of any intelligent control, over men with a low standard of living, and a narrow horizon of desire, can never end in anything but disaster, whatever be the avocation or pursuit to which such a system is applied. Most disastrous of all must it be when applied to that industry and pursuit which comes before every other in the progress of nations. Unlimited licence to sub-let and to sub-divide, and to multiply down to the level of a potato diet—a perfect jungle of sub-tenures—one set of lettings beneath another, and single "rigs" below the lowest—all let to the highest bidder—all except the first, from year to year only—and all interposed for long and indefinite periods of time between the Owner and any possibility of improvement or even of regulation—such a system was perfectly adapted to banish Mind, in all its higher faculties, from the business of agriculture, and from the building up of Society upon foundations even tolerably safe. Ownership lost all its virtue along with all its opportunities, and all its power. And all this system was purely native—purely Celtic. The Middleman holding tracts of lands for Life or Lives, and living on the competitive rents of very poor and very ignorant people, all struggling for a bare subsistence, is the nearest possible modern representative and analogue of the old Irish Chieftain nourishing a crowd of Septs as his servitors and retainers, and living in his turn upon them, by their help in inter-tribal wars, and in peace "by coign and livery," "cosherings and cuttings." The abuses of the system adopted by the Middlemen were multiplied and intensified by the abuses which grew up like weeds among all below them. There was one hideous practice of Tenants of Ireland, unheard of in any civilised country in the world, to which they were stimulated by the high prices of wheat during the many years of war towards the end of the last, and the first quarter of the present century. This was the practice of burning the land—setting fire to the finest grass lands, whereby the best mineral and vegetable ingredients of the soil could be used up and carried off in a few years of enormous and exhausting profits. In vain had the Irish Parliament passed one enactment after another to prohibit and punish this barbarous waste. It was only one of a thousand other mischievous practices arising out of the paralysis of the powers of Ownership. Laws are useless when they cannot be enforced, and they never can be enforced when the power to practise and to compel obedience is not in the hands of those who have a motive and an interest in doing so.

Like many other noble words that are used without thought, the word Custom has suffered degradation. It has a venerable sound—reminding us of harmless ancestral usages, loved, regretted, and commemorated. It has its own place, too— and a very high place—in the most civilised systems of Jurisprudence and of Law. Neither oral nor written Covenants between men, however definite, can express the whole of the conditions which they imply. Many of these conditions may be, and indeed must be omitted,—not at all because they are inapplicable, but, on the contrary, because their application is of necessity understood. Customs so universal or so general, as to occupy this rank, are not opposed to Covenant or Contract as the basis of all relations between men in matters of business. They are essential parts of every system of Contract, in so far as they are evidence of things mutually understood. In the oldest Charters in Scotland there are many references to customary Use and Wont, to be ascertained as a matter of fact, in the determination of the most important rights; as, for example, in the extent and boundary of lands, or in the extent and limits of the privilege of fishing. But nothing can be more different from this high idea of Custom than that other idea which consecrates under the same name every stupid practice and every abuse which may creep in and establish itself among the ignorant or the weak.

The wonderful burst of Industry which transformed the whole face of Scotland in the course of the Eighteenth Century, and especially during the latter half of it, could never have arisen if her ancient Law had not been kept pure and uncontaminated from such debasement. Everything that takes from Knowledge its initiative by depriving it of Opportunity — everything that discourages Enterprise by accumulating against it unknown elements of uncertainty—is a barrier—often an insuperable barrier—to improvement. Fortunately for Scotland the rights recognised by Charter on the one hand, and conveyed by Covenant on the other, had been kept clear and definite. If the property conferred on Corporations was longer left without improvement, or if it had been wasted and dispersed, this result had only arisen because Corporate Bodies can never in such matters represent, except very imperfectly, the natural influences and motives which animate Individual Owners, and which make their aspirations and desires coincident in the main, and in the long-run, with the public interests. No such law was ever thought of for them, as the law which was ultimately passed for Burghal Owners, laying down an universal and unbending rule that nothing should be let except by roup, and at the highest rates determined by competition. On the contrary, in a memorable Act passed at a memorable epoch in the national history, Parliament had called upon all Landowners to remember that in the disposal of their lands they held, and were free to use a large and a wide discretion over the choice of their Tenants. Upon the loyal exercise of this power, the Monarchy had relied in its long contention against the most formidable political dangers. Upon the wise and enlightened exercise of the same power the Nation now again relied, not less securely, for its advance from famines and poverty to comfort and to abundance, and from comparative barbarism to a high and advancing civilisation. As in the Sixteenth Century Landowners were called upon not to let their farms and "rooms" to men ignorant of their duty to the National Government, so now, in the dawn of the Industrial Ages, they were trusted not to let their lands to men ignorant of, or deaf to the new duties, the new demands, and the new opportunities of their day.

On the other hand, as the progress of agricultural knowledge had been slow even among the educated classes, it could not fail to be much more slow among those who had no education except that of tradition and routine. It was not possible, and it would not have been wise, if it had been possible, to bring about too suddenly the immense changes which were absolutely required. Nothing but the free play of individual motive,— of knowledge, of enterprise, and of personal relations,—could have worked with the elasticity, and with the variety of application, which such circumstances eminently demanded. And never, perhaps, in the history of any country was a more signal illustration given of the inestimable value, on the one hand, of a strict and clear definition of all legal rights, and, on the other hand, of perfect individual freedom in the handling of them. In the beginning of the century, by far the largest part of the country, not only in the Highlands and in the Borders, but also in the Lowlands, was unenclosed, unimproved, and cultivated, or rather wasted, by groups of Tenants whose relations with each other were an insuperable obstacle to every reform. At the end of the century all this had been reversed. By far the largest part of the country had been or was being enclosed, and improved, or for the first time reclaimed. The farms had been generally let to individual Tenants, free to change and to adapt their management without let or hindrance from slower "neighbours," or from more ignorant or more obstinate partners.

And all this great change—great in itself, but greater still from the opening it gave to a continuity of progress—had been effected without any disturbance, or commotion, or serious discontent. At one time in the wilds of Galloway alone, there is some record of bands of men going about the country pulling down the newly erected dikes, just as in much later times bands of men in the West of England went about breaking the new machines which were another of the instruments of advancing agriculture. But this excitement in Galloway was transitory and local, not unconnected with the Celtic origin of the "Galwegians," who in the days of the early Monarchy were always addressed as a separate people from the Scots. But here, too, as elsewhere, the work of improvement was speedily resumed, and went on with that sure and steady pace, and with that silent and peaceful development, which are the sure indications of healthy organic growth.

And this is exactly what it was, and what the progress of Nations must always be, if it is to be great and lasting. It was not a mere burst of speculation like the South Sea Bubble, or even as the Darien Scheme. It was a general awakening of Mind, directing stronger Muscle, and taking advantage of new and boundless horizons of Opportunity. All ranks and classes—all orders and conditions of men—took part in it. It was a general advance all along the line. The rising industry of the Towns was ready to absorb the overflowing idleness of the country. The rising activity and the increasing knowledge of the agricultural classes were ready to supply all markets as they had never been supplied before, and to feed as they had never been fed before, all who came from Potato patches to enlist in the ranks of industry. Many of those who did so were continually returning to their old homes with sums of money which enabled them to take their place among the new Tenants of single, undivided, and therefore unwasted, Farms. All values were rising, partly from a change in the value of money, but mainly from a rising demand which even an increasing volume of production could not adequately supply. Muscle was among the articles which had a rapidly increasing value, and this was one of the many simultaneous adjustments, due to natural growth, which made all the changes fit into each other, and work with so little friction or disturbance.

Great distress had arisen in the Seventeenth Century from the displacement of the military population out of the Border Counties, after the Union of the Crowns, because at that time the progress of industry had not, either in town or country, reached a point which enabled it to afford employment. But in the Eighteenth Century, after the Union of the Parliaments, the ranks of the Industrial Army were never full. Every recruit was welcome, and every soldier was paid far better than ever he had been paid before, even by the most successful raids for cattle. So early as 1730-35, Captain Burt found that about Inverness every young fellow with any genius for his trade or business, and with any spirit of enterprise,[1] was looking and going for employment to England or to the Low Country. All over the Western Highlands the rising industries of the Clyde were the great centre of attraction. They were like a powerful magnet waved over an area full of particles of iron. Even when smothered in earth and sand, these particles will respond to such attraction,—heaving aside the inert particles around them, and moving like Ants in an Ant-hill, until the whole grainy mass seems alive with creatures. Such was the effect produced, only more slowly and

---

[1] Burt's *Letters*, vol. i. p. 112.

more gradually, by the magnetic attraction of the wages offered in Greenock, Paisley, and Glasgow,—and all over the country in works of Reclamation—to the men who had been gathering in the glens and hills of Dumbarton and Argyll. The Minister of one of these Highland Parishes tersely and graphically describes the condition from which this great opening relieved them, when in his Statistical Report he says, " Idleness was almost the only comfort they enjoyed."[1]

It is a striking illustration, too, of the close inter-communion between all classes in Scotland during this great period of national advance, that when we look into local records we find that Landowners had often much to do with the rise of Towns, whilst there are conspicuous examples of the dwellers in Towns taking the lead in agricultural improvements. Thus, for example, the earliest germ and nucleus of the present Town of Greenock lay in a little Village called Crawfordsdyke, part of the Barony of Crawfordsburn, which belonged to a family of the name of Crawford. Immediately after the Revolution the Proprietor appointed the grandfather of James Watt to be his Baron-bailie—a position at that time of great local influence and importance. In like manner, Greenock itself, then a separate but adjoining village, was on the property of Sir John Shaw, whose heirs and representatives are still in possession of the Estate, and whose interests have ever since been

[1] *Old Statistical Account*, Parish of Lochgoilhead, vol. iii. p. 185.

identified with the rising fortunes of this great Seaport. The quiet bit of sandy shore which is now covered with its Docks and Quays, was then known as "Sir John Shaw's little Bay."[1] The new centres of industry which were then rising in Scotland needed at that time not only the encouragement of such Landowners, but also their influence and protection in their contests with the oppressive monopolies of the older Royal Burghs, such as Dumbarton and Glasgow.

On the other hand, turning from the West to the East of Scotland, it seems to have been a Lord Provost of Edinburgh, who, about 1688, set the first example of the most fundamental of all agricultural improvements, in dividing and enclosing his estate of Prestonfield close to that city.[2] This, however, he did, not in his capacity of Provost dealing with Burghal Property, or "Common Good," but in his capacity of a Private Owner, in the exercise of those full rights which such Ownership always carried and implied. No doubt those lands, almost touching the old walls of Edinburgh, must have been previously grazed by the cows of some definite or indefinite number of persons, each paying some "grass mail" for the poor support in summer of some still poorer cattle. But common use did not constitute common Property. The ignorant usages of an ignorant time were not stereotyped by

---

[1] Smiles's *Lives of Boulton and Watt*, pp. 83-84.

[2] *Old Statistical Account*, Parish of Duddingston, vol. xviii. p. 362. The name of this gentleman seems to have been Sir Magnus Prince.

being converted into legal rights standing in the way of every kind of progress. And yet, in the result, the exercise by the Provost of his rights of private Ownership over these lands, was an immense gain to the citizens of Edinburgh. The meat market and the milk market were at once better supplied. Cows which barely gave two or three pints a day, during a very small portion of the year, were replaced by cows which gave perhaps eight or ten pints a day, and for a much longer period of time. The measure of this public benefit was indicated by the correlative share of it which was secured by the Proprietor. It became gradually known all over Scotland that by virtue of enclosure alone, land near Towns rose in rental by more than a third or $33\frac{1}{2}$ per cent., which meant that the total produce rose on at least a corresponding scale. Land was never so well and so fruitfully "municipalised" as when it was owned as the private property of an intelligent and enterprising Citizen.

On the other hand, the not less important function discharged by individual Ownership in mitigating the hardness, and modifying the rapidity of changes so great, was not less signally illustrated on another Estate contiguous with that of Prestonfield. This was the Estate of Duddingston—embracing the southern slopes of Arthur's Seat, and the hollow which lies between that hill and the heights crowned by the Castle of Craigmillar. The most tragic scenes in the tragic life of Mary Queen of Scots make all that land classic ground in the history of Scotland. It is almost startling to find that for the long period of sixty three years after the enclosure of Prestonfield, the lands of Duddingston, so close to the Scottish Capital, continued to be held by a number of poor Tenants, on the Runrig system, with all the pastures common and unenclosed, and with all the arable land miscropped and exhausted under the same barbarous usages which still linger in the remotest and poorest Parishes of the Hebrides. It was not until 1751 that the Estate was brought under the conditions of agricultural civilisation by the enclosure of the lands, the separation of the farms, the erection of better houses, and the introduction of a better husbandry. All this was done at last under the powers and rights of Ownership by the Abercorn family; and so well and wisely done that the Minister reporting in 1796 could describe the change as not less happy for the Tenants than for the Proprietor and the Country.[1]

We may well wonder, sometimes, at the stupidities of men which so long prevented them from putting the gifts and opportunities of Nature to those methods of use which seem to us now so obvious. But our wonder may well be greater still when we find that new stupidities, in our own day, and after all the enlightenments of experience, are scolding at the knowledge, and at the enterprise, and at the achievements, by which in our fathers' time

[1] *Old Statistical Account*, vol. xviii. pp. 362-4.

the older stupidities were replaced. Among these new stupidities there is none so great as the modern revolt against enclosures. These are equally necessary, and equally the symbol of all improvement, whatever be the purpose to which land may be applied after it has been enclosed. It is equally necessary to enclose land whether it be used as Allotments for the poorer classes, or for Farms of all sizes for men having various amounts of capital, or even whether it is to be kept wild and uncultivated, for the purposes of public recreation. It may have been one of the stupidities of former generations not to foresee the importance which would come to be attached to this last purpose from the enormous growth of Cities. But their growth was so gradual, and the want of open spaces was for generations so little felt, that this particular failure in foresight is not really any great matter of surprise. However this may be, the preservation of certain areas of ground for public Parks near great Towns has now become a most rational and even a most necessary use. It affords, however, no justification for the denunciation of Enclosures which has become loosely popular. This denunciation rests upon nothing but a vague jealousy of all individual appropriation, and against all the improvement which depends upon it. As such it is a sentiment more ignorant and barbarous than any of those that retarded the progress of Agriculture during the stagnant ages. Some of these had, so far as mere sentiment is concerned, a far better justification. The ruinous customs of Runrig, for example, rested originally on a sentiment of justice and of fairness as between the individual shareholders in a Township—a feeling that every one should have his chance and his turn of the best and of the poorer bits of soil. Hence the custom of innumerable sub-divisions, and of the yearly disposal of them by lot. But though the sentiment was good, the ignorance was profound. Men did not then know that the worst land might be made into the best, if it became the interest of any individual to make it so. Nor did they consider that the very best land would become as bad as the very worst by the continued cropping of it by men who had no motive to improve. But none can plead these ignorances now. In our time, therefore, any feeling against Enclosures which are the indispensable foundation of all agricultural improvement, is simply a return to barbarism, far worse than any old failure of our fathers to rise above the knowledge of their times. It is a sentiment in favour of the right of everybody in general to keep the country waste, lest anybody in particular should profit by its reclamation.

In 1756 there was published an elaborate and indeed a sumptuous Work on the Agriculture of England, which in not a few things is even now ahead, if not of the science, yet at least of the practice of our own day.[1] Nowhere is there to

---

[1] *A Complete Body of Husbandry*, by Thomas Hale and others; a fine folio.

be found a more clear and forcible exposition of the place which Enclosure occupies as the one preliminary condition of every possible improvement, both of the land and of the people who live upon it. The authors declare as the result of their own observation and experience that "Whatever pretences may be made of the oppression of the poor by the enclosing of Lands, this is certain, that they nowhere are so happy as where the land in general is under enclosure, and nowhere so miserable, poor, ragged, and idle, as in those places where most of the land lies in common." Again they say, "Upon the edges of all great commons we see a set of miserable cottagers. Hunger is in their faces, and misery upon their backs: they idle away their time in tending their own and other people's cattle, and breed their children to this poor employment."[1]

Most fortunately for Scotland "Commonties," in the full sense of that word, had almost entirely disappeared before the close of the last century. Moors, and "outfield" pastures used as a common grazing by the joint-tenants of one farm—these, indeed, remained in abundance all over the country. In all the backward parts of it they remain still. But these are not Commons or "Commonties," as they were called in Scotland, in the English sense of the word. "Commonties" were areas of land over which an indefinite number of persons had various and indefinite rights of use, founded only on customs of ancient origin. Farm

---

[1] *A Complete Body of Husbandry*, Book III. chap. ii. pp. 100-101.

grazings open to nobody except to the legal Tenants of the farm, and used by them under no other rights than those conveyed to them from the Owner by Lease or otherwise, were indeed, in one sense, "common" grazings. But they were totally different in their nature from Commonties. They could be divided, enclosed, reclaimed, planted, or otherwise dealt with, at the will of the Proprietor whenever an existing Lease expired. And even during an existing Lease they might be similarly dealt with by bargain and agreement between the Owner and the few Tenants who were exclusively concerned. "Commonties," on the other hand, could only be divided and reclaimed by some Judicial process. But the Judicial process provided by the Law of Scotland for dealing with them, was less expensive and troublesome than any which had been provided in England. They never seem to have existed in Scotland to anything like the same extent as in England. The clear and sharp definition of all rights and tenures, which the system of Leases had established with the earliest civilisation of the Kingdom, had tended to keep out confusion. But it is curious and instructive to observe how, in the Border Counties, where centuries of continual war had unsettled everything, and where large areas of land could not be secured for a twelvemonth from devastation, the natural results of promiscuous, hap-hazard, and indefinite usages of Occupation, had precisely the same effects as those so forcibly denounced in England by the universal voice of all impartial observers. In the excellent Report on the County of Dumfries, rendered to the Board of Agriculture in 1794, the strongest language is used in condemnation of the "Commonties" which had existed there, and of the impediments which even the more favourable Law of Scotland had placed in the way of the abolition of them.[1] "Commonage" is declared in that Report by a competent observer "to be so inimical to all improvement of land, and a source of so many moral evils affecting the whole community, that they ought to be abolished everywhere by a general enactment."[2] But this was quite unnecessary, so far as Scotland was concerned. All difficulties and impediments disappeared before the obvious interest of almost all who were locally concerned. Commonties soon completely vanished from the map of Scotland; and nothing remained to be dealt with that even savoured of the same evils, except those ignorant methods of cultivation in Runrig which were pursued by the Tenants of Township Farms.

It is well to remember, however, that, even in this very mitigated form, the principle and the practice of stifling individual interests, and personal aptitudes, in their application to the most important of all industries, was specially dangerous in Scotland because of the great amount of intelligence and of enterprise which were needed to reclaim her rough and encumbered soil. It is impossible to read the account, given in the Report

[1] *Reports*, vol. ii., Co. Dumfries, p. 55. [2] *Ibid.* p. 56.

of 1794 on the County of Aberdeen, of the tremendous effect produced by a few "ill years" or bad seasons at the close of the previous century, without seeing that not over the Highlands alone, but over a very large proportion of the whole of Scotland, Famine had been always standing at the door. Very widely indeed that gaunt Figure not only stood at the door, but entered within the House. It was said of the "ill years" referred to, that, in addition to all those who were only kept from starvation by collections at the churches, there were more than 200,000 people who were wandering mendicants begging from door to door.[1] This represents a terrible percentage of the then population of Scotland. The County of Aberdeen was depopulated. The land was waste; and not until after the new burst of Industry had begun, and an appeal was made to individual skill, enterprise, and capital, in the holding of undivided farms, was the country redeemed from its desolation.

Neither was it enough that the Tenants should all be men with single holdings, and freed from the common interest of ignorant partners in the perpetuation of senseless usages. This was not enough, unless the new Tenants were fitted to take advantage of their new position, by having themselves risen above the old level. Accordingly, nothing is more striking in the accounts we have of the condition of the country before the Union, than the testimony they bear to the failure

[1] *Northern Rural Life*, p. 46.

which followed the letting of land to men who had neither knowledge nor capital. Many Proprietors after the Famine had no opportunity of exercising any effective power of selection, because there was no competition. They were glad to let their land to any applicants who could take it, even in the smallest portions, and with the poorest qualifications. They were tempted to break down their farms into minute holdings at from £2 to £5 Rent. The Occupants made a little money by knitting stockings. They could eat potatoes. But they were ignorant of agriculture. The result was that, in 1794, wherever these small holdings prevailed, the condition of the Occupiers was described as having become gradually reduced to "the degraded state they held at present."[1] Next followed the great scarcity of 1740, and again the repetition of famine in 1782, which affected with special severity the County of Aberdeen.[2] But by this time the new knowledge had begun, and the general rise of Industry had been well established. As usual under such conditions, both Migration and Emigration followed, and a race of new Tenants, with the requisite skill and capital,—selected by the Owners—holding undivided Farms,—and encouraged by adequate Covenants, joined the broad and rapid stream of national advance.

[1] *Reports*, vol. i., Aberdeenshire, p. 51.   [2] *Ibid.* pp. 57-8.

CHAPTER IV.

THE FRUITS OF MIND.

It was not in Agriculture alone that the great principle of giving free scope to individual Mind, and to individual Capital, which is its fruit, became the prime agent in the advancing prosperity of Scotland. It was equally conspicuous and equally powerful in the opening of her Trade and Commerce. In a former chapter[1] I have referred to the engrossing Monopolies which had been given by early Charters to the old Royal Burghs of the country. Those who have been accustomed to think of Fiscal Protection as specially associated with the interest of Landowners, have little idea how universally this system originated with the only popular Bodies which existed in the Military Ages, or of the extravagant lengths to which commercial exclusiveness was carried on their behalf. For centuries, and by repeated Statutes, the whole Trade and Commerce of Scotland were placed in the hands of a few Communities of ancient date, to the absolute exclusion not only of the whole agricultural classes, but to the exclusion also of all other Towns and Villages which had arisen from time to time in situations favourable for some particular kind of

[1] Chapter ii. p. 86-88.

industry. The "liberties" granted to the old Communities were Monopolies in the only correct sense of that word—the sense, namely, in which it means the absolute prohibition of all selling and buying by all persons who do not belong to the privileged Community, so that even their own money and their own goods are made useless for purposes of exchange except through the narrow circle of the Monopolists.[1] Not a single quarter of corn,—not a single beast of any kind,—not a single cask of wine,—not a single fleece of wool, nor hide of cattle, could be lawfully imported, or even bought and sold, except through the hands of the privileged Freemen of the Royal Burghs. Within the Burghs themselves the Magistrates assumed and exercised the right of regulating and fixing the prices of all kinds of goods, and especially of bread and provisions generally. This was done in the assumed interest of the Community.

Nothing is more remarkable in the History of Scotland than the manner in which this wide, deeply rooted, and oppressive system was gradually invaded and destroyed by the natural action of individual interests, without any previous change of abstract opinion against the general policy on which the system had been ignorantly founded. So late as the reign of Charles I. in 1633, a fresh Act was passed renewing, reviving, and enforcing the older Statutes, and whatever had become more or less obsolete in these Communal Mono-

---

[1] It is a vulgar error to apply this word to the possession of articles which are limited in quantity. If all who have such articles are free to sell them, and all are equally free to buy them, then the possession is not a monopoly.

polies over the whole Trade and Commerce of the Nation.[1] This was too much. There was an immediate and strong reaction from the growing energies of individual enterprise and industry. The first great breach which was effected in the system, came through the undermining action of the new Towns and Villages which had no old Charters, and were not included within the charmed circle of the Royal Burghs. The inhabitants of these places could not practically be prevented from buying and selling such articles as they were able to make, or—if they were near the sea—to import. Then came the supporting action of the Landowners on whose Estates these new Towns were rising. They had risen and were growing under the powers and rights of Leasing, of Feuing, and of Heritable Jurisdiction, which these Landowners held by Charters erecting their Estates into Baronies of Regality, or into simple Baronies with powers only a little less extensive. Hence these new Towns and Communities were called Burghs of Barony and of Regality. For several centuries there had been more or less of a perpetual struggle on the part of the Royal Burghs to enforce their monopoly, and to crush the newer Towns as nests of Smugglers. On the other hand the great Landowners who held Baronies and Regalities, were naturally interested in the prosperity of the new Towns which were rising under them, and thus became insensibly, but very practically, interested in the extension of individual

---

[1] *Act. Parl. Scot.*, vol. v. p. 48 (1633), c. 24.

liberty, and consequently in the freedom of Trade. Accordingly when legal questions arose, and the Royal Burghs prosecuted other Towns for violation of their monopolies, the Landowners sometimes appeared in support of the defence.

The Act of 1633 was too violent to be borne. At last, in 1671, a case arose which brought matters to a head. Falkirk was a Burgh of Regality built on the Estate of the Earl of Callendar. But it was within the area of Monopoly claimed by the Royal Burgh of Stirling. It was prosecuted for allowing its inhabitants, who were " unfreemen," to engage in trade. The case attracted great attention. The Barons of Regality took up arms in a body in favour of a wider liberty. The Duke of Lauderdale himself, who was interested in the rising Town of Musselburgh, was induced to come to Edinburgh to watch the case as it was argued before the Court of Session. It soon appeared that the questions raised touched the whole policy of the Kingdom, and could only be settled by the Legislature itself. A suggestion to this effect by Sir George Mackenzie was taken up by the Lords of Parliament, whose duty it was to prepare Bills; and the result was the Act of 1672,[1] which effected a temporary compromise between the interests of individual freedom and the old Monopolies in the hands of a few popular Bodies. Parliament declared that the Act of 1633 had extended those monopolies to a degree

[1] Act. Parl. Scot., vol. viii. p. 63 (1672), c. 5.

"highly prejudicial to the common interest and good of the Kingdom." Nevertheless, the monopoly of the Royal Burghs was for the future kept up as regarded both the export and import of many articles of foreign produce, except in so far as private persons of all ranks might import them for their own domestic use alone. On the other hand, the export and sale of all agricultural produce and all native commodities was made free to all the subjects of the Realm. The new Towns, the Burghs of Regality and of Barony, were made free to trade in all manufactures of their own, to export all home produce, and to import many articles required for "tillage or building;" whilst the retail trade of Markets was made absolutely free.

This was a tremendous breach in the exclusive privileges of the old Burghal Communities, and it was the opening of a very wide door for the free action of all individual interests. Accordingly, against the ever widening consequences of this Act the Royal Burghs, which alone were represented in Parliament, carried on an unceasing struggle and protest, loudly calling for its repeal. They did succeed in getting some new Acts passed after the Revolution, fencing and guarding, by new provisions and penalties, the exclusive rights which still remained to them as regards the imports of foreign produce; and at a later date their interest in Parliament, backed by the influence of traditional feelings and opinions which were not yet theoretically abandoned, were sufficiently strong to secure a Clause in the Treaty of Union with England, providing for the security and continuance of their privileges as they then stood. But too much freedom had now been granted to keep out the continued and unceasing pressure of individual Mind. The Courts of Law in all doubtful cases ruled in favour of freedom in the true sense of that word, the sense, namely, of individual liberty. The natural right of every man to exercise his own faculties in the free disposal of his own means and property, became too wide an instinct to be compatible with even a faint survival of the Communist Monopolies. Yet it may well be regarded with surprise, that, so far as the Statute-Book was concerned, they survived down to our own day. It was not until 1846 that an Act was passed formally abolishing them, and this was passed as the result of an inquiry by Royal Commission, which reported that practically they were already dead.

Every step in the long process of self-education through which the Nation passed in this question of Trade Monopolies, is full of historical and of political interest. There are two documents which throw especial light upon that process, which are separate from each other in date by no more than 35 years. The first belongs to the time of the Commonwealth—the second belongs to the time of William III. The Protector, as is well known, contemplated and for a time effected, a complete Union between England and Scotland, both being under one Government, and represented in one United

Parliament. It is to the credit of the Royal Burghs of Scotland that a majority of them seem to have voted for Cromwell's policy, which included as one of its main advantages, complete freedom of commercial intercourse between all citizens of the Commonwealth. Struck by the poverty of Scotland and the heavy deficit on its revenue below the cost of its administration, he sent down an experienced Commissioner [1] to inquire into the subject, and especially into the condition of the Royal Burghs. His Report, rendered in 1656, gives an authentic and a very striking account of the almost abject poverty of the country, and of the miserable narrowness of its Commerce. He saw at once that much of this scantiness of Trade was directly connected with the backwardness of Agriculture, and the consequent want of any products to exchange. This condition of Agriculture again he ascribed to the ignorance, poverty, and slothfulness of the people. With a curious insight and perspicacity, he pitched on the most striking symbol of all the waste he saw, and pointed to a "lazy vagrancy of attending and following their herds up and down in their pasturage." [2] There was consequently no trade from the inland parts. There never had been much; but what remained was limited to the seaside, and was confined to a few Ports on the East coast, and in or near the Estuary of the Clyde. Glasgow

[1] A Mr. Tucker from the Office of Excise in London.
[2] *Miscellany of Scottish Burgh Records Society*, 1881: Tucker's Report, p. 16.

had then only twelve vessels, the biggest of which were 150 tons burden, and most of which were mere boats. They traded to Ireland with small coals in open boats of from four to twenty tons, taking back meal, oats, butter, with barrel staves and hoops. There was a limited trade with France and Norway—coals, plaiding, salt herring, and salmon being the chief articles, for which they got some condiments and prunes. Dundee had suffered severely from the Wars. Her trade had declined, but "though not glorious, yet was not contemptible." She had ten vessels in all, the biggest 120 tons. Ayr was in a sad condition, from the silting up of her river and harbour. "The place was growing every day worse and worse."[1] Newark (now Port-Glasgow) had "some four or five houses besides the Laird's house of the place." Greenock was just such another, only a little larger —the people all fishermen and sailors trading to Ireland and the Isles in open boats; yet in spite of all this leanness in the land, Cromwell's agent had the perception to see, and did not omit to mention the "Mercantile genius" of the people.

Such was the description of a stranger, coming from a wealthier country in 1656. But thirty-five years later we have the description of the Royal Burghs of Scotland given by themselves. They had spent many of the intervening years in vain endeavours to enforce their monopoly against all

[1] *Miscellany of Scottish Burgh Records Society*, 1881: Tucker's Report, p. 28.

their countrymen, and in alternate contests and negotiations with the Landowners who were encouraging the new, unprivileged, individual Traders who were rising everywhere. The Restoration of the Monarchy had brought with it the immediate abandonment and revocation of all Cromwell's policy, including Free Trade with England. This great outlet was lost to Scotland—to all her Towns whether " free " or " unfree." All the more was personal energy and character required for success in the narrowed and restricted paths of industry. The old Royal Burghs did not advance. At last, in 1691, they appointed a Committee to inquire and report on the condition, revenues, resources, and difficulties of every one. A tabulated series of questions were addressed to each. The result was a series of Reports of the highest interest in History and in Politics. One broad result stares us in the face—that almost everywhere the privileged and monopolist Burghs were stagnant or declining, whilst the new Towns which had no privileges, and were even heavily handicapped in the race by having to fight against Communal Monopolies, were as universally prosperous, and were rising every year in wealth and in importance. Mind, set upon its mettle, was everywhere triumphing over routine and usage :—Mind, in the selection of new sites—Mind, in the advantage taken of special opportunities—Mind, in seeing new openings—and everywhere, Mind freed from the stupid levelling of arbitrary Guilds.

Nothing can be more striking than the evidence to this effect. One of the questions asked of all the old Royal Burghs concerned the number and condition of the New Towns of Barony and Regality which existed within the area of their Monopoly. The list given is a list of many of the most important Towns now existing in Scotland. The Royal Burgh of Renfrew enumerates no less than nine new Burghs of Barony and Regality within "their precincts," even the smallest of which had "a much more considerable trade" than themselves. Among these nine we find Paisley, Port-Glasgow, Greenock, and Gourock. The rising trade of all these places was, if possible, to be suppressed, and the Royal Burghs universally refer to it as "highly prejudicial" to their own interests and industry. Even Glasgow was at that time declining—with nearly five hundred houses "waste," whilst those still inhabited had fallen nearly one-third in the rents they fetched. The best houses in Glasgow were at that time worth no more than £8, 6s. a year in Sterling money. Glasgow bitterly complained of the same neighbouring Towns, and of some others, which so vexed the soul of Renfrew. In particular, the little village which was growing up on the shores of "Sir John Shaw's little Bay," Greenock, was described as having "a very great trade both foreign and inland, particularly prejudicial to the trade of Glasgow."[1]

[1] *Miscellany of Scottish Burgh Records;* State of Burghs, etc., p. 72.

And yet in the midst of these stupidities we have a few evidences that even the Communal Mind was opening to the lessons of experience. In a few cases men began to see that the action of the human Will is subject to certain natural laws, and that when enactments run counter to these, or do not take due note of them, such enactments, however virtuous in motive, are purely mischievous. Thus in 1688, the Convention of Royal Burghs had awakened to the fact that the Sumptuary Laws had been "very prejudicial" to them.[1] It was turning out that what were called the luxuries of the rich were inseparable from the comforts and necessities of the poor. Costly things were only costly because they were much desired, and because much was consequently given to those who could find, produce, or make them. And a great part of this cost went of necessity to the Muscular Labour, which was the contribution of the poor. Again, the Royal Burghs were beginning to find out that even within their own "precincts," individual enterprise was breaking through the incubus of their communal restrictions. Individual citizens and Burgesses, seeing the success of their neighbours in the "unfree" Towns, were entering into partnership with them in various enterprises and speculations. It is worth while to listen for a moment to the words in which this conduct of men in the free disposal of their own faculties, and of their own property, was denounced by that spirit of tyranny which is never

[1] *Miscellany of Scottish Burgh Records :* Preface, p. 32.

more oppressive than when it is wielded in the supposed interest of a local popular majority. "The Convention being resolved no longer to suffer the privileges of Royal Burghs to be abused and encroached upon by their own Burgesses, who, by joining stocks with unfreemen, inhabitants in the Burghs of Regality and Barony, and other unfree places, both in point of trade and shipping, whereby those unfreemen receive all imaginable encouragement from freemen in Royal Burghs to trade, and that the said freemen do voluntarily and with their own hands destroy the privileges of the Royal Burghs —therefore"[1] the Convention denounced new pains and penalties against all such persons—as disloyal to the Community to which they belonged.

Here was an aperture in the armour of Burghal monopolies which the irrepressible energies of individual interests were quite sure to widen. Partnerships could be easily concealed, and the only result of enforcing inquisition into the use to which men might put their own money, would have been, and doubtless was, that the most enterprising Minds would seek refuge in the new Towns. With them, therefore, the contest was hopeless, and it soon ceased altogether. But for many years after this date, and even after the Union, the exclusiveness of the Guilds in the supposed interest of the Skilled Labour, and of the Retail Trade of the old Burghs, continued unabated. It was

[1] *Miscellany of Scottish Burgh Records:* Preface, p. 40.

reserved for this system as it prevailed in Glasgow, to afford the most signal illustration of its antagonism to the laws of Nature. The site of Glasgow had been chosen without any view to industry even of the earliest and rudest kind. It had not clustered under a Rock Fortress, like Stirling or Dumbarton. It had not arisen beside a natural harbour, like Dundee or Aberdeen. It had not grown up out of a fishing-village, like Greenock or Rothesay. Its nucleus was not even a feudal Castle. Its position had been determined by the Cathedral of St. Mungo, and was originally a mere hamlet of "the Bishop's men" living under the protection of a great Archiepiscopal See. It was not among the number of the most Ancient Royal Burghs of the Kingdom. In the Fifteenth Century its importance was increased by being made the seat of a new University. But this was done through the same influence and agency of the Church to which the Town owed its own foundation. Glasgow was itself, therefore, nothing more than one of the Burghs of Barony on a Church Estate. Two of the Old Royal Burghs, Rutherglen and Dumbarton, long domineered over it, as now Glasgow tried to domineer over Greenock and Paisley. It is true that it stood near the river Clyde, towards which its houses gradually straggled. But the Clyde at that point was distant from the sea, its course was very shallow, and it was being perpetually silted up with shifting sandbanks. This was one of the causes of its decay in Cromwell's time.

Only through the new openings which came with the Union did it begin to revive again. But, as a Seaport, it never could have reached its present position without the operation of the Steam Dredge, through which ships of the heaviest burden have long been able to ascend the river, and to lie beside its quays. During the last forty-six years very nearly forty millions of tons of material have been removed from the bed of the Clyde by the Steam Dredge— a mass which would form a conical mountain 513 feet high, with a circumference at the base of one mile and a half.[1] Yet it is a memorable fact that when the future Inventor of the new Steam Engine, without which dredging on this gigantic scale would have been impossible, came to reside and to open a shop in Glasgow, he was persecuted as an interloper and a poacher on the domain of the Guild of Hammermen. James Watt was then probably known there as an ingenious Mechanic, but he must have also been known as the grandson of one of the earliest Bailies of the "unfree" Town of Greenock, that most presumptuous union of the villages of the Crawfords and the Shaws. The Hammermen declared that from the competition of such an "unfree man," the whole Community would "suffer skaith." A man on whom Nature had bestowed, in richer measure than it had ever been bestowed before, the very individual and the very special gift of mechanical genius, and whose discoveries were des-

[1] I give these astonishing facts on the authority of Mr. James Deas, C.E., kindly communicated to me through Dr. Marwick, Town Clerk of Glasgow.

tined to raise Glasgow to be one of the greatest Cities of the world, was actually driven from her Burghal "precincts." Fortunately the University had precincts of its own which were outside the "liberties" of the Guilds. Within that sanctum this patient and laborious Mind wrought out the great problem on which its heart, as well as its intellect, was set. It thought and pondered, and weighed and measured, and tried and tried again, until at last the moment of Inspiration came, and one of the most tremendous agencies in the material world became tractable as a little child. It was tamed, yoked, and bound to every variety of human service —an immense contribution indeed, not only to the Common Good of Glasgow, but to the Common Good of all Mankind.

The same natural play of instinct and of motive which had led the Landowners with such immense success to foster individual liberty and enterprise, in the hands of their own Villagers and Feuars, now led them also to rely more and more on the same great principle as equally applicable to their agricultural Tenants. For this purpose the first step to be taken was that, wherever possible, on the expiry of old Leases, their farms should be re-let to individual Tenants. Such Tenants became at once freed from the trammels of Communal Usage, and could move out of the ruts in which the wheels of progress were jammed up to the very axletrees. They could —but were they sure to do so? Here again there was an education of experience—analogous to that which only very slowly and very gradually educated the Towns in the lessons of the new Industrial Age. It soon turned out that neither the mere circumstance of undivided holdings, nor the additional circumstance of very long Leases, were enough of themselves to secure an improving Agriculture. The reason is obvious. If the sources of all Wealth are Mind, Materials, and Opportunity, it is clearly not enough to have only one, or only two of these sources opened. Materials are useless, and so is Opportunity, and so are both together, if the appropriate qualities of Mind to make use of them are wanting. Significant indications are given in the Reports so often referred to, of the steps of experience through which the Owners of land were taught how best to secure the improvement of the soil. Thus in the Lennox, the perpetual tenure of Feu for a fixed annual payment, had been given over various areas of agricultural land to men who thereby became small Owners, and had all the inducements to improvement which Ownership is reputed to give. But neither the accumulations due to Mind in the past, nor those aspirations of Mind which regard the future, were present to take due advantage of the Material and of the Opportunity. These Feuars belonged originally to the old unimproving class. They had no conception of educating their children for any other employment than that on which they and their fathers had maintained existence. Consequently they went on sub-dividing their lands among a progeny as ignorant and unimproving as themselves. "They thought it a disgrace that their children should be anything but Lairds."[1] This sub-division went on increasing until the little possessions had become so small, in 1794, that some of the Owners could not afford to keep a horse. Then we have the usual sickening detail of constant over-cropping, of "nothing being laid out on improvements, and of the land being scourged to the last extremity." The whole produce could hardly support the families that depended upon it, even with the addition of what was procured by the unremitting labour of the wife and children in spinning and a little weaving.[2] This is an exact description of the results of a similar condition of things now common among the Peasant Proprietors of parts of France, as described by such eye-witnesses as Mr. Hamerton, Lady Verney, and many others.

The lesson against feuing agricultural land was hardly needed. Land feued is land sold. Feuing is merely one form of total alienation. A "Superior" parts with all the powers and rights of Ownership, except that of receiving a Rent charge. The Feuar becomes the Proprietor. On the other hand, the evidence furnished by the Report of 1794 on Dumbartonshire, is in favour of what are now called Allotments—that is to say, small areas of land let to Labourers and Tradesmen who were intelligent. These were reported to be by no means ill cultivated or unimproved.[3] On the contrary,

---

[1] *Agriculture of Dumbartonshire*: Reports, vol. ii. p. 14.
[2] *Ibid.*
[3] *Ibid.* p. 15.

they were reported to be as far advanced as any part of the County—at a time too, when the Common Good of the Burgh was lying comparatively waste. On such Allotments the full benefit of individual interest was at work, coupled often with knowledge above the average of that possessed by the old class of Tenants. Feus are an excellent tenure for purposes of Building, and Scotchmen generally will not build on any tenure less secure and permanent. But there is no reason which should induce a Proprietor to give off agricultural land on this tenure. If he wishes to sell, it is best to sell out and out. But the example of those old feus to small Owners in Dumbartonshire is an excellent illustration of the general principle on which all improvements depend.

There was, however, another case in which the teachings of experience were more practically important. Leases of great length are another panacea amongst those who have had no experience, which is often recommended with much confidence. But this also was tried, and with the same result, depending exactly on the same principles. It appears from Professor Walker's Work, published in 1808,[1] that Archibald, third Duke of Argyll, the friend of Culloden, had been induced to give some very long Leases of large farms in Mull—Leases for "three nineteens," or a period of fifty-seven years. He expected the Tenants "to set a pattern of industry and improvement" on such length and

[1] *Economic History of the Hebrides*, vol. I. p. 68.

security of tenure. But the expectation was not fulfilled. When the Leases were half expired the farms were found to be as little improved as any on the Island. The same experiment had been tried in the Island of Islay by Mr. Campbell of Shawfield, who, in 1720, let all his Estate on Leases of the same long duration, with the result that in 1764 that Island had undergone no improvement—with one solitary exception. Flax had been introduced, and became a source of industry and advantage to the Island. But this one exception was the result, not of the long Leases, but of the only compulsory clause which had been inserted in them by the Proprietor, which was a clause binding the Tenants to cultivate flax.[1] It thus appeared that the only one item of improvement which had been effected during more than half a century was due, not to the Mind of the Tenant, but to the Mind of the Proprietor— to his forethought, and to his knowledge—in binding men who were comparatively ignorant, to begin a new industry, which of themselves they never would have thought of.

In this one exception to the general result we see the whole secret and the whole philosophy of the only method by which it was then possible to improve the agriculture of Scotland—to arrest the increasing impoverishment of her soil, and to lift her rural population out of the poverty and sloth in which they lived. It was the exercise, in a new direction, of the same Power to which the Parlia-

---

[1] *Economic History of the Hebrides*, vol. i. p. 68.

ment of Scotland had often appealed before, not only to secure a Tenantry loyal to the Government, but also to secure such rural improvements as were then known. Educated men were to direct the energies of men less instructed. Mind was to keep its power over Muscle. Very long terms of Lease, during which this power was to be suspended, could not but be mischievous. Most fortunately for the country, few Proprietors had been induced to try an experiment which could not be stopped during the long period of nearly sixty years—although it might be quite evident before one-half that time had expired, that it must end in total failure. In the great majority of cases they had granted no other Leases than those of the ordinary duration of "one nineteen," and at the end of every Lease they inserted stipulations in the new Tacks binding the Tenants to execute certain specified improvements. These, of course, expanded with the expanding knowledge of the day. Proprietors were themselves only in course of being educated; and some were before others in appreciating and accepting the advancing knowledge of a new science. In some points they were almost as slow to break with ancient Usages, and to perceive the mischief of them, as the most ignorant of their Tenants. The heavy dues exacted for "Thirlage," or the maintenance of Mills, were a great evil, and they were not wholly abolished till recent years. But the stipulations in Leases became more and more enlightened and important in their effects. They began generally with stipulations for the making of enclosures, and for the building of better Houses than the old hovels, which were as universal in the Lowlands as in the Highlands. But this rudimentary step of providing for enclosures speedily involved corresponding stipulations for the uses to which enclosed land was to be applied. There were clauses to forbid old habits which were ruinous. There were clauses prescribing new methods which were fruitful—clauses forbidding continuous cropping with Cereals—clauses enjoining an alternation with the new Green Crops—clauses insisting on the use of Sown Grasses—and on the application of due quantities of manure. With the growing knowledge of the cultivating class, and the yearly proofs experienced of increasing produce and of rising values, the necessity for such detailed stipulations gradually abated. The "rules of good husbandry" became a legal phrase, having a definite meaning, and susceptible of judicial interpretation. A class of Tenant farmers arose having themselves ample knowledge, sufficient capital, and technical skill. In proportion as the permanent accommodation and apparatus required for scientific agriculture became more costly, it became more and more the universal habit in Scotland that the Owner should supply that accommodation and apparatus along with the land itself. In some cases part of this work was done by the Tenant on stipulated conditions—he making his own calculations for repayment, either by comparative lowness of rent, or by comparative length of Lease—or by both combined.

It is not often that we can enjoy in human affairs the sharp and clear processes of demonstration which are the glorious reward of Physical Research. Yet such—and not less certain—are the proofs now afforded by the history of Scotland in favour of the Powers and Agencies through which her Agriculture was reformed during the latter half of the Eighteenth Century. By all that had happened before the change—by all that ceased to happen wherever it was effected—by all that continued to happen wherever it was hampered or delayed,—it is proved to demonstration that terrible evils and dangers were inseparably bound up with the older system, and with the ignorant habits in which the whole of it consisted. This is one kind of proof. But there is another kind. By all the benefits which the change immediately conferred—by all the increase in these benefits which arose in proportion as it became developed—by all the sacrifice of them wherever it was still delayed,—we can see without the shadow of a doubt, that the new system was founded on Natural Laws, on the recognition which they demand, and on the obedience which they reward. Nature takes no cognisance of stupidity in the sense of allowance or of remission. She does take cognisance of it in the way of punishment. Chronic poverty and frequent famines had been, as we have seen, the punishment in Scotland of the ignorant wastefulness of its traditionary agricultural customs. So now when Mind had been awakened, and when its energies, wielded by individual men, had been turned with better knowledge to the improvement of the soil, Nature took notice of it by a lavish increase of her fruits. It is a striking fact that the "ill years"—the bad seasons—of 1781-2 were the last which afflicted any large part of Scotland with severe distress and the danger of famine. In those years the new knowledge, and the new class of Tenants who were able to make any use of it, were as yet established only in some parts of the country. Everywhere else the old usages were still supreme—the Runrig cultivation—the promiscuous grazing—the wretched Cattle—the not less wretched Oats and Bear. The consequence was that over no less than fifteen of the Counties of Scotland, a population of not less than 111,521 souls were only rescued from starvation by charitable collections.[1] After this date down to our own times there have been bad seasons again and again recurring at about the usual intervals—but never have they had the same effect—except in the few remaining fastnesses of the ancient ignorance. These fastnesses have chiefly been in the Hebrides, and in a few Districts of the Northern Highlands —always where, only where, and in proportion as, the old stupidities have resisted and survived.

But the story of this resistance is so curious and so instructive that it must be shortly told.

We have seen how in 1739, under the advice of Culloden, the first great step had been taken on the Hebridean Estates of the Argyll family—that of

[1] *Memoirs of Sir John Sinclair, Bart.*, vol. i. p. 90.

redeeming the class of Sub-Tenants from their servitudes to the Tacksmen under whom they universally held at Will. In some cases they were themselves raised to the position of Tacksmen—in all cases they were freed from indefinite exactions. We have seen, too, how shocked Culloden had been by the wasteful and barbarous husbandry he witnessed in Tyree. But on the other hand he did not see his way to any immediate or compulsory change in these methods of cultivation. He probably thought that self-interest, now called into play under new conditions of security, would be enough to bring about reform. Wielding the powers of Ownership, he had abolished one deeply-rooted and most ancient custom—the custom of indefinite Servitudes. He did not know, or perfectly understand, that nothing but the same powers, wielded with like determination and like intelligence, could uproot those other Servitudes—as old and as destructive—under which the people were chained and bound amongst each other in a perfect tangle of obstructive usages.

Culloden and all that generation passed away, with his two friends, Duke John and Duke Archibald (Lord Islay). The struggle was unceasing to get the people to amend their culture. Then came the Potato—then the Kelp. Subsistence became comparatively easy, and was sometimes abundant. But all this came to a people unprepared by previous habits, or by any new aspirations, to profit by it. Nothing was saved or stored. They lived, and ate, and multiplied. From the date of my Grandfather's succession in 1770, he issued ceaseless instructions for the improvement of the people. He insisted in his Leases on enclosures, to save the arable lands from constant invasion by whole herds of useless horses and lean cattle. He insisted on better Houses. He tried his best to prevent the systematic waste of Barley by illicit distillation. He tried to establish Fisheries. He tried to stop the destructive habit of breaking up pasture on Sands which were liable to be blown. When Kelp became an important resource he left so large a part of it to the workers that they held their land practically for nothing, because the whole rent, and often much more, came out of Kelp. His rent from 13,000 acres of land did not amount to more than the saleable value of the Barley crop alone. All other produce,—potatoes, lint, sheep, milk, butter and cheese, poultry, eggs, etc., were not counted at all as contributing to rent, because the Proprietor said "he wished the Tenants to live plentifully and happily." It was all in vain—as regards any permanent improvement. Plenty is a relative term. Produce which was plenteous for a population of 1676 persons in 1769, would not be plenteous to a population which had risen to 2776 in 1802. In that year the condition of the Island alarmed his agent, Mr. Maxwell of Aros, an excellent and able man who was maternal grandfather of the late Dr. Norman Macleod. His Report is a repetition of the worst accounts to the Board of Agriculture in 1794.

Subdivision had reduced the holdings to starvation point. The Cows did not produce calves above once in two or three years. Troops of Horses, used only for dragging seaweed at one time of the year, preyed all the rest of the year on the exhausted pastures. Hosts of Cottars living only on the wages of Kelp-burning oppressed the unfortunate Tenants. The quality of the Barley was deteriorating rapidly. Ignorance of all husbandry, and stubborn attachment to the old customs, offered "arduous obstacles to the improvement of the Island." The additional One Thousand people who had grown up in recent years could not be supported. My Grandfather had begun to entertain the proposal to help them to the Colonies. But in 1803 there arose, as we have seen, that panic against Emigration described before. The old Duke seems to have deeply shared in it. His soldierly spirit was stirred, too, in favour of the men who had enlisted in the Fencible Regiments which were about to be disbanded at the Peace. He determined to try a new plan. He resolved to break down and cut up several of the larger Farms falling out of Lease, and to settle as many of the people as he could on smaller but separate Holdings of a size calculated to support a Family with ease. But one essential part of this scheme was enclosure —individual possession— the abolition of promiscuous waste in the form of Runrig. He employed a professional Surveyor to lay out the new "Crofts," which were to be capable of supporting not less than 16 Cows.

This most benevolent scheme was met by the most obstinate resistance on the part of the people. Rather than give up the wasteful habits of Runrig, they declared they would rather go to join the emigration which Lord Selkirk was then leading to North America. The Duke's agent at the time was a Highlander himself, intimate with the condition and habits of the people. Yet he writes almost in despair with their infatuated blindness to their own obvious interests, and to the value of the reforms which had by that time become accepted by every educated man. He suggested to the Duke a postponement of the plan. Yet time was needed to make even a beginning, and the powers of Ownership were once more asserted to insist on the abolition of a system so destructive and so dangerous. By firmness, and by assistance given in fencing, the division and individuality of the arable lands was at last effected. The grazings only continued to be used in common, but even on these the amount of stock was carefully fixed and apportioned to each man.

Now followed a most remarkable series of facts. The old Field-Marshal died in 1806. In one respect his policy was entirely successful. The separation of holdings—the individualisation of the arable areas—resulted, almost automatically, in a great increase of produce. But it had another result which was not foreseen. It facilitated and gave a new impulse to further subdivision. Under the Runrig system the introduction of an additional shareholder required assent. In settling this there were at least some difficulties to be overcome in the way of subdivision. Under separate holdings of the arable area these difficulties were much diminished. Increasing produce and a greater freedom in subdividing, were at once taken advantage of by a people whose intelligence was not developed in proportion to its opportunities. Nothing but the continued exercise of the powers of Ownership in fighting a watchful and uphill battle against inveterate habits, could have been successful. Instead of this there was an almost complete abandonment of all control. There came a Reign— not of Law, or of Mind—but of what in medical language is called "Amentia." My Grandfather's Successor[1] lived for thirty-three years—during the whole of which time the powers of Ownership may be said to have been suspended. He was a perfect type of the kind of Landowner who was adored in Ireland—one who never meddled or interfered with the stupidities of Custom. Celtic usages were allowed their course. Subdivision went on at a redoubled rate, and population kept up even more than pace. In 1822 the Farms which had been held by small Tenants ever since Culloden's time were crowded with a population of 2869 souls; whilst the newly divided farms, five in number, held no less than 1080 more. There had been a bad season in 1821. The Cattle were almost starved, and there were many cases of great misery among the people.

[1] George, Sixth Duke of Argyll, succeeded 1806, died 1839.

Once more, Kelp came to the rescue. There was an extraordinary supply of it, and this, with wholesale insolvency admitted and allowed, tided over the crisis for a time. Next came another tremendous blow. The whole Kelp Trade rested on Fiscal Protection, and on two special taxes alone. One was upon Spanish Barilla—a Plant growing not in the sea, but on the land, and rich in the Alkalis which seaweed afforded. The other impost was the tax on Salt—a tax most oppressive to numberless industries, and specially injurious to the Highlands, through the impediments thrown in the way of the trade in fish. From common salt, which is a salt of Soda, the same important Alkali could be made into other combinations. Both these taxes were repealed—one in 1823, the other in 1826. The trade of the Kingdom as a whole was immensely benefited. But the special, and the only manufacture of the Hebrides, and of the adjacent coasts, was destroyed.

In all other countries when Mines are exhausted, or when Mills are closed, or when any other local industry is extinguished, the people who had been so employed invariably move off to other fields where their labour can be made remunerative to themselves, and useful to the world. But the Hebrideans never thought of this. There is, nevertheless, no suspension of the laws of Nature for the special and exclusive protection of any particular set of men, merely because they belong to a particular race, or because they live in an Island, or because they speak a particular language. Failing the Kelp trade, they still held on by the Potato. The consequence was that the "ill years," which must every now and then recur, always smote them with the misery and famine which had in former generations smitten the rest of Scotland. In 1836-7 there was terrible misery all over the Highlands wherever the old system still survived, and especially in Skye. We have an account of it, and of the causes which produced it, from an educated Highlander,[1] who writes with that high intelligence of his race which never fails to be conspicuous wherever Highlanders are lifted above the level of the old Paternal Customs. I need not repeat his story. It is a mere duplicate of the course of events which we have followed in Tyree. Everything that had been done in the panic of 1803 against emigration, had simply ended in aggravating the evil. Even the making of the Caledonian Canal, begun in the same year, from which much was hoped, had done no permanent good. The Skye men had indeed worked at it. Whilst the construction of it had lasted, between 300 and 400 of them had earned from £3500 to £4000 in the half year. But there was no change of habits—no elevation in the standard of living. On the contrary, it was becoming lower and lower from the wretched husbandry, and from the stimulated growth of population. The one Parish of Kilmuir had in 1736

[1] Mr. Alexander Macgregor, Licentiate of the Church of Scotland. *Quarterly Journal of Agriculture*, No. XLII., vol. ix.

only 1230 souls. Even this was far above the population it had supported in the Epoch of the Clans. This is repeatedly and emphatically stated by Mr. Macgregor, and it reminds us that even then the population of the old Military Ages had been far exceeded. Yet nineteen years later, the population had risen to 1572. In 1791 it was 2060. In 1831 it was 3415, and in this year of renewed famine 1836-7, it amounted to about 4000.

It will be observed that this exorbitant increase went on after the Kelp trade had been destroyed. There was nothing whatever to justify, or account for such increase except an ever-increasing dependence on the Potato, and a corresponding lowering of the conditions of life. There was not the slightest advance in agricultural knowledge or industry. On the contrary —no account given by wandering Englishmen or by Low Countrymen, which may be thought highly coloured by anti-Celtic prejudices, can exceed in wretchedness the account by this descendant of the Clan Gregor in respect to the industrial habits of the Skyemen among whom he lived so late as 1838. The women alone did all the harrowing; whilst every implement and every method of cultivation were alike barbarous and ineffective. Next came the final blow—the Potato disease of 1846. By that time the population of Tyree had increased to about 5000 souls—an increase probably without parallel in any purely rural district in the world. It may bring this abnormal multiplication more strikingly home to us, when we observe the fact that this single Hebridean Island added to its population during about 80 years a greater number of souls than were added to the population of the Cathedral City of Glasgow during all the generations which elapsed between the War of Independence and the Reformation.[1] It did this under the stimulus of a manufacture which rested wholly on Protective Duties injurious to the rest of the community—under the influence of a mindless contentment with a very low diet—and of an indulgence, not less mindless, in instincts which are natural in themselves, but which, like all other natural instincts, require the control of an enlightened Will. The love of offspring is a natural instinct which we share with all creatures. But educated men do not anywhere encourage their children to build hovels round their home, without reference to adequate means of maintaining a civilised existence. Even among the Birds of the Air, and the creatures of the Field, there is a wonderful, and even a mysterious law by which a wholesome dispersion is secured, and limited areas of subsistence are kept from being overstocked. It is a curious fact, quite common in the Highlands, that small areas of arable land which can never be enlarged from the nature of the country, are frequented by a single pair of Partridges, producing a single covey every year, which, even when never shot, never remain to multiply. It is true that Man has

[1] *History of Glasgow*, by George Macgregor, 1881, Appendix, p. 530.

powers and resources which the lower animals have not. It is true that with every new mouth that is born, two new hands are born to feed them. But it is not true that the two hands have power in all circumstances to earn new subsistence. Sustenance cannot be sensibly increased upon St. Kilda. Nature intervenes and kills off the children by a horrible and mysterious disease. Even those that remain live largely upon charity ; and are now said to exhibit the moral deterioration which such dependence always causes, when it becomes habitual. This is an extreme case. But it is very little more extreme than the case of other Hebridean Islands. The love of Race is another natural instinct. But educated men do not cling to spots of birth when wider regions invite to wider duties, and to more fruitful works.

Sooner or later Nature finds out the sins and blindnesses of all her children. We know what were the results of the Potato famine in Ireland, where it fell on a population which had never been redeemed from a terrible continuity of Celtic usages, and had never enjoyed the opportunities afforded to the people of Tyree, by the abolition of Middlemen, by the formation of separate holdings, and by rents kept down to a low rate on purpose to let them live with exceptional ease. The same effects resulted where all these opportunities had been afforded, but where they had not been put to the right use by minds adequately prepared. There was imminent danger of starvation. It was prevented by charity—the charity of Proprietors generously aided by the charity of the Public. This charity was rendered effective in the Hebrides by the comparatively limited area of distress. The rest of Scotland suffered great losses in one article of produce and of sale. But no part of Scotland suffered any danger of famine, except those parts of it where the old mediaeval ignorances had been suffered to survive. There never was so clear a lesson. Conviction was forced on the poor people of the Island of Tyree, and they addressed to Sir John M'Neill, who was then at the head of the Board of Supervision for the Poor, an earnest and even a passionate petition asking for assistance to emigrate to Canada. I have nowhere seen a more forcible and more conclusive plea set forth in favour of this remedy.[1] It fell to the lot of my Father and myself to respond to it. At great cost we enabled upwards of a thousand people to go where they could put to use the admirable elements of character which never fail to be exhibited by Highlanders when they move out into the stream of the world's progress. When I visited Canada and the United States in 1879, I had the warmest invitations from Highlanders who had emigrated; and the accounts of success were universal.

I take but little merit to myself, that in the face of proofs so ample, and of results so terrible, I determined—with due regard to local circumstances, and to a past which could not be too

---

[1] See Appendix II. p. 328.

suddenly reversed without hardship—to return to the principles which—starting everywhere from the same conditions—had secured the wealth, the comfort, and the civilisation of the rest of Scotland. Subdivision was stopped. Existing subdivisions, when vacant from death, insolvency, or migrations, were never put up to competition, as they would have been under Middlemen. They were invariably added to the holding of the nearest neighbours who could take them. Some new Tenants from the Low Country were brought in, who could show new methods, and introduce some circulation of ideas into a stagnant air. By the steady prosecution of this process during forty years, some approach has been gradually made to the condition of things which was aimed at by the old Field-Marshal. With the increasing size of holdings, comfort and prosperity have steadily advanced. But the tendency to revert to ancient habits reappears from time to time; and the encouragements of a very ignorant sentiment " out of doors " has lately led to an attempt to go back through the paths of violence to the ruinous practices of the past, in spite of all reason, and in spite of a long and a terrible experience.

I have spoken of the wonder that must often strike us when we look back on the slowness of Mankind, in opening their eyes to the most obvious facts of nature, and to conclusions of the reason which now appear to us quite as obvious as the facts. There is one signal example of this connected with the history of a large part of Scotland, which applies not to the poorer, but to the more educated classes, and especially to the Landowners. An immense area of the Western and Northern Highlands is occupied by high and very steep mountains. We have seen that only little bits of them were ever put to any use at all under the old system, and even those bits were used for only about six weeks in the year. For several generations it had been known in the Border Highlands that such mountains were most valuable grazings for sheep, which could be fed in thousands upon their steepest surfaces, and could remain on them all the year round. Yet it was only very slowly and very late— that it dawned upon Farmers, or upon Landowners, that the Highland mountains could be put to the same use, and could be thus redeemed from all but absolute waste. The enormous addition made by this discovery to the natural produce of the country, is very apt to be forgotten now, because of the great ignorance prevalent on the extent of area which was thus, for the first time, made contributory to the comforts and sustenance of mankind. On my own estate there is one Mountain which, with its spurs and peaks, and shoulders, occupies more than 20,000 acres. Of this great area only about 500 acres are arable, and many of these have been reclaimed and enclosed at great cost, within the last fifty years. Of the rest, probably not more than 1000 acres would be available for Cattle. All the remainder, at least 18,500 acres, are very steep,

BEN MORE, MULL, VOLCANIC MOUNTAIN.

and many of them either actually, or almost, precipitous. No other animal except Sheep could, or ever did, consume the grasses which clothe these surfaces more or less abundantly. Yet they can and do feed some 8700 Sheep, without interfering with the comparatively few Cattle which were ever reared in the olden time. If, now, we look at an Orographical Map of the Highlands, we shall find that this case is the typical case of the Western Highlands and of the Northern Highlands, embracing the larger half of the Counties of Inverness, Ross, and Sutherland. Sir John Sinclair calculated that before the introduction of sheep-farming, the whole produce exported from all the Highlands did not exceed £300,000 worth of very lean and poor Cattle. Under Cheviot Sheep he shows that the same area would produce at least twice the value of mutton, or £600,000, besides all the Wool, equal to a further sum of £900,000. This Wool, again, when manufactured, would represent a value of at least £3,600,000 of Woollens. The total difference therefore between the produce of the Country under the new system as compared with the old, was as the difference between £600,000, and £4,200,000—this difference being all added to the comfort and resources of Mankind.[1]

It does seem almost incredible that Highland Landowners and Tenants should have been so slow to find out an application and a use for the Moors

---

[1] *Agricultural Reports*, vol. iv. p. 185: Northern Counties.

and Mountains they occupied or possessed, a use
which in reality constituted as much the addition
of a new country as the recovery of the Bedford
Level from the Sea. The Mountains round Moffat
in Dumfriesshire are hardly less steep or less high
than the Mountains round Loch Maree in Ross-shire,
or round Loch Laxford in Sutherland. The Highland
Mountains had even an advantage over the Border
Mountains, that they were nearer to the Gulf-
stream, and snow lay less long upon them. Yet the
stupidities of Custom and Tradition were so difficult
of removal that Sheep-farming spread as slowly
as the Potato, or the manufacture of Kelp. No
doubt the new Sheep farming involved some local
displacement of population, because Sheep could
not be supported without access to low ground,
which was sometimes occupied by "Clachans,"
liable to periodical distress and famine. But this
displacement of population was far less than that
which had been involved all over the Low
Country by the abandonment of Runrig, and
in the Border Counties by the Sheep-farming
which had superseded the Moss-troopers. Neither
again did it involve necessarily in all cases very
large farms. The Highland Counties have at
this moment a much greater variety of holdings in respect to size, than the most thriving
Lowland Counties. Neither again did it involve
any general substitution of Lowland farmers for
Highlanders. Some of the earliest sheep farmers
were Highlanders who had acquired capital by

LOCH MAREE, ROSS-SHIRE.

industry. Others were Lowlanders who brought knowledge of management, and imparted it, to the immense advantage of the country. It remains therefore a wonderful example of the slow progress of new ideas that the Highland Proprietors adopted Sheep-farming on the hills so slowly and so late as they actually did. Although it began as soon as 1768, it was not universally applied to the wasted areas till as late as 1823.

But there is another phenomenon, even more wonderful, which is equally common—and that is, the coming back of old blindnesses—the revival of old errors—and even the passionate return to practices which Nature has condemned. Yet this phenomenon has its analogue in the material world as well as in the World of Mind. It is now universally admitted that Development, or Evolution, does not always work in one direction. It works downwards as well as upwards. As Tennyson expresses it—"Thronèd races may degrade."[1] There is even reason to believe in a constant force tending to revert to earlier and ruder stages of existence. Whether this be so or not, the fact is certain that there are many creatures that fall from a comparatively high, to a comparatively low, organisation. The freedom—nay the very organs—of locomotion are abandoned and cast away. Even the noble faculty of vision is lost. The creature becomes fixed to a bit of rock, or to the shells and exuviæ of dead things. So it is with Man. At the beginning of this

[1] *In Memoriam*, Canto 128.

Work I have referred to the influence exerted over our longings and desires by the pressure of modern life—the "fumum strepitumque Romae"—the strain of Work in the pursuit of Wealth—or the not less trying strain of Mind in a speculative age in the quest of satisfying Truth. All this tends to throw a most false glamour on the ages which have passed. The old tastes for a Wild Life return upon us, inherited through many generations.

Most of us know the feeling. It is pleasant to return to childhood, and the pleasures of imagination. I never read any detailed account of so-called "primitive" life in any of the happier climates of the world, without at least some passing feelings of desire to join in its freedom and pursuits—to live in Pile Dwellings on the lagoons of a Coral Sea, or in huts on the tops of trees—to watch the Birds of Paradise in the Forests of New Guinea—to shoot reedy arrows at the great Ground Pigeon—or to hunt for the wondrous hatching-mounds of the Brush Turkey. Not less attractive to other tastes would it be to go back to the Epoch of the Clans,— to sail, and to fight, and to spoil in beautiful Galleys, with all their bravery of war. It is perhaps less easy for civilised men to think with any envy of the old Celtic habits—of the wattled huts, jointly inhabited with the cows and calves—of the perpetual atmosphere of Peat-reek—of all the hardest labour left to women, and of seeing them yoked to Harrows as described by Mr. Macgregor, writing as late as 1838. But imagination has a wonderful power of winnowing out all facts that are disagreeable, and of resting only on those which have a flavour of the picturesque. We have seen that not only the charm and glamour of these old habits, but the actual delight of exercising the powers of "Chiefery" with which they were inseparably connected, had been strong enough to corrupt the noble chivalry of Norman Barons, so that even a man near in blood to Robert the Bruce had descended to the level of a mere "Wolf of Badenoch." We have seen how, in a much later day, another conspicuous example of the same influence had been displayed by Sir James Macdonald, who was known in the Palaces of the Kingdom as a most polished and accomplished Knight—but who, when he returned to Islay or Kintyre, became the bloody and the fierce Macsorlie. In our own time it has too often an influence not indeed so formidable in action, but hardly less corrupting in opinion. Harmless in the form of mere sentiment and poetry, it ceases to be harmless when it perverts History and loosens the hold of Mind over the rights and obligations upon which every Society must be built.

In this form it acts as a solvent upon Opinion which is the root of Law. It subordinates the Reason to Fancy—it elevates the ignorant Declamation of the Platform over the responsible decisions of the Bench. This is a return to the power of "Chiefery" not in its ancient and nobler form but in a new and debased embodiment. It is a reversion, as Darwin expresses it, in Biology, to an old and ruder type. It is however worse than this. It is a mere travesty and corruption of that violence against which the Monarchy and the civilisation of Scotland had to wage for centuries one long continuous war. It is the true modern analogue of the worst Anarchy of the Clans.

It is curious to observe the different direction which this kind of sentiment has taken in regard to the country formerly inhabited by the Border Clans. That country has been infinitely more changed and more depopulated than the Celtic Highlands. The vast stretches of moorland, and the long vista of vacant Glens which strike the eye on the borders of Dumfriesshire and the Upper Wards of Lanarkshire, are far more desolate of human habitation than any similar areas in the Highlands possessing equal possibilities of reclamation. But more than this: the greener and lower Valleys which are so beautiful in Selkirk and Roxburgh, are almost entirely destitute of the smaller Holdings which are abundant and successful all over the Counties of Argyll and Inverness. How does true Poetic Sentiment deal with the memory of the days when these Valleys were full of a military population—when a few powerful Chiefs could summon at the shortest notice armies of 10,000 men? It sings of those days indeed. But the Singer does not pretend to wish that they should return. Let us listen for a moment to the melodious words in which the great Minstrel of the Borders recalled the Military Ages of that pastoral land in which, when a child, he lifted his little hands to the lightning in a raging Thunderstorm,[1] and shouted with excitement "Bonny, Bonny!":—

> "Sweet Teviot! On thy silver tide
>   The glaring bale-fires blaze no more:
> No longer steel-clad warriors ride
>   Along thy wild and willowed shore;
> Where'er thou wind'st, by dale or hill,
> All, all is peaceful, all is still,
>   As if thy waves, since Time was born,
>   Since first they rolled upon the Tweed,
> Had only heard the shepherd's reed,
>   Nor started at the bugle-horn." [2]

This is delightful and legitimate. But more than this would be childish. Scott himself became a Landowner in that very country—and latterly he possessed no inconsiderable Estate. He built a Baronial Hall. But he did not restore a Cottier Tenantry. He enclosed and planted. But he planted Larches. He did not invite the Workmen making high wages in Hawick or Galashiels to come back to starve on patches of corn and of potatoes along the once populous "Haughs" of Tweed. The unreality on which much of this kind of sentiment is founded was never more curiously illustrated than when the Government chose as the Head of a Commission appointed to inquire into the Small Tenants of the North and West, a Scotch Peer[3] whose own Estate is situated among the long "cleared" sheep pastures of the Southern Highlands, and in a locality

---

[1] Lockhart's *Life of Scott*, vol. i. p. 83.
[2] *Lay of the Last Minstrel:* Canto Fourth, 1.
[3] Lord Napier and Ettrick.

which is specially described by Sir Walter Scott in *Marmion* as a perfect picture of solitude and depopulation.[1] This distinguished Scotchman has given elaborate advice to Highland Proprietors for the extension—not merely of small Holdings—but of the special form of these which is least advantageous—that of Joint or Township Farms. There is nevertheless not the slightest reason to believe that he himself or any of his brethren, would consent to cut up any portion of their great sheep grazings, or of their comfortable and single arable Farms, for the purpose of restoring the population of the Military Ages. Many Owners in the Lowland Counties now wish that they had, as the Highland Counties have, more small Farms, and fewer of the largest class. But no man who knows anything of Agriculture, or of the influences which promote its progress, would ever recommend the revival of the old Township System. In my own experience I have always found that the moment any "Crofter" becomes exceptionally industrious and exceptionally prosperous, he earnestly desires, above all things, that his grazings as well as his arable land, should be fenced off from those of his neighbours, so that he may have the exclusive use of his own faculties in the better tillage of his land and in the better breeding of his stock. The multiplication of small Farms, indeed, such as will profitably employ the whole industry and capital of individual men, is

---

[1] *Marmion*: Introduction to Canto Second. St. Mary's Lake.

an object most desirable. But the conditions of success vary with every locality, and can only be determined by local knowledge. It cannot be settled by a vague desire to revive the usages of a time which has passed away for ever.

Sentiment, however, must never be surrendered to those who have little knowledge and no balance. Such are the men who are very apt to claim it as their own, whilst instructed men are too apt to leave it in their hands. Sentiment can be strong as well as weak—healthy as well as sickly, manly as well as mawkish. It can fix its enthusiasms on what is really good, as it too often does on what is only picturesquely bad. The cruelties, treacheries, disloyalties, and brutalities of the Clans were mere developments of corruption, due to the divorce between them and all settled Government and Law. They represented nothing but anarchy in their relations with the Nation and the Kingdom, and nothing better in their relations with each other. But the root and the principle of their organisation was that of a Military Tribe, recruiting from all directions,—practising obedience,—acknowledging authority,—and loving its hereditary transmission from those who had first afforded guidance, conduct, and protection. This is a constructive, and not a destructive or anarchic principle. It needed only to be turned in a right direction to become one of the steadiest of all foundation-stones for the building up of a great structure in the light and air of a higher civilisation. It was thus that in the transition between the two Ages, the broken fragments of a hundred Septs enlisted under the Banner of the Black Watch, and began the immortal services of the Highland Regiments. Yet this is only a late and picturesque incident in a long series of events. Nothing is more striking or more poetic in the history of Scotland than the slow and arduous processes by which the rough energy of the Military Ages was transformed under the ages of industry and of peace. Malcolm Canmore had begun the transformation by his own Union with the Daughter of another blood. Robert the Bruce continued it by the welding of broken Races in the heat and fire of Battle. Between the War of Independence and the Union of the Crowns it was one long, continuous, constant, struggle. But by slow and steady steps the work was done, and Scotland became a Nation with a noble and a settled Jurisprudence. Our Kings became our only Chiefs: our Country became our only Clan. Her Law, the best symbol of her History, and the best expression of her Mind, became the only authority to which we bowed, and the only protection to which we trusted. Under its shelter man could have confidence in man, because there was no fear of that which even the old Celts ranked with Pestilence and Famine—the breaking of the Bonds of Covenant. In this high field of Human Energy,—the establishment of that confidence in Law which is the nearest approach we can ever make to the methods of the Divine Government,—Scotland may well be proud of the old beginnings, and of the steady growth, of all her National Institutions.

Among these Institutions there is one of purely native origin which, perhaps, as much as any other, is a striking embodiment of this principle, and a splendid illustration of its effects. I refer to her Banking system. Barter, as we all know, is the earliest form of Exchange, and under that system if the Seller can bring his produce to a market, and the Buyer can carry it away in safety, no higher kind of security is required. Then comes Money as an abstract representative of Value, immensely facilitating Exchange, by providing an article with which, and for which, everything can be got from somebody. Lastly comes Credit, the highest and the most powerful of all agencies for promoting the intercourse of men. It is the highest because it is most purely the work of Mind—the most absolute expression of confidence in the universal authority of Law. In other countries the intervention of the State has been required to establish Banks, and the work assigned to them has been lauded as among the highest efforts of Statesmanship. In Scotland an immense network of Institutions for the universal diffusion and organisation of Credit, has been spread, as it were, by a natural growth indigenous to the soil. In Scotland there is a Bank for about every 4000 souls of the total population. Ten of them represent a paid-up capital of above Nine Millions sterling, and Deposits to the amount of more than Eighty Millions; their

Branches are all over the country. Thus everywhere men are able to take advantage, not only of their savings, but of the credit in which they stand for their character in business—that is for their honesty, their industry, and for all the mental aptitudes which give promise of success. The whole of this vast system of Credit is founded upon confidence in the Law—constituting a Wages Fund co-extensive with the possibilities of Industry and of Knowledge. It would all crumble at the touch of Anarchy. Under the confidence which this Reign of Law ensures, Mind in all its forms, whether of enterprise, or of invention, or of organisation, or only of patient perseverance, has made an entirely new world of Scotland. It has reclaimed her soil, it has deepened her rivers, it has built her commercial navies, it has brought into her harbours the products of the most distant regions, and it has redeemed her own people, immensely multiplied, from chronic poverty and frequent famines.

There must be something wrong with ourselves, and not with the Order of Nature, or with the Designs of Providence, if we can find none of the pleasures of the Imagination, and none of the gratifications of Sentiment, in changes such as these. Nothing can be more certain than that we are but accomplishing part at least, and an essential part, of our mission in the world when we turn the desert into the fruitful field. Nothing can be more certain than that it is our duty to put our Talents out to Use, and not to hide them in a napkin. Most of these Talents have their poetic side. Slothfulness is not one of the Christian virtues, even when it is passed amidst picturesque surroundings. The Hebrew People were not devoid of Poetry or of Sentiment, and yet their Songs and their Prophecies are full of the imagery derived from the improvement of the soil, as well as of the precious and beautiful things which were brought in Commerce by the ships of Tarshish. With them the Olive, and especially the Vine, were the symbols of cultivated fertility; and in connection with the Vineyard, in particular, we have the most touching and passionate allusions to all the care and labour bestowed upon Enclosures as the best type and symbol of the work needed in the higher cultivation of the soul. The "fencing" of land, and the "gathering out the stones thereof," and the "planting" of it, and the building "in the midst of it,"[1] are as apposite a description of the work of Reclamation in Scotland as it was of the same work in Palestine. The taking away the "Hedge thereof," and the "breaking down the wall thereof" are used as the best Images of utter Desolation,[2] whilst the ravages of the wild creatures which fences are intended to exclude are similarly used to typify the invasions of the sacred fields by the arms of Heathendom.[3] There is too, in the Book of Proverbs, a striking description of the ignorant and lazy habits which had afflicted

[1] Isaiah v. 2.   [2] *Ibid.* v. 5.   [3] Psalm lxxx. 12, 13.

Scotland: "I went by the field of the slothful, and by the vineyard of the man void of understanding; and, lo, it was all grown over with thorns, and nettles had covered the face thereof, and the stone wall thereof had been broken down. Then I saw, and considered it well: I looked upon it, and received instruction. Yet a little sleep, a little slumber, a little folding of the hands to sleep: so shall thy poverty come as one that travelleth; and thy want as an armed man."[1] Yet, beyond all question, the "prunëd vine" is a much less picturesque object than the Briers and the Thorns which ignorance or violence may allow to choke it. On the other hand, the clustered grapes,—and the winds passing over fields of corn,—and the flocks browsing in perspective upon great plains,—and the sheep herded on the mountains—are all pictures full of poetry—far higher than that which circles round the deeds and the pursuits of half-barbarian Man.

We cannot go back to the Primitive Ages, whatever else we do. We must live in our own time, and we must put to culture and to use, such talents as come to us from the inheritance of the Past, and from the opportunities of the Present. It is a delusion to suppose that the sin of covetousness belongs specially to the later ages of the world. The naked Savage covets more of his beads, or of his bits of iron, as much as the civilised Man covets some new indulgence. Modern Industry has its own dangers, and its own evils, but the

[1] Proverbs xxiv. 30-34.

truth is that the pursuit of Wealth under the conditions of civilisation, having in it more of Mind than the same pursuit under conditions of Barbarism, tends to be better and higher in its moral character. There is less in the mere getting, and more in the intellectual interest belonging to the processes through which the getting comes. The Machine Maker thinks as much of the perfection and accuracy of his work, as of the price he gets for it. The Shipbuilder thinks most of the fine "lines"—of the speed, and capacity, and strength of his ships. The Skilled Workman rejoices in his manual dexterity, and takes a pleasure, purely intellectual, in the triumph of his hands—in the straightness of his furrow — in his mastery over some difficult and intractable material. One of my earliest recollections is of the laborious and conscientious pains bestowed by my Father, as a Mechanic, on the high finish of the articles he produced—on the perfect symmetry of form—on the joinings which the finest touch could not detect —on the harmonies of colour and of substance. Throughout all the Kingdom of Labour—using that word, not in its vulgar but in its highest meaning, as including above all the Labour of the Brain—there is a Hierarchy or Gradation of rank corresponding to the degree in which the mere getting of Value is subordinate, and the production of excellence is predominant. The lowest rank must be assigned to the most purely mechanical— such as Commission Agencies—in which there is no skill, although the work may be useful, or even necessary, as part of the machinery of Distribution.

And most assuredly in this Hierarchy of Labour the work of the Improver and Reclaimer of Land stands very high in the variety and dignity of the motives which come before the mere love of gain. Time may be on his side, but generally it is time belonging to a somewhat distant future. A single successful voyage, one single turn of the market, may make and has often made the fortune of a Merchant. One happy thought flashing on the Brain of the Inventor, may reward him at a stroke with abundant wealth. But the fruits of the Earth cannot generally be multiplied so quickly, and we see by the history and experience of the past, how difficult it has been to exercise the foresight, and to submit to the immediate sacrifices, which the laborious steps of a reformed Husbandry have demanded of those who live by it. The love of Agriculture is among the original instincts of our nature—as distinct from others as, in early ages, is the love of the Chase, or, in all ages, the love of Decoration. And amongst these original instincts it is unquestionably the highest and the best, both from the simplicity of its character and from the beneficence of its effects. With advancing education it suffers no decay. On the contrary, it charms and elevates the mind in proportion as it exercises us in our great commission over Nature, and brings us into closer contact with those "abodes where self-disturbance hath no part."[1] The sentiment which prefers to these attractions the far off echoes of the Spear and Shield, or the alternating indulgence of fierce activity and of selfish idleness, is a sentiment unworthy alike of true Poetry, of true Religion, and of true Philosophy.

I have spoken of the natural causes which lead to forgetfulness of the work of Ownership in the Agricultural Improver—causes connected with the very completeness of that work, and with the total obliteration of the older surfaces which have been reclaimed. These are causes which lie in mere ignorance and want of thought. But, strange to say, this ignorance or forgetfulness has been stereotyped, and as it were enshrined, in doctrines which profess to be scientific. In this matter the Formulæ of Political Economists have been even more feeble than in the definitions of Wealth and of its Sources. Ricardo's famous definition of Rent is a perfect example of that delight which men are apt to have in formal propositions spun out of their own brains, which have little or no correspondence with the facts of Nature. Abstract ideas are the high prerogative of Man, and he could not get on for a single day without them. All Language is built upon them, and the rudest Savage who can convey intelligence to his fellow is exercising the same power which may one day lead on his descendants to the peaks of science. Men practised Logic before the days of Aristotle, and the Inductive Philosophy

[1] Wordsworth.

before the days of Bacon. Political Economists are quite right to reduce within the terms of some abstract definition, if they can, those facts of human history and the nature of human transactions, which are the sources of Rent. But there are bad abstractions as well as good,—abstractions which do not take in more than a fraction of the facts, and that fraction perhaps the least significant of all. They may be true in a sense, and yet be valueless. That is to say, they may reproduce and represent with vividness some mere circumstance connected with particular results, and yet miss completely the essential conditions on which these results depend.

Ricardo's definition of Rent, as pruned and shaped under the fire of criticism by later writers, is not only true, but it is a truism. The Rent which any given piece of land will fetch is precisely the excess of its value over another piece of Land which is too poor to fetch any rent at all.[1] But we may well ask, like Eliphaz the Temanite, when we hear such a definition as this, "Should a wise man utter vain knowledge, and fill his belly with the East wind?"[2] This definition is true, not only of the rent of land, but of the rent of all other things which fetch a price for hire. The admirers of it sometimes boast that the mere statement of it has all the force of

---

[1] Professor Fawcett expresses it thus: "The rent of any land is the difference between its net produce and the net produce of land which pays a merely nominal rent."—*Manual of Political Economy*, 6th Ed. p. 117.

[2] Job xv. 2.

a self-evident proposition.[1] This, however, becomes very doubtful praise when we observe that the same self-evident character follows the definition when it is applied to the hire of a Costermonger's Donkey as much as when it is applied to the hire of a Farm. The value for hire of any particular Donkey is obviously the value of its labour above that of any other Donkey which will fetch no price at all for hire, but which works just enough to pay for its own feeding. So in like manner the Rent of any given House is the excess of its value for hire above that of some other House which would fetch no rent at all, but which is used by Paupers as a Hovel. In this form the proposition is true, but it is also barren. All the corollaries which have been drawn from it in later speculations, are not logical consequences at all, but are built up on verbal fallacies imported into the definition by the careless use of ambiguous words. It certainly does not prove, or tend to prove, that the Rent of agricultural land is no element in the cost of Production,[2] because whatever may be the truth in this matter, the Formula gives us no analysis of Rent, and tells us nothing of its sources or of its composition. It is not very easy to see how the hire of a Steam-Plough would be part of the cost of Production, whilst the hire of a drain or of a fence would not. Yet the hire of such improvements is a large element in Rent. Still less does the Formula prove that all the growing values

---

[1] *Progress and Poverty*, Book III. ch. ii.
[2] Fawcett's *Manual*, p. 126.

in all the Products of Labour, tend to become absorbed in the Rent of land—a proposition in itself absurd, and opposed to all observation and experience.[1] The proportion of gross or total produce which goes to Rent is not greater, but, on the contrary, it is smaller, as Agriculture becomes more scientific. Nothing like one-third—the old Scotch proportion in rude ages—of the gross produce, now goes to Rent. One-sixth or one-eighth is more near the average proportion. More than before goes to Muscular Labour; more goes to the breeder of Horses; more goes to the maker of machines; more goes to the seller of manures, and, in average times, more to the Farmer. The increase of Rent arises entirely from the enormous increase of total produce, and from a corresponding increase of demand. This is the reason why high rents are a sign of general prosperity.[2] If the sixth or the eighth of the total produce be only ten shillings, then the total produce per acre must be as low as £3 per acre or £4. This indicates wretched crops, or a poor market, or both. If, on the other hand, the rent of land be sixty or eighty shillings an acre, it proves that the total produce must be at least £18 an acre or £24—indicating abundant crops, and a good market. Both of these are the signs of general activity and increasing wealth among all classes. "A low rent," says a well-informed writer, "is always an index of the poverty of the land, a thriftless and unscientific

---

[1] Henry George, *passim*.

[2] I speak, of course, of Rents freely offered by free men, and usually paid.

method of culture, or a want of enterprise on the part of both Landlord and Tenant."[1] The inference that all values are absorbed in Rent is absurd. But whether true or false, such inferences as these have no foundation whatever in the Ricardo Formula, in so far as that Formula expresses a self-evident proposition. It has this self-evident character only when it is kept strictly to a purely quantitative relation. It defines Rent only as regards its amount or quantity, and in no other relation whatever. The moment it pretends to explain Rent in any other of its many relations to the Past, or to the Present, the Ricardo Formula passes beyond its province. It is a definition dealing with quantity alone—and dealing with that element in Rent in a form so elementary that its boasted self-evidence may freely be conceded. It measures even quantity by a standard of comparison which is of no practical use whatever. It assumes a Zero line—the existence of land which will afford no Rent at all, or only a Rent which is nominal. It then announces the profound conclusion that all higher Rents are to be measured in respect to quantity by their elevation above this Zero line. This is a theoretical but a self-evident truth, even if we dispute as a fact (as well we may) that there is any land except naked rock, which will yield no Rent whatever.[2] But this self-evident truth is as naked as the only land which answers to

---

[1] *Judicial Records of Renfrewshire*, by W. Hector, 1876, p. 319.

[2] The most naked mountains in Scotland will hold a few sheep, and every sheep affords a rent.

its description. It tells us nothing of any practical or even of any speculative value.

By a curious coincidence I first heard this Ricardo Formula for defining Rent, set forth, many years ago, by Lord Macaulay—the only illustrious descendant and representative of the Clan on whose reclaimed lands I had been born and bred. He had evidently very little practical knowledge of the many economic elements which determine Rent, nor probably had he ever thought of tracing the Historical elements which explain its origin in the Past. On the other hand, at that time I had not myself studied the subject theoretically; whilst, practically, I had a good deal of instructive and significant experience. I recollect noticing the evident intellectual pleasure with which he expounded a Doctrine which can be so neatly expressed, and which assumes to set forth in so small a compass one of the most complicated of all the facts of History and of Life. Not less distinctly do I remember the sense of emptiness—the painful contrast, as it struck me, between the self-evidence of the Definition, and the sterility of it—not only as regarded any practical application, but even as regarded any satisfying theoretical analysis.

This is but one example out of many of those methods of handling which have brought Political Economy into its present disrepute, as not only a "Dismal Science" but as a Body of Doctrine either actually deceptive or at least to a very large extent misleading. No doubt part of this eclipse in popular estimation, arises from nothing but ignorant rebellion against some truths which are as certainly ascertained as any other truths whatever. For this evil the only remedy, other than discussion, will be found in those practical results of evil which must always follow, sooner or later, from kicking against the pricks of Nature. This was the teaching, for example, as we have seen, which led men at last, in Scotland, to recognise the folly of Sumptuary Laws —of Laws forbidding men to sell or buy except through certain Corporate Monopolies,—and of Laws which pretended to regulate the price of anything. But Ignorances and Rebellions of this kind, affecting our obedience to those Supreme Enactments which are enforced by the high pains and penalties of Natural Consequence, are not the only cause of the wide revolt which now assails the teaching that passes under the name of Political Economy. Another cause is to be found in the fact that this teaching has been often most defective, and, not seldom, even thoroughly erroneous. One grand defect in it has been the comparative neglect, and sometimes even the complete elimination, as not belonging to its Province, of those agencies of Mind which are in reality the ultimate sources of all that is done, or enjoyed or suffered, in Societies of Men. In undertaking to reduce the growth of Nations, and the progress of Mankind, to causes as rigid and mechanical as those which govern the Material World, it has missed the highest offices which it is its duty to discharge. Political Economy, properly treated, ought not to be a Dismal Science. It ought not to present results emptied of all adequate recognition of the work done by Mind, and Heart, and Will. To pretend to explain the origin, or the growth, or the distribution of Wealth—to explain anything, indeed, of the past history or present condition of Man, without full recognition of these great moving Forces, is like pretending to explain the cylinders, and the tubes, and the valves of a Steam Engine without any reference to the properties of Steam, and without any reference to the mechanical Invention by which its pressures are generated, concentrated, and brought to bear on Use. Against this kind of science, falsely so called, continual resistance and revolt is both inevitable and just. On the other hand, when the Science which deals with all these things, comes—if it ever does come—to be properly handled, and when all the facts of our complicated nature are marshalled in their due rank and order, it will be a Science full of all the interest, and of all the poetry, and of all the pure intellectual delight, which must belong to the contemplation and the analysis of Nature in the noblest of all her Provinces.

Nothing, for example, can be more interesting or instructive than to trace in the light of History the sources and the origin of those relations between men which directly or indirectly exist in all regions of the civilised world between Owners and Occupiers of the Soil. We need not fill our bellies with East Wind in artificial definitions of Rent which have nothing to do with either its origin or its nature. There is really no difficulty in arriving at a definition which is not artificial, but natural,—a simple description of facts,—and one which nevertheless immediately suggests questions leading up to higher and higher aspects of the truth. Rent is that which one man pays for the temporary possession, or exclusive use, of anything that is not his own, but is the permanent property of another. Rent is the price of Hire. As regards this essential and definite characteristic, it matters nothing what the thing thus hired may be. In common parlance Rent is usually applied to the Hire of land, or of Houses, or of Mines, or of Fishings, but is not usually applied to the Hire of Horses, or of Carriages, or of other moveable property. Each of these different things has its own peculiar kind of use, and each special use holds out to us some special inducement to hire it. But no peculiarity in the nature of the use constitutes any distinction in the principle of Hire. That principle is the same in all cases in which we pay for the temporary possession of anything that belongs to another. What we pay for, when we hire anything, is the Exclusive Use or Possession of it, for a time. And the price we pay for this Exclusive Use is paid to the man who himself possesses it, and has the power of lending it. What we owe to him in the form of Hire, or Rent, is due to him because of his exercising in our favour his right and power of lending. If we want to have the Exclusive Use of a Horse, or of a Cow, or of a Cabbage Garden, or of a Vineyard, or of a Farm, we must hire this exclusive right for a time, if we cannot buy it out and out.

If we go further and ask how the Owner came to have that right of Exclusive Use which many other men can only afford to Hire, we shall find that there is no difference in principle between the different things over which this right has been acquired. It is true that the land of the Cabbage Garden, or of the Vineyard, or of the Farm has not been the creation of Muscular Labour. But neither have Cattle, nor Sheep, nor Horses been the work of Muscle. The breeding of them is the work of Nature, under the direction to some extent of a selecting Mind, and even this only rendered possible by the right of Exclusive Use over at least some grazing land. And so, although land is not in itself the produce either of Muscular or of Mental Labour, yet the Exclusive Use of any part of it has always been originally acquired by the work of Mind. To seek the origin of this exclusive Right of Use we must go back to the Conquering Tribes from which we are all descended. And then, again, to explain how they came to conquer, we must always go back to some time, whether within the area of History or beyond it, when the Men of Muscle surrounded some Man of Mind, lifted him perhaps on their shields and shouted, " Be thou our acknowledged Strongest."[1] In our own country

---

[1] I borrow this from Thomas Carlyle, but I do not recollect the Work in which it occurs.

this tracking of the ultimate sources of Ownership leads us along no doubtful path—no mere faint indications interpreted by theory and speculation. The footprints are revealed to us in no dim light of mere tradition, but in the full blaze of History. We see men crowding under the banner of powerful Chiefs, and seeking "rooms" of land under their protection, because of the security it held out to them for Exclusive Use. We see our early Kings, with the consent of Barons, Clergy, and People, acknowledging the power of those Chiefs as a Power which had been established long before, and tendering to those who held it a new Form of Record as a reward for new, but immortal, services. Poetry and Sentiment could hardly have a better subject. The Recording Instruments may have been long lost—they may be now reduced to pulp in damp cellars, or in neglected Charter-Chests—or they may have been happily preserved with their old Parchments, and their old stately Seals. But whether surviving in this form or not, they live in the continuous transactions of perhaps a thousand years. That which men have been holding—that which they have been buying and selling during all these centuries—has been the Tenure which these Instruments record. Over the whole of Scotland every morsel of land which is owned or hired for the exclusive use of any man, is held by him in virtue of the Rights of Predecessors in Title dating from before the times of Malcolm Canmore, or from the years of contest that were closed at Bannockburn.

The aptitudes of Mind are infinite—or at least as various as all the varieties of circumstance in which the Human Species has been placed since it was born into the world. Nothing can be done without it—everything that has been done, has been done by it. In early ages, courage and conduct in War has been the form of mental energy most effective. But this is generally a compound of many qualities. The influence of some men cannot be explained. It is magnetic. In their presence other men become excited with a fire which is not their own. Without such Minds, mere numbers are of no avail —for the units become as incoherent as grains of sand. Such men become the Founders of Nations because of the confidence they inspire—of the ideas they represent—and of the Institutions which they inaugurate. One of the very first works which they accomplish is, the establishment of supreme and exclusive dominion over some portion of the Earth's surface for themselves and for their immediate followers. This right of Exclusive Use is subdivided and partitioned in a thousand ways. But in its essence and in its principle it is everywhere the same. It is, in its very inception, the fruit of Mind, and it affords the only fulcrum on which Mind can exert its higher powers over the Increase of the Earth during the more peaceful ages which follow, and are the rewards of, Conquest.

Examples have not been wanting in our own day, which exhibit the power of one gifted Mind so to discipline the forces of mere Muscle, and the labour of comparatively mindless men, as to lay the foundations of a civilised State. General Gordon was unquestionably one of those men—whose heroic nature represents, as Muscle never can represent, those supreme forms of "Labour" on which all Wealth, and Comfort, and Law depend. And it is remarkable that when he was first ruling as Governor of Khartoum, one of the most immediate and striking effects of his dominion, was a revival of that cultivation of the soil which is inseparable from individual appropriation, or Exclusive Use. Tracts of land which had been desolate for generations, became cultivated again, simply because the Owners were secured under his dominion against the inroads of men who would not respect the rights of Exclusive Use. If General Gordon had been a Native Ruler, or a Native Chief, having extensive Territorial rights over the Soudan, and depending for the maintenance of his power upon native revenues, the private Owners to whom the fruits and rights of Ownership had been thus restored, would have been only too glad to yield to him no inconsiderable share of these fruits, which could not be enjoyed except under the protection he afforded.

There may be other cases in which the individual appropriation of land, and the acknowledged right to its Exclusive Use, has arisen from other causes. Indeed, it may be said with truth to be a universal and apparently a necessary fact in every portion of the Globe, and with every branch of the human family. One of the most prominent Socialistic theorists[1] who now denounce it, is himself one of a small group of men—less than one quarter of the population of London—who claim Exclusive Use over the whole State of California, embracing about ninety-nine millions of acres, or 156,000 square miles of plain and valley, of mountain and of hill. No part of this vast territory is open to all mankind—except upon the conditions imposed by this small community. But like all other communities in like circumstances—like all the colonies of our own Empire—they not only practise the individual appropriation of land among their own citizens, but they recognise it as the foundation of their prosperity. What they all want is Settlers; and what all Settlers want is land on which they can exercise their industry for their own benefit and the benefit of the world. Some evidence of truth is always afforded by the universal instincts of Mankind. The celebrated test which has been put to very doubtful use in Theology, has nevertheless its own sphere of legitimate application—"Quod semper—quod ubique—quod ab omnibus."[2] The most experienced travellers in Africa tell us that there is no portion of that vast Continent which is not claimed in Ownership by some Tribe, and the invasion of which by others would not be resented and resisted by those who thus claim its Exclusive Use. If there be any

---

[1] Mr. Henry George of San Francisco.

[2] What has been held always—everywhere—and by all men: the test of Catholic orthodoxy, laid down by St. Vincent of Lérins, A.D. 434.

portions of the Earth's surface where individual appropriation might be less absolutely necessary than another, as regards the means of subsistence, it would seem to be in those happy Islands of the Eastern Archipelago where wild and native trees bear the most nutritious fruits, and the vegetable world holds out the most lavish inducements to an idle communal existence. Yet I find in an interesting account of New Guinea by a Highlander who has devoted himself to Missionary Work in the Pacific, the following instructive passage respecting that immense Island:—"Far up the distant mountain sides, in the clear atmosphere of morning, we saw the smoke made in the Bush by cultivators of yams. The Teachers assert that every acre of soil along this part of New Guinea has its Owner."[1]

There is no Political Economist, to whatever School he may belong, however narrow may be his formulæ, and however narrower still may be his use and his interpretation of them, who does not at least confess with his lips that "Labour" must be held to include every kind and form of Human Energy. Yet very few writers have really digested this truth,—have taken adequate account of it in their reasonings,—or have attempted to follow it to all its consequences. The great difference between the wages of Skilled and of Unskilled Labour is one

---

[1] *Work, and Adventures in New Guinea.* By James Chalmers, 1885. This distinguished missionary is a native of Argyllshire, and was educated in the Parish of Inveraray.

of the most rudimentary facts of Life which indicate the value of the mental element even in its simplest forms. The simplest of these forms is that in which some special faculty of Perception is united in the same person with the Labour of the Hands. But all the higher forms of Mental Energy are, for the most part, not united in the same person with the Labour of the Hands. It is the value and effect of these higher Energies of Mind which are most habitually forgotten, and in almost all Treatises on questions of human Progress the word Labour gradually slips down—and down—in its use and signification, until practically it means nothing but the Labour of the Hands, with the more or less implicit addition, only of the various degrees of mere technical or manipulative skill. "The producing Classes"—"The produce of Labour," and many other similar phrases, are perpetually used as if Muscle only were concerned in the sources, or in the increase, or in the diffusion, of Wealth. Nothing can be more erroneous, and yet the error has never been sufficiently exposed. The Modern Socialist School are especially forgetful of Mind in all its highest and most operative powers, and are especially jealous of those facts—the most certain perhaps of all facts—which establish the natural, ineradicable, and far-reaching inequalities with which these powers have been bestowed by Nature on individual men. All the writers of this School dislike and avoid the subject, and, when they do deal with it, show how very little they recognise or appreciate the real facts of Nature.

The most signal example I have seen of the measureless difference between these facts and the Socialist appreciation of them, is the example to be found in some words of Mr. Henry George: "I doubt if any good observer will say that the mental differences of men are greater than the physical differences."[1] Here we have a comparison made between two things which are absolutely incommensurable. It may be quite true that the tallest Giant ever known is scarcely more than four times as tall as the smallest Dwarf. It may be true that the average difference in height between men does not exceed one-sixth, or one-seventh of the whole stature. It may be true that the scale of difference in muscular strength—in the lifting of weights, for example— is a scale not much wider in its extremes. But most certainly it is not true that even in those lower manifestations of Mind which constitute mere manual dexterity and skill in handicrafts, the differences between men, are like mere bodily differences, either in kind or in degree. A short man may be as good for all manly work as a tall man—or an ugly man as a man of the most perfect form. But in Mechanics, or in Chemistry, or in Art, the corresponding differences of skill make the whole contrast between work which is useless or effective—healing or poisonous—hideous or of surpassing beauty. To Be, or Not To Be— this, and no less, is the question which may depend,

[1] *Social Problems*, p. 69.

and often does depend, upon the degrees of Faculty with which the eyes are directed, or the hands are moved. Still more futile is this comparison of physical distinctions as any illustration of the differences which separate one man from another in the higher faculties of the Mind. The difference between a dull man and a man of genius—whatever the particular line of that genius may be—is a difference so immense as to be immeasurable. The scale is one which reaches from Zero to a practical Infinity. Moreover, it is a scale of difference applicable above all to those kinds of Work on which Society is founded, and by which its progress is determined. There is no scale that can measure the difference, in actual working value, between the Mind of James Watt and the Mind of the most skilled Workmen whom he employed to make, first, his Models, and then, his Engines. But great as this difference is, it is perhaps exceeded by the difference between the average faculties of ordinary men, and those rarer gifts which in the early stages of Society are concerned in founding its Organic Structures, and in establishing its Opportunities of Growth. Yet as regards physical powers, there is often little or nothing to distinguish between such men; and certainly no physical difference could even be a symbol, however imperfect, of the differences of level on which they stand.

It is one of the regrets of my life that I once had a long interview with General Gordon when I did not even know who he was. It was before the time of his greatest fame, but when in a very distant region he had done enough to indicate what manner of man he was. There was, however, nothing in his outward appearance to arrest attention. There was no aspect of command. There was no look of genius in his almost cold, grey eye. There was no indication in his calm manner, of the Fires of God that were slumbering underneath—of the powerful yet gentle nature which was equally at home in the "confused noise" of Battle, in the teaching of poor children, or in the comforting of a deathbed. Yet General Gordon was one who even then had saved an Empire, and had rescued, by his own individual example and force of character, a whole population from massacre and devastation. Not, perhaps, very tractable in council—sometimes almost incoherent in speculative opinion—he was, beyond all question, a born Ruler and King of men —one who in early ages might have been the founder of a Nation—the Chosen Leader of some Chosen People on the way from intertribal wars and barbarism to peace, and Government, and Law. To say of such men as Gordon that the difference between them and the common herd, is no greater than the difference between men of the biggest and the smallest size of body that may be picked off the street, is to betray a profound ignorance of the causes and the forces which have governed the history of Mankind. Nor does it need such an extreme case to illustrate the fallacy. The varieties of Mind are infinite, and the pre-eminence of one over another in some special faculty—some single gift—may, and often does, make the whole difference between victory and defeat — between triumphant success and total failure, in the race of individual life, and in the struggle between Tribes and Nations.

The protection of the Powerful has been in all ages the earliest shelter for the beginnings of industry and of wealth. In our own country we have traced these beginnings from before the dawn of History—when Power was establishing itself through all the various gifts and aptitudes which made some men Kings, and Chiefs, and Leaders, by clustering round them all who could not otherwise defend themselves. The Exclusive Use of land, whether by small groups or by individual men, has always been absolutely necessary for the production and enjoyment of even the simplest of its fruits; and this Exclusive Use could not be had without coming under the protection of those who had become Owners, who could defend their Ownership, and who could defend also those to whom they let it, or lent it, for a time. Rent, originally and historically, was the price men were too glad to pay for this protection. This element in Rent is still expressed in every Lease by words which in one form or another have been continuously used for 700 years, and which embodied in language understandings which were necessary and universal. They are words which convey the promise that Tenants will be protected in their Exclusive Use "at all hands, and against all mortals." Sometimes the words were shorter—"against all deadly." This was the Occupier's Tenure. This was his Security. This was the one fundamental advantage for which men owed, and gladly paid, some portion of Produce, or of their own Muscular Labour, or of both.

But from very early times another element was added to the benefits for which Produce and Services were paid. Owners lent not only the Exclusive Use of land, but also the cattle by which the land was stocked. We have seen that this form of what on the Continent is called "Metayer," was common over the whole of Scotland under the name of "Steelbow."[1] Next came a further change—another addition, or rather another great group of additions, to the benefits for which Rent was paid. These additions included, in the first place, all those exercises of Mind and of Authority by which ignorant and wasteful Usages were abolished, and all those by which the new methods of husbandry were taught and first established. They included, in the second place, all that we now know under the head of Reclamation and Permanent Improvements,—operations which have in all cases far exceeded the capital value of the Land before they began. The Burst of Industry

---

[1] Among the Celts of Ireland this footing seems to have been equally common, and the Landlord's share of produce was two-thirds, one-third representing Rent for use of land, and another third for the stock also lent. *Manners and Customs of the Ancient Irish*, by Professor O'Curry, vol. i. Introd. p. 122.

which I have described as having begun to transform the face of Scotland during the latter half of the last century, did not end with a Burst, but has been continuous and increasing ever since. On this point I can speak from personal experience. Some parts of the "Old Coast Line" on which I have described the operations of Lord Frederick Campbell, were still left unreclaimed when I began the work of Ownership forty years ago. I found that the cost of bringing them into the condition of arable land was not less, and sometimes exceeded, £25 an acre. As in its unreclaimed state the land was not worth 5s. an acre of the coarsest pasture, this outlay represents one hundred years' purchase of its original value. Sentiment,—of one kind,—has often led me to desire to see, even if it were only for a moment, the aspect of our country when, before the days even of the Picts and Scots, it was covered by magnificent and continuous Forests—where not a stick has grown within the memory of Man, or within the records of authentic History. But as this revival cannot be, Sentiment—of another kind—has led me lately to dig up the trunks of the Caledonian Forest, and to cover with corn-fields some areas which have been for many centuries under bog. One of these seems to have been a glade shaded by giant Oaks. Here again my experience has been that the outlay is far beyond—sometimes forty and fifty times beyond—the capital value of the land as it stood when I began. But reclamations effected thus suddenly, and by one single operation, are few in comparison with those other reclamations which have been gradual and continuous during many generations — each successive work bringing up the condition of the land to the standard of knowledge existing at the time. I have found that in the West of Scotland, where there is a very heavy rainfall, and where great areas of country are far from Tileworks, the mere re-drainage of old cultivated land cannot be thoroughly done, at the present or recent prices of Muscular Labour and of Material, at a less cost than from £10 to £12 per acre; and this alone is very frequently more than twenty years' purchase of the former rent.

But there is another kind of outlay connected with modern husbandry which has been on an enormous scale, the work of Ownership in Scotland, especially during the last forty years. Up to about that time, over the greater part of the country, it had been one of the customary stipulations in Leases that the Tenants should erect new Houses, with such assistance as in each case might be agreed upon. This stipulation was connected with the abandonment of Township Hovels, and of Runrig Tillage. The new class of Houses, although an immense advance on the old huts of Wattles and turf, were generally built of stone without lime and with roofs of thatch. Comfortable and commodious as these Houses often were when compared with the squalid dwellings which had preceded them, they still left much to be desired when compared with the advancing tastes and knowledge of the day. Accordingly, in almost all cases, Tenants taking farms during later years, have offered their new rents upon condition of getting the farms furnished with new Houses, both for themselves and for their Cows and other stock. On this branch of the Work of Ownership, I can also speak from a somewhat large and long experience. It is quite impossible to graduate the outlay on Houses according to the scale of Rent. Certain requirements apply equally to a Farm of £100 a year, and to a farm of £500 a year. I have rarely succeeded in building a "Steading" or complete set of Farm Buildings, under at least five years' outlay of the improved rent. Nine and ten years' outlay is common; and in the case of small Farms of between £100 and £200, the outlay has been as high as sixteen years of the rent. The general result is that the capital represented by Ownership in Scotland is seldom less than from forty to fifty years' rental, and is very often a great deal more. The average capital of Tenants is certainly less than five years of the rental per acre. I have elsewhere[1] specified the case of one farm in which the capital of the Owner represents the sum of £7046, whilst that invested by the Tenant would represent, on a liberal computation, not more than £966. The results of any improvement which such a Tenant can make upon his farm must be always

---

[1] *Nineteenth Century*, No. 106, Dec. 1885. "Capital and the Improvement of Land."

in greatest measure due to sources which he did not contribute. He is trading on the capital, on the previous improvements, and on the ancient Ownership, of other men. Yet there are politicians and economists who recommend that a Tenant who builds a new Piggery or a new Silo, at the cost of some fraction of a year's rent, should be allowed to deprive Owners of the rights which flow from centuries of Tenure and of outlay, by selling the occupancy which has been lent to them for a time upon stipulated conditions.

These facts, and a host of others correlative to these, open up an immense subject. If writers on Political Economy and on Social problems of any kind, would not only say, but would practically remember that Labour means every form and kind and degree of Human Energy, and most especially all those kinds which were the earliest and are the highest, their "Science" would not be the dismal, lean and erroneous teaching which too often it has been found out to be. Abstractions from which everything has been subtracted that ought to have been included—arbitrary selections and as arbitrary rejections among the elements contributing to great results—slovenly analysis, and complete forgetfulness of essential things which are by way of being left to be understood,—all these sources of error leave but a poor and beggarly account of the inexhaustible riches and Poetry of Nature, in the true history and progress of Man. The multitude of mental agencies, and of powers—the complexity

of the sources, and of the opportunities of work
—dating back through many centuries, with which,
and upon which, every man trades in Scotland
who hires any land belonging to another— but none
of which are due to the hirer—are but the type of
a general truth, affecting more or less all callings
or employments. When Men are taught that
they ought to have the "whole value of their own
Labour," they are never taught to count and
estimate all the factors which go to make up the
total value of results to which, perhaps, their
own contribution may be the smallest. They do
not think of the Capital which is the savings of
Mind, of the Organisation which is the invention
of Mind—of the Enterprise and Confidence which
are the expectations of Mind—of the Law which
is the embodiment of Mind,—on all of which the
whole of their own opportunities have absolutely
depended. And yet these considerations are
not founded on theory or speculation. They are
founded on indisputable facts, and are brought
to light as facts by the very simple process of
analysing with care and accuracy the conditions of
our own life, and the meaning of the commonest
words in which we instinctively express them.

The great interest and value of the history of
Scotland regarding all these matters, lie in its
splendid continuity. Like the days of the Poet,
our generations have been "bound each to each by
natural piety."[1] From the days when her early

[1] Wordsworth.

Sovereigns, in the Eleventh and Twelfth Centuries, gathered round them the Barons and Knights and the Burgesses of the Kingdom, and gave them new Instruments recording and defining the rights and powers which they had even then immemorially enjoyed—from the time when Robert the Bruce emerged triumphant from the War of Independence, and transferred these rights and powers from men who had been faithless, to men who had been faithful to their Country—from the time when he rewarded by a fresh and noble Tenure those who had stood by his side from Methven Bridge to Bannockburn,—the history of Scotland has been one long and steady development of the Reign of Mind in Government and in Law. The amalgamation of Races—the blending of interests—the fusion of Classes—the freedom of trade—the local movements of population in the rise of new industries,—these have been the lines of its long rough but steady march from extreme poverty and rudeness, to great wealth, and great achievements in every walk of intellectual exertion.

There are drawbacks and limitations to progress in all Nations, and it would be alike foolish and dangerous to forget them. But it is certainly not true that the immense increase of Wealth in Scotland since the Union has been an increase not widely distributed over the bulk of her population. The wages of her artificers, by no means the highest in skill, who are now employed on the Industries of the Clyde, amount very often in a single month to more money, with ten times the purchasing power, than the whole yearly income enjoyed by their fathers a hundred years ago. The same contrast is presented in every walk of life. The Houses and Cottages which all Owners have been building for Tenants during the last fifty years, are palaces compared—not only with the huts of the corresponding classes in the Military Ages, but compared even with the Houses lived in by powerful Chiefs not longer than a century and a half ago. The multiplication of Villas and Houses of a high class along all our shores, and round the old centres of our great cities, represents an immense aggregate of comfortable means among all the classes engaged in Trade and Commerce. The condition of our great cities is justly attracting attention, and much remains to be done for them in lines of action which cannot be too earnestly considered. But the more carefully we look into the Past, the more we shall be thankful for the general direction of the path in which, as a Nation, we have been led.

No man was more deeply versed in the literature of the Past—in the details of life during the Military Ages—than the late Mr. Cosmo Innes. He did not escape altogether from that curious form of Sentiment which tempts us all at times to long for a Wild Life, and to wish that our wild land had remained for ever unreclaimed—that our mountains had remained for ever waste. Under the influence of this strange glamour, which, as we have seen, never has any power as regards the Lowlands, he has allowed himself in one passage to take strange liberties with History and with Logic. He suggests that all the wild surfaces of our Country were not really intended to be conveyed by Charter, because in those days they were not really thought of. Yet in another passage of the same Essay, when dealing with the express words of these Charters, which carefully and exhaustively enumerated every variety of surface within the boundaries of an Estate, he explains that these enumerations were introduced *ob majorem cautelam*[1]—or, in other words, from the very excess of thoughtfulness. Of course this—the only irrational passage in all the writings of a very learned man—is the only one ever quoted by the irrational and the sentimental. Yet I know few writings more rich in evidence of all the leading facts and inferences which have been set forth in the preceding chapters—those especially which show us at once the connection and the contrast between the past and the present condition of our country. The original identity of Celtic Institutions with those of the other Northern Nations—differing only in the longer survival of early customs, and in the want of any code to define or fix;[2] the gradual adoption of Saxon Laws, not as alien or as the result of conquest, but because there was nothing definite to be displaced, and because those laws were in their nature " the most approved—the most civil;"[3] the

---

[1] *Scotch Legal Antiquities*, compare p. 45 with p. 155.
[2] *Ib.* pp. 97-8.   [3] *Ib.* pp. 95-6.

extent of exactions imposed upon the people during the Military Ages;[1] the fractionally small portion of the country which was cultivated at all, this portion being confined to a narrow strip on the river bank, or beside the sea;[2] the miserable use to which even those small areas were put that were grazed at all—just serving to keep the cattle from starvation; the constant quarrels arising out of the common use of pastures;[3] the great excess of population which arose in the Glens over the number which the country could support with its own produce " or honestly ;"[4] the enormous waste involved in the neglect and utter vacancy of vast areas of mountain land—stretching, on one Estate, across the whole of Scotland from sea to sea, and yielding literally nothing to represent " the thousands and millions of sheep which graze them now;"[5] the beginnings of improvement in the obligatory stipulations imposed on Tenants by Owners in the terms of Leases, so early as 1511;[6] the enforcement of all such stipulations by the penalty of removal or dismissal from the Estate;[7] the safety of the evidence that the small cultivators and sub-tenants, now called Crofters, were then Tenants at Will;[8]—all these, and many other kindred facts, testify, first, to the rude and barbarous condition of our ancestors, and, next, to the powers and processes by which their children have been raised

---

[1] *Scotch Legal Antiquities*, p. 276. [2] *Ib.* pp. 154-5.
[3] *Ib.* p. 268. [4] *Ib.* p. 269. [5] *Ib.* p. 263.
[6] *Ib.* pp. 250-2. [7] *Ib.* p. 252. [8] *Ib.* p. 251.

to an acknowledged place among the most civilised nations in the world. The contrast is indeed astonishing. "Always on the verge of famine and every few years suffering the horrors of actual starvation"—such are the words in which this careful Historian describes the old condition of the Highlands.[1] There is no wonder that he is roused to something like enthusiasm when in the case of a particular Estate,—that of the Campbells of Cawdor in Nairn,—he sees and describes all the poetry of a most blessed change :—"The woods now wave over the grey Castle with a luxuriance of shade which its old inhabitants never thought of. Above all, the country round, of old occupied by a half-starving people, lodged in houses of 'faile,'[2] disturbed by plundering neighbours, and ever and anon by the curse of Civil War, is now cultivated by an active and thriving Tenantry, with the comforts which increasing intelligence and wealth require and supply."[3] This is a beautiful vignette. But, again, this is only a little bit out of a wide landscape, which carries into the mind, through the eye, certain convictions in which we cannot be deceived.

And so it happens again that Mr. Cosmo Innes when, in another Work, he finds himself in contact with the actual records of old times, and with the picture they present of life and manners, was, as we all must be, recalled to the realities of historic truth. In closing his Preface to that instructive

---

[1] *Sketches of Early Scotch History*, p. 424.
[2] "Faile," turf.   [3] *Sketches*, p. 436.

record of life on a great Highland Estate during three Centuries, which is contained in the Book of Taymouth, he expresses his general conclusion in these remarkable words:—" While there is enough of romance in the glimpses here opened of the rough life of the 'good old time,' it is pleasant to think that while much is changed, every change has been for the better. The country which these papers show us in so wild a state of lawless insecurity has for the last two centuries steadily improved, and the process has not been more marked in the face of the country than in the moral and physical condition of the people and their social happiness." Yet this is spoken of a district in the Highlands from which there was as large a movement of population, in connection with the Industrial Age, as from any other portion of the country.

Among the many delusions which a false sentiment has promoted there has, perhaps, never been a delusion more complete than that which imagines that in early Celtic Customs or traditions, as distinguished from the corresponding Customs and traditions of the Teutonic Nations, there was any element which, if it had been left alone, would have built up some Polity better for the mass of the people than the Polity which actually arose, out of the amalgamation of the races, in England and in Scotland. As it so happens, we have historical evidence on this subject, more ancient, more continuous, and more conclusive, than on any other subject whatever connected with the rise of civilisation in any part of Europe. In an earlier chapter I have already referred to the curiously narrow and local, but attractive culture of the early Celtic Church. It is beyond question that the Monks and Priests of that Church had some culture and some letters in a literature purely Celtic, at a time when the other modern European nations were either sunk in utter barbarism, or at least were so little advanced as to have nothing of the same kind. But from this very fact we have an amount of evidence in respect to the condition and habits of these Celts, which we do not possess in respect to any other European race whatever at the same date. In the *Annals of Ireland by the Four Masters* we have a continuous Chronicle which is supposed, on good grounds, to be substantially authentic from the Second Century of the Christian Era. Even if this very early date be doubted, there seems to be no doubt whatever that these Annals are authentic from at least the Fourth Century, and they are continuous down to the middle of the Seventeenth. They present to us all the chief incidents of each year which were considered worthy of record by men of the most educated and intelligent class in Ireland. The result is to show that not only were the whole conditions of Society barbarous in the sense of being rude, rough, and violent— but that they were barbarous in the sense of being exceptionally savage, and without a trace of amelioration or of progress towards better things.

There may be a high interest attaching to Warlike Tribes—if their Wars have in them even the germ of contests animated by nobler passions than the mere thirst for blood, or the mere triumphs of revenge. But we may turn over page after page of these *Annals* without seeing even one solitary symptom of the crystallising forces which begin the Organic Structures of Civilisation. Every page is a sickening repetition of intertribal battles, murders, and devastations. Taking only the period before the English Conquest by Henry Plantagenet, we have the record of about 700 years. Not one single step can be traced through all those centuries in the path of progress. On the contrary, the country was getting worse and worse. And yet there was Poetry and Sentiment—of a kind. One of the most curious features of the Monkish Journals is the constant bursting of the narrative into verse— couplets and quatrains of rhythmic utterance. Few of us can judge of any beauty which may belong to them in the Erse. But we can all judge of the meanings and passions which inspired them. There are some allusions to Nature—to the Sea—to Rivers—to Mountains—which are poetic. But the animating spirit is almost purely ferocious—with nothing of the higher sentiments which we understand as Patriotism. No deeds of massacre, however dreadful, are ever narrated with rebuke—still less any acts of mere plunder—unless, perchance, any of these should have been directed against Ecclesiastics. Then indeed the culprit "King" or Chief is denounced as a monster, and some rival

King or Chief is incited—in piteous or in furious appeals—to punish him with death and with the devastation of his country. Thus in the year 733 we are told in the *Annals* that a Celtic King had ventured to practise upon some Church or Convent one of those exactions, "Coigny," which were universally practised against all the laity. He had forcibly taken some "refection" from a Church called "Cill-Cunna." For this offence another King was incited by "Congus, successor of Patrick," to take bloody vengeance on his too hungry rival. As usual there was a great battle. On the way to it the avenging King bursts into this characteristic poetical effusion :—

> "For Cill-Cunna, the Church of my Confessor,
>   I take this journey on the road;
> Aedh Roin shall leave his head with me,
>   or I shall leave mine with him."

And then we have the result chronicled thus :—

> "The slaughter of the Ulidians with Aedh Roin by
>   Aedh Allan, King of Ireland,
> For their Coigny at Cill-Cunna he placed soles to necks."

This last image may be very beautiful and poetic in Erse, but in Anglo-Saxon it requires explanation. Accordingly the meaning is given in a note by the learned Editor, as follows :—" This is an idiom expressing indiscriminate carnage, in which the sole of the foot of one body was placed over against or across the neck or headless trunk of another."[1]

[1] *Annals*, vol. i. p. 331.

It would be easy to fill whole chapters with extracts of the same kind. Many of them would exhibit the misery of the people. One of them celebrates a battle of which it is specially recorded "Great the carnage of Fir Feini," which is explained to be the "Farmers"[1] or Cultivating Class. Down to the very latest date in these Annals the same spirit is exhibited. The glory of a great Irish Chief who died in Rome so late as 1616, is celebrated in the last pages of the last volume. He is praised as "a warlike, valorous, predatory, enterprising Lord."[2] The truth is, that the Celtic race, like many others, were first lifted above themselves by contact and mixture with other blood. By themselves they had not only failed to advance, but they had fallen back. They had declined from the doctrines and the practice even of their own Brehon Laws. The Colony which they sent out to Scotland in the Sixth Century, rose, and has risen, in exact proportion as it became thoroughly mixed and fused with the Teutonic people. England gained immensely by both the Conquests which were effected over her. Scotland gained quite as much by the more peaceful but equally effective processes through which Saxon and Norman blood established itself even in the remotest Highlands. Ireland has suffered not from the Conquest, but because the higher Rule and Law were so long limited to the Pale. No corner of Europe needed so much that work of com-

---

[1] *Annals*, vol. i. p. 334.   [2] *Ibid.* vol. vi. p. 2375.

plete amalgamation which has given all its strength and power to the British people.

There is, however, one fruitful branch of the national life of Scotland to which I cannot now direct any adequate attention, but to which I must shortly refer in closing. This fruitful branch is that which consists in the life and labours of men of the Celtic race, who have moved out from their native hills and glens, and have given the benefit of high culture, or of a rich and imaginative character, to their country and to the world. Two examples of this kind are impressed upon my memory by circumstances which have left an indelible impression. Many years ago I was speaking to Lord Macaulay on the subject of the Indian Code of Criminal Law, to which, in his own earlier life, he had devoted his learning and his genius. He had occasion to mention the difficulties of the work—the deep questions of Jurisprudence which it involved, and the sources from which he had sought and found assistance. Amongst these he mentioned especially the name of a man of whom at that time I had never heard—one of those who work unseen in our Civil Services, and to whom the Nation very often is indebted for far more than it ever comes to know. This was Sir John M'Leod, a native of Skye, and one of the smaller Proprietors in that Island. Lord Macaulay was not a man to lavish praise indiscriminately. His mind was critical, and he had of necessity in his own nature a very high standard in judging of intellectual powers. It was therefore with some surprise that I heard Lord Macaulay speak in almost enthusiastic praise of this little-known descendant of the old MacLeods of Skye, as having one of the most profound, sagacious, and philosophic minds he had ever met with.[1] When I came to know Sir John M'Leod as I afterwards did, I found in him the perfect type of a highly cultured son of the Celtic race—modest, refined, dignified,—and speaking English, after some forty years' service abroad, with as strong a Gaelic tone and accent as if he had never left his Estate in Skye.

But I recall another example somewhat different in kind. A curious habit of the Highland people serves to conceal sometimes the part they have played in the highest walks of human enterprise. This is the habit of changing their name—dropping one and assuming another. During the Military Ages they did so perpetually, as we have seen, when they enlisted under some new Chief, and joined some other Clan. In assuming the name of their new associates they kept up that theory and flavour of blood-relationship which in nine cases out of ten had no other foundation whatever. Sir Walter Scott tells us that one of his friends, shooting in the North, had a native guide assigned to him under the name of Gordon. But he recognised the man as having served him in a similar capacity some years before in another place under the name

---

[1] "The very rare talents" of J. M'Leod is the expression used by Macaulay on another occasion, as quoted in Trevelyan's *Life*, vol. i. p. 413.

of MacPherson. On asking the man whether he was not the same, and whether his name had not then been MacPherson, the composed reply was, "Yes, but that was when I lived on the other side of the hill."[1] It is less known, however, that this habit has always been very general when Highlanders leave the hills and settle in the Low Country. The native Celtic name is dropped, and some Lowland form is adopted which is supposed to be a translation or an equivalent. It was thus that during the scarcities and distress which afflicted the Hebrides during the last years of the last century — about 1792 — a family of the name of MacLeay migrated from the Islet of Ulva, one of the broken fragments of the volcanic Island of Mull, and settled at Blantyre, near Glasgow. The name they took was Livingstone, and their illustrious grandchild was the great African Traveller and Missionary. The purity of the true old Celtic race cannot be safely determined by name or language. Long centuries of foreign dominion, and of intercourse and inter-marriage, leave it very doubtful where we can find, even in the Hebrides, anything like an unmixed descent. But having had the honour of a somewhat intimate friendship with David Livingstone, I always regarded him as an example of the purest Celtic type. Rather below the medium stature, broad, sturdy, and with an evident capacity for great endurance, the special feature which attracted notice was his

[1] *Quarterly Review*, vol. xiv. p. 301.

very dark hazel eye—an eye so dark as almost
to suggest a Southern or an Eastern origin.
Great self-possession and dignity of manner were
blended with a curious mixture of gentleness
and determination. Nothing in Nature escaped
his observation; and shortly before his death I
had a letter from him, written in Central Africa,
alluding to a peculiarity of growth in a tree at
Inveraray which I had not before noticed, but
which he must have noticed in silence when we
were together. He was another instance of a
man like General Gordon, with a special gift and
a special inspiration, which in all human probability would never have been developed if he had
been born in the life passed by the old Sub-tenants
in Ulva. Burning a little Kelp, digging a few
Potatoes, or even herding Cattle in the summer
Shealings which looked down on

"all the group of Islets gay
That guard old Staffa round,"[1]

is a life which it is difficult to rank at its proper
level as compared with that which he actually led
—a life in which he became to millions of the human
race the first Pioneer of Civilisation, and the first
Harbinger of the Gospel.

The blood and the race which in our own
day have produced two such men — one from
the class of Chiefs, and another from the class
of ordinary Clansmen, must have the very best
stuff of human nature in it. But that blood

[1] *The Lord of the Isles.* Fourth Canto, x

and race is not confined to those who still retain the Gaelic speech. The larger and the more cultivated part of it is spread over the wide Dominions of the British Crown. It is one of the many sources of our Imperial strength and wealth. The Low Country of Scotland is full of it. The Colonies are full of it. The Indian Services have always been full of it. The Army and the Navy have had abundant reason to be proud of it. It was trusted by The Bruce in the thickest of the Fights he fought. But its whole pride, and aim, and object must continue to be those which that great King promoted—the object of living and working in harmony with the other elements which have built up the Scottish Nation, and in obedience to those Natural and Moral Laws which are the only solid foundation of all Human Institutions.

The progress that Scotland made after union with England, was a progress without a parallel in any of the older Nations of the World. Yet that progress was not due to anything she derived from England in the way of Laws and Institutions. These were all her own. She kept them at the Union, and guarded them, with a noble, because a grateful, care. We were jealous about them, not from any narrow or provincial feeling,—but because our fathers had told us of the noble works done in their days, and in the old times before them. The one great benefit which Scotland did owe to the last and happiest of her many unions, was nothing more than access to larger fields of exercise—to wider openings of Opportunity. She rose to the immense prospects of this new horizon because of the Mind and Character which had been developed under the long discipline, and through the fiery trials, of her own stormy history. The wonderful start she made in the race of intellectual and industrial Life, was due to that history—to the older unions effected during it—to the doctrines it had embodied—to the energies it had developed—to the great principles of Jurisprudence which had worked under the sanctions, and with the authority, of Law. Scotland, therefore, at the Union, did not break with her own Past. On the contrary, she kept it, and cherished it, as the richest contribution she could make to the growth of One Great Empire, and to the Polity of One United Kingdom. Let her keep it still—and always in the same spirit, and with the same great end in view.

APPENDIX.

APPENDIX I.

VOL. II. CH. I. P. 35.

LEASE OF FARM IN MULL, signed by DUNCAN FORBES of Culloden, as Commissioner for John Duke of Argyll and Greenwich, 1739.

Att Stonyhill the Eighteenth day of Aprile one thousand seven hundred and thirty-nine years, And

It is contracted, agreed, and finally ended betwixt the partys following, viz. :—Duncan fforbes of Culloden, Esquire, Lord President of the Session, as having power from his Grace John Duke of Argyle and Greenwich, Heretable Proprietor of the Lands and others after specified, To the effect after mentioned, Conform to Commission dated the twenty-fourth day of March one Thousand Seven hundred and Therty-eight nine years, Registrat in the Books of Session the ffourth day of Aprile and year foresaid, on the one part, and Hugh McLean, Rachell McCarter, Donald McDonald, John McLean, Duncan Beaton, and Archibald McCarter, *all present possessors of the Lands and others underwritten,*[1] on the other part, in manner following—That is to say, The said Duncan fforbes, as having power in manner forsaid, *has sett and in Tack and assedation Letton,* Like as He by thir presents, *with and under the conditions and for payment of the Tack Duty aftermentioned,* Setts and in Tack and assedation Letts *to them and their heirs and such partners as they shall from time to time assume upon the Death or ffaillure of any of them in manner herein after mentioned*[2] (*Secluding all other Assigneys and Subtennents*), All and Haill The one penny half penny Land of Bunessan, with houses, biggings, yeards, parts, pendicles, *and universall pertinents thereof whatsomever used and wont,*[3] lying in the Division of Ross, Island of Mull and

---

[1] Showing that the new Leaseholders were of the old class of cultivators, probably sub-tenants.
[2] Showing that new Lease regulated, and strictly limited any admission of co-partners in the farm.
[3] Showing admission of " use and wont " in ascertaining facts.

Sheriffdom of Argyle, *by the proportions following*, viz. :—To the said Hugh McLean *one-half ;* To the said Rachael McCarter *one-sixth ;* To the said Donald McDonald *one-twelfth ;* To the said John McLean *one-twelfth ;* To the said Duncan Beaton *one-twelfth ;* and to the said Archibald McCarter *one-twelfth :*[1] And That *for the space of nineteen full and compleat years*[2] from and after their entry thereto, which is hereby Declared to have been and begun at the term of Whitsunday one Thousand and Seven hundred and Therty-eight years ; and *so furth to continue in the peaceable possession of the said Lands during the space foresaid :* Which Tack above written The said Duncan fforbes, as having power in manner foresaid, Binds and obliges the said Duke, his heirs and successors, *to warrand to them and their foresaids att all hands and against all deadly as Law will :*[3] For the which Causes and on the other part the haill forenamed persons Bind and oblige them Conlly. and Sevally., their heirs, Exctrs. and Successors whatsomever, *Thankfully to content and pay* to the said Duke and his above written, or to his or their assigneys or Chamberlains in his or their names, *the Sum of One Hundred and Seventy-Six pound Scots money*[4] at the term of Martinmas yearly, AND THAT IN FULL SATISFACTION OF ALL HEREZELDS, CASUALITYS, AND OTHER PRESTATIONS AND SERVICES WHATSOMEVER, WHICH ARE HEREBY DISCHARGED,[5] *Except the Services of Tennents for Repairing Harbours, mending Highways, or making or Repairing Milnleads for the generall Benefite of the Island,*[6] with Therty pound money foresaid of penalty for ilk term's failled and annual rent of the said Tack-duty from and after the term of payment during the not payment : Declaring The first year's Tack-duty was payable at the term of Martinmas one Thousand seven hundred and therty-eight years, and that the Tack-duty is to be paid yearly at the term of Martinmas for all the years contained in this present Tack : And furder, The haill forenamed persons *Bind and oblige them and their foresaids to possess the Lands and others above written with their own proper stock allenarly,*[7] As also To ffree and Releive the s^d Duke and his foresaids of all Cesses, Ministers' Stipends, School-

---

[1] Showing great inequality in shares – recognising facts.
[2] Showing fixed limit of time.
[3] The usual clause of Warrandice—conveying security for Exclusive Use.
[4] Showing fixed rent in money.
[5] Showing the terms in which Servitudes were abolished.
[6] Showing the specific services retained, as of public utility.
[7] To prevent Debt, and secure Tenants with sufficient means.

masters' Sallarys, and all other burdens imposed or to be imposed upon the lands above mentioned: And it is hereby expressly Provided and Declared That in case one year's rent or any part thereof shall remain unpaid when another year's rent becomes due, Then and in that case this present Tack shall *ipso facto* become void and null without any process of Declarator to follow on the said Contravention: And it shall be Leisume and Lawfull to the said Duke and his foresaids to Lett the Lands above written of new as if this present Tack had never been made or granted; *Providing also that in case any one or more of the Tennents above named shall faill in their Circumstances so as they shall not be able to hold their proportions of the said Lands, Or if upon the Death of any of them there shall not be a fitt person to take up their possession, The remaining tennents shall either take the share or shares of the person or persons so failling amongst them during the residue of this present Tack, Or shall find and assume a fitt Successor or Successors to him or them, for whose answering the prestations Incumbent on them as Succeeding to a Share or Shares of this present Tack the remaining tennents shall be answerable:* In performance of which the haill forenamed persons not only bind and oblige them and their foresds., But also in payment of the above rent at the terms and in manner above mentioned: And both partys Bind and oblige them and their foresaids to perform the premisses *hinc inde* to others, under the penalty of Eighty-five pounds money foresd., to be paid by the party ffaillier to the party performer or willing to perform by and attour performance: And Consent To the Registration hereof in the Books of Councill and Session or others Competent to have the strength of a Decreet of any of the Judges thereof Interponed thereto, That Letters of Horning on six days' charge and all other Exect[s] needfull may pass hereon in form as effeirs, & yrto. Constitute

Their proct[s], etc. In witnes whereof their presents, consisting of this and the two preceeding pages of Stamped paper, written by David Marshall, writter in Edinburgh, are Subscribed as follows, viz[t]: By the said Duncan Forbes Att Stoneyhill the said Eighteenth day of Aprile one thousand Seven hundred and thirty-nine years Before these witnesses, Ronald Dunbar, Writer to the Signet, and David Forbes his Serviter, Inserter of the place, Date, Witnesses' names and Designations to the said Duncan Forbes his subscription.

(Signed)	(Signed)
RONALD DUNBAR, *Witness*.	DUN. FORBES, *Comr*.
DAVID FORBES, *Witness*.	

APPENDIX II.

PETITION FROM POOR PERSONS IN TYREE FOR AID TO EMIGRATE.

Unto Sir JOHN M'NEILL. 1847.

The Petition of the undersigned Cottars and small Crofters on the Island of Tyree,

Humbly sheweth,

That since the making of kelp ceased, and particularly since the failure of the potato crop, the inhabitants of this island have been in a state of great destitution; and, were it not for the benevolence of the proprietor, and the aid afforded by the relief board, they would inevitably have starved. That hitherto they have been employed by the proprietor at drainage and other works, during the winter and spring months, before the land was cropped, and during the summer they were supported by the funds of the relief board. That this latter resource being now at an end, your petitioners' prospects, on looking forward to the ensuing summer, are in the extreme dismal, and the more so, as the only prospect of ultimate relief to which they so fondly cling is denied them—that of emigration—which your petitioners neglected to take advantage of while in their power, probably supposing that the relief funds were to last, or that the potato would be restored. That, to add to their further grievance, your petitioners are led to understand that those averse to emigration from the West Highlands are using every possible means to prevent it, and that statements are made publicly that the poor can be supported by employing them in the improvement of waste land. Those who advocate such are certainly actuated by other motives save that of philanthropy, and display the grossest ignorance as to the resources of the country, particularly as regards this isolated island, where there is no fuel, and not an inch of waste land which the inhabitants could not drain and trench in a few months. That your petitioners would now most earnestly request, that if possessed of the bowels of compassion, such as were your forefathers, or value the lives of your countrymen, you will not credit the statement of those inimical to our best interest, but examine individually into our circumstances, and the condition of the island, when they have no doubt you will have sufficient proof afforded of the fallacy of such statements, and the injury and cruelty done us by such misrepresentations, which may perhaps be the means of the Duke's withholding his bounty, and depriving us of the power of participating in the enjoyments and comforts, they are from day to day informed, their friends in Canada enjoy to such an extent.

> May it therefore please your honour to take the miserable consideration of your petitioners into consideration, and use your influence with Her Majesty's Government, or His Grace the Duke of Argyll, to provide for them the means of emigrating; and your petitioners shall ever pray.

(Signed by 136 heads of families representing 825 souls.)

FINIS.

www.ingramcontent.com/pod-product-compliance
Lightning Source LLC
Chambersburg PA
CBHW031858220426
43663CB00006B/681